THE PLANTFINDER'S GUIDE TO
ORNAMENTAL GRASSES

THE PLANTFINDER'S GUIDE TO
ORNAMENTAL GRASSES

Roger Grounds

DAVID & CHARLES
Newton Abbot

TIMBER PRESS
Portland, Oregon

PICTURE ACKNOWLEDGEMENTS

Karl Adamson 21, 33, 52, 60, 70, 82, 104, 120, 142, 146 Neil Campbell-Sharp 57, 92 top left, 92 top right, 93 bottom, 93 top left, 93 top right, 147 Roger Grounds 1, 3, 8, 12, 16, 18, 23, 27, 34, 43, 51, 66, 88 bottom, 88 top, 136, 148, 149, 155, 157, 158, 173 Noël Kingsbury 101, 103, 107 Wolfgang Oehme 99, 100 Marie O'Hara 2, 6, 11, 17, 22, 24, 25, 26, 28, 30, 35, 36, 37, 39, 40, 42, 44, 45, 46, 48, 54, 55, 56 bottom, 56 top, 58, 62, 64, 65, 67, 73, 74, 76, 78, 80 bottom, 80 top, 85, 91, 103 top, 110, 114, 115, 116, 119, 123, 124, 128, 129, 131, 132, 135 top, 144, 145, 152, 154, 159, 161, 162, 167, 184, 186 Piet Oudolf 86, 96 Howard Rice 148 Patrick Taylor 94

Illustrations on pages 13, 14 and 15 by Coral Mula

NOTE: Throughout the book the time of year is given as a season to make the reference applicable to readers all over the world. In the northern hemisphere the seasons may be translated into months as follows:

Early winter	December	*Early spring*	March	*Early summer*	June	*Early autumn*	September
Midwinter	January	*Mid-spring*	April	*Midsummer*	July	*Mid-autumn*	October
Late winter	February	*Late spring*	May	*Late summer*	August	*Late autumn*	November

First published in the UK in 1998 by David & Charles Publishers,
Brunel House, Newton Abbot, Devon
ISBN 0 7153 0638 3
A catalogue record for this book is available from the
British Library.

First published in North America in 1998 by Timber Press Inc.,
133 SW Second Avenue, Suite 450, Portland, Oregon 97204, USA
ISBN 0-88192-451-2
Cataloguing-in-Publication Data is on file with the Library of Congress

Printed and bound in France by Imprimerie Pollina S.A., n° 73933

Photographs page 1 *Ampelodesmos mauritanicus*; page 2 top left *Cortaderia selloana* 'Sunningdale Silver' with *C. s.* 'Pumila' and *Miscanthus oligostachys* 'Purpurascens' behind; bottom left *Imperata cylindrica* 'Rubra' with *Stipa tenuissima* behind; bottom right *Miscanthus sinensis* 'Kleine Silberspinne'; page 3 *Hordeum jubatum*

Contents

Introduction

A wind of change is blowing through our gardens and through the fields of garden design and landscape architecture. The view that control is the essence of gardening is giving way to a more relaxed concept in which the plants are allowed to live together in mutually compatible communities. And with this change the ornamental grasses which have fascinated me for so long and whose praises I first sang 20 years ago are at last coming into their own and finding their true place in our gardens.

I find it surprising that they have taken so long to be appreciated. It may be that one of the things that has deterred gardeners is the great edifice of strange words used to describe the parts of their flowers. This specialized vocabulary is called for because the flowers of grasses, being wind-pollinated, are quite different from those of more familiar garden plants. But this should deter no one from growing grasses, for the decorative parts of grasses can well enough be described in familiar terms as heads or panicles, and the parts that correspond to flowers as spikelets.

The aim of this book is to discuss ornamental grasses and how they may be used in the garden rather than to look at the botanical niceties that distinguish one from another. For this reason they are discussed in relation to the qualities either of foliage or flower which they contribute to the garden, or in relation to their usefulness in a particular situation. The first half of the book is devoted mainly to a description of those grasses that may reasonably be expected to flourish in most gardens, needing little more than ordinary earth and sun. Those with more particular requirements are discussed in their appropriate chapters in the second half of the book — shade-lovers in the chapter on woodland and shade, those with a requirement for moisture in the chapter on wetland and waterside, and so on. It is in this second half that various approaches to the uses of grasses in gardens are discussed. An alphabetical listing of ornamental grasses by botanical name is provided in Appendix III.

It may puzzle some readers that nurserymen's catalogues may seem to give contradictory descriptions of the flowers of some grasses. It's all a matter of timing. The floral parts of *Sesleria heufleriana* form a dense, cylindrical spike which is of a green so dark that it is sometimes described as black, but later in the season the spikelets protrude their anthers so that it looks as though the whole thing is decked out in tiny white prayer flags, when the cylindrical spike might well be described as white. Where such conflicts of description arise I have tried to describe both aspects. There is a similar problem with the measurements of heights, because grasses tend to go on growing, elongating the stem sections between the nodes, after flowering. The heights I have given are those at flowering time.

I have endeavoured to include all those grasses that I consider gardenworthy, though in a world in which there are so many grasses, most of them beautiful in one way or another, it is difficult to draw a line between those that are ornamental and those that are not. On the whole, by ornamental I mean those grasses that are showy either by virtue of the profusion of their flowering or by the colour of their leaves, or both.

I hope this book will open the eyes of others to the beauty of ornamental grasses, which have so much more to offer than the static flowers of traditional border plants, and to the variety of ways in which they can be used in the garden. Most of all, I hope it will encourage others to find as much pleasure in them as I do.

Stipa (Calamagrostis) brachytricha, a highly desirable grass.

Part One Introduction to Grasses

1 The Fascination of Grasses

Gardening is a broad river with many currents: besides the main streams of formality and informality there are the lesser currents of wild gardening and natural gardening. Other currents have surfaced and submerged again, though not without trace; close-boskage shrub gardens, a fashion for foliage and, later, heathers and conifers. But one current, scarcely perceptible at the start of the century, has persisted, gathering force with the passing years and now apparent as the coming tide. Ornamental grasses are the signature plants of the new English garden.

What is magical about grasses is their intimacy with the natural world – the way they reflect its every mood, catching the sunlight in their flowers and seedheads or holding the morning dew suspended, changing with the passing hours, ebbing and flowing with the seasons, burgeoning in the spring, maturing in summer, burning with tints of autumn fire and then becoming mere spectral shapes against the watery winter sun. Spangled with raindrops or rimed with frost, they have a poise and presence unsurpassed by any other plants. Their beauty lies in their linearity – the lines of their leaves, their stems and the branches of their flowerheads. Such linear effects make a complete contrast with the rounded shapes of more familiar garden plants, and the two used together complement each other to perfection.

Lacking the brightly coloured flowers of the familiar, broad-leaved flora of our borders, grasses are grown for their structure, for the subtleties of their shape, form and texture, for the translucency of their flowers and seedheads, and for the movement they bring into a garden, for they stir with the slightest breath of air, toss in every storm, and resume their serenity once the wind has gone. Theirs is a lasting beauty that lingers across the seasons, for their flowers lack the fleshy petals of everyday garden plants, which by their very nature must soon decay; the true flowers of grasses are tiny but are surrounded by bract-like structures which retain their form as they dry, while the flowers themselves are replaced by seeds, the seedheads remaining beautiful for weeks or even months.

Grasses have not only beauty and variety to commend them but also ease of cultivation. Given ordinary earth and a place in the sun, most are extraordinarily drought-tolerant and need little care beyond an annual grooming.

PIONEERS OF GRASS GARDENING

Probably the first grass to have been grown in gardens at least in part for its ornamental value would have been Job's tears (*Coix lacryma-jobi*), which was common in monastery and herb gardens in the 14th century. Its large, hard seeds were not only decorative but were also used in the making of rosaries. The now ubiquitous reed canary or ribbon grass (*Phalaris arundinacea* 'Picta') is mentioned in many herbals of this time as being cultivated for its brightly coloured leaves, and was probably the first variegated grass to be brought into gardens.

The first known example of a grass being listed specifically as an ornamental occurs in the 1782 catalogue of John Kingston Galpine, who was a seedsman and nurseryman of Blandford in Dorset, England. What is interesting is that the grass was not an exotic but merely an English native, *Stipa pennata* (feather grass). Another century would pass before William Robinson was to list, among other perennials in the first of many editions of his classic *The English Flower Garden* (1883), some 30 ornamental grasses, while in *The Wild Garden* (1870), that precursor of so many modern trends, he gives a list of British native grasses suitable for what he called 'naturalization'. Robinson, always at war with the formality of Victorian gardening, advocated their use in wild gardens and in informal beds.

Gertude Jekyll, whose career waxed as Robinson's was waning, used ornamental grasses frequently and is really the first writer to discuss how grasses should be used in the garden. She liked to place big grasses as specimens by water, used the common woodrush (*Luzula sylvatica*) as a covering for woodland floors and liked to work blue lyme grass (*Leymus arenarius*) into plantings of glaucous grey and blue foliage.

Influential though Jekyll and Robinson were, it was really the German nurseryman Karl Foerster who started the tide of interest in ornamental grasses. Foerster, a pacifist, linked the health of the world with gardens and favoured the concept of what he called *Durchgebluht*, meaning bloom throughout the year, a concept that he demonstrated in his own nursery. It was Foerster who realized the importance of grasses to all-season gardens, for it is they that give a garden structure and interest in the autumn and winter. Like Robinson, Foerster was a great champion of the plants he believed in and he wrote some 30 books, the most important of which is *Eintritt der Graeser und Ferne in den Gaerten* (Introducing Grasses and Ferns into the Garden), which was published in 1957. Unfortunately, this book has never appeared in English.

Foerster exerted an enormous influence on the generation of gardeners and designers who followed him, two of whom have become as influential as he. One was Wolfgang Oehme, who met Foerster and was influenced by his ideas of all-season gardens. The other was Roberto Burle Marx, who studied in Germany and was much inspired by Karl Foerster's advocacy of natural plant associations. It was they who took his ideas to the Americas.

As Roberto Burle Marx worked in South America, largely using tropical plants, his influence has not been much felt in Europe other than in his use of multi-coloured lawns. Wolfgang Oehme's influence, however, has been more pervasive in Europe. He studied horticulture and landscape architecture at the University of Berlin and when he moved to the USA in the 1950s he was appalled to find that ornamental grasses were virtually unheard-of there. Meanwhile, Richard Simon, an American, graduated from Cornell University in 1956 and then worked for a time in a Swiss nursery, where he met Kurt Bluemel. Three years later Kurt Bluemel came to America and worked in the Simon family's famous Bluemount Nurseries. Together Bluemel and Oehme persuaded Simon to grow grasses at Bluemount, and it became the first American nursery to offer a collection of ornamental grasses.

Four years later Bluemel left Bluemount to start his own nursery. He worked for a time with Wolfgang Oehme but in 1975 Oehme joined forces with James van Sweden to form the design team Oehme, van Sweden Associates, Inc. and Bluemel continued on his own. When visiting landscapers saw his fields full of grasses they realized the impact that grasses can have when grown *en masse*.

Meanwhile, at Leer in Germany, Ernst Pagels was breeding miscanthus to produce earlier-flowering forms. By crossing *Miscanthus sinensis* 'Gracillimus' (maiden grass) with larger miscanthus Pagels produced a whole new race of free-flowering hybrids of intermediate size, many coming into flower as early as late summer. These have done much to create the current interest in grasses.

Miscanthus sinensis 'Morning Light', an outstanding new cultivar recently introduced by the United States National Arboretum.

But the story does not end there. New grasses are still being collected from remote corners of the globe, while the process of raising and introducing new varieties gathers pace. In the USA Kurt Bluemel, in addition to introducing outstanding new varieties of his own, has been responsible for marketing new grasses introduced by Longwood Gardens and the US National Arboretum. One of the most remarkable is *Stipa* (*Calamagrostis*) *brachytricha* (Korean feather reed grass), collected by Dr Richard Lighty on a trip to Korea sponsored by Longwood Gardens. *Miscanthus sinensis* 'Cabaret', 'Cosmopolitan' and 'Morning Light' were collected by Dr John Creech and Sylvester March, staff members of the US National Arboretum, while in Japan in the mid-1970s.

The grasses of tomorrow are already being tested. In the USA, Barry Yinger has on trial a variety of *Miscanthus sacchariflorus* with brightly gold-variegated leaves and beautiful red culm sheaths, while Greg Speichert is testing, among others, a Chinese sedge that looks much like *Carex muskingumensis* except that it is electric blue. In the UK the newly discovered white-variegated *Trisetum flavescens* 'Peter Hall' looks promising, while I myself have recently found a gold-variegated *Miscanthus floridulus*, to be called 'Gilt Edged'. And who knows what gems are still to be discovered, for the world of ornamental grasses has hardly begun.

2 The Biology of Grasses

For the human race the true grasses are the most important of all plant families, for they provide the cereals which are the staff of life for most of the world's population. They also provide the forage grasses on which meat and dairy cattle are raised, the starches which are the basis for alcohols, the sugars on which confections are based, the essential oils used in many perfumes and the reeds for wind instruments, while in warmer climates bamboos, which are true grasses though woody, supply almost all needs from the cradle to the grave.

From a botanist's point of view the grasses are one of the most fascinating of families. Though they are generally known as the *Gramineae*, the name *Poaceae* is to be

The golden spikelets of *Stipa gigantea* exposing the pollen-producing anthers.

preferred for two reasons. The first is that in modern usage all family names end in *-ceae*, *Gramineae* being a relic left over from the early days of plant classification. The second is that the family name is usually derived from the first genus in that family to be named, which in this case was *Poa*, as authored by Linnaeus. While not the largest of families – the *Compositae*, *Leguminosae*, *Orchidaceae* and *Rubiaceae* are all larger in terms of species and genera – the *Poaceae* exhibits almost endless diversity within an essential uniformity of structure, and it is this which has enabled it to be one of the most successful of all plant groups.

Along with the *Liliaceae*, *Orchidaceae* and others, the *Poaceae* belong to the monocotyledonous class of flowering plants – that is, that subdivision of the plant kingdom whose seedlings produce only one cotyledon or seed-leaf. The *Poaceae* is itself divided into five sub-

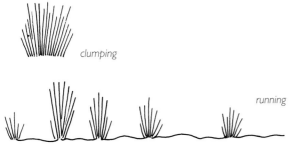

Fig. I Root type

families, the *Bambusoideae*, the *Arundinoideae*, the *Pooideae*, the *Chlorioideae* and the *Panicoideae*, which are themselves further divided into tribes, though these subfamilies and tribes need not concern us here. Below these come genera, species, varieties and some lesser classifications with which most gardeners are familiar.

PLANT FORM

The *Poaceae* account for more of the world's plants than any other family, and their conspicuous success is chiefly due to their simple yet infinitely adaptable architecture. The roots, which may make up as much as 90 per cent of a grass's body weight, are fibrous, shallow and extensively branched. They are extremely efficient, making most grasses highly drought-tolerant. The leaf mound springs directly from the roots, and the positioning of the buds from which this growth springs in relation to the soil surface determines the form of the leaf mound. If the buds occur just above the soil surface the grass will form a tussock; if they occur at soil level the grass will assume a stoloniferous or sward-forming habit; if they are below the soil the grass will have a rhizomatous or running habit.

The positioning of these buds is crucial to the success of the grasses since it places them out of reach of the teeth of browsing animals, and indeed of the blades of mowers, and makes it relatively easy for the grasses to produce new shoots (tillers) to increase the girth of the plant or replace lost leafage. Such tillers readily produce roots and are self-sustaining almost from the start. As a grass plant gains in girth it becomes in effect a bundle of genetically uniform individual plants, making it easy to produce large quantities of the same grass.

From a gardener's point of view it is useful to have a simple classification of the mound form of grasses. The first determinant is root type and this is classified as either clumping or running (Fig. 1). Clumping grasses form tight, dense mounds which increase girth steadily but do

not spread aggressively. Running grasses spread by means of vigorous rhizomes. A few grasses are intermediate between the two.

The leaf mound shapes (Fig. 2) may then be defined as follows to indicate their form and characteristics: tufted, mounded, upright, upright-divergent, fountain-like, arching and trailing.

LEAVES

To many people it is the leaves of grasses that distinguish them from other flowering plants, these leaves having parallel veins. They are narrow, arranged alternately in two rows on opposite sides of the culm, or stem, and employ essentially the same ground plan as the leaves of other monocotyledonous plants, that is, a division into blade and sheath. However, in the grasses the blade is clearly differentiated from the sheath, which wraps around the culm, by the presence of a ligule (little tongue). This is a small, shield-like fringe clasping the culm above the point at which the blade falls away from the sheath. Ligules are unique to the grasses, though similar organs are found in one or two other genera. Their function is not understood.

What distinguishes the grasses and gives them their structural strength is the way in which the sheath and blade combine to form a single structural unit from which the growing point arises surrounded by a cylindrical nest of concentric protective sheaths. Herein lies another reason for their success, for whereas in most plants the

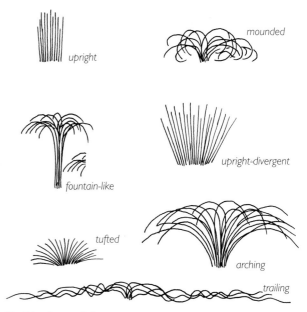

Fig. 2 Leaf mound shapes

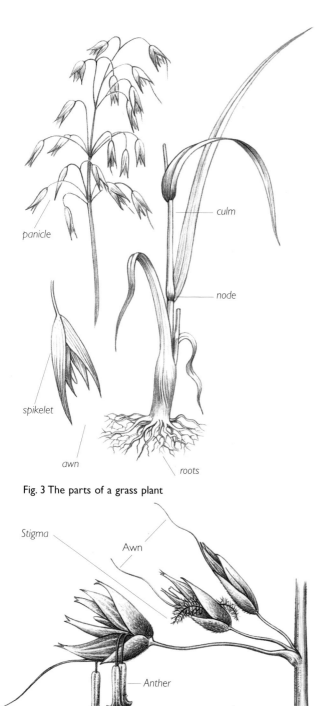

Fig. 3 The parts of a grass plant

Fig. 4 The pollination of grasses Although the spikelets of grasses normally contain both male and female organs, any one spikelet will only expose either its stigmas or its anthers at any one time. Later, once the anthers have shed their pollen, that spikelet will expose its stigmas, and the one that first exposed its stigmas will expose its anthers.

tissues responsible for cell division and therefore growth occur at the tip of the leaf or shoot, in the grasses that area is located at their base deep within the concentric protective sheaths. This is why grasses can be grazed or mown and will still continue to grow, whereas in plants whose growing point is at the tip of the leaf or shoot no further extension is possible if that tip is removed.

STEMS

The stems of grasses are mainly cylindrical and hollow except at the joint or node – the point where the leaf is attached – although solid stems do occur in a few genera. They are mostly unbranched, the bamboos being the most conspicuous exception. During the vegetative phase of growth the distance between the nodes is kept short, only elongating as flowering approaches. The nodes are generally slightly swollen and the stems may change direction at the node rather as the upper arm and lower arm change direction at the elbow. In a few grasses the nodes become conspicuously swollen and may act as a food-storing bulb or corm.

THE FLORAL ORGANS

The flowers of grasses are different in structure from those of more familiar broad-leaved plants as, being wind-pollinated, they do not need the showy, colourful petals which are used by other plants to attract pollinating insects. Theirs is a simple structure through which the wind can pass, shaking pollen from the anthers and blowing it onto receptive stigmas. The pollen of grasses is highly specialized and unique to the *Poaceae* family, one of its most notable attributes being that it produces a wide range of antigens whose twin purposes are to prevent self-pollination and to facilitate the recognition of a suitable mate. It is these antigens which cause hay-fever in susceptible people.

The flower of a grass (Fig. 4) consists of an ovary at the tip of which are three stamens and two stigmas, and at the base of which are two lodicules. The stamens are the male organs and produce pollen; the stigmas, which are feathery in design, are the female organs which in due season become receptive to pollen. The lodicules have no sexual function themselves but inflate at flowering time, thereby opening the floral envelope and allowing the anthers to emerge to scatter pollen. They then deflate, causing the floral envelope to spring shut. It remains shut until the stigmas are receptive. In some grasses there is some sexual segregation of the flowers,

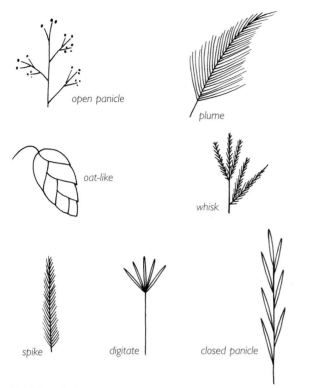

open panicle

plume

oat-like

whisk

spike

digitate

closed panicle

Fig. 5 Panicle form

those producing only anthers being known as sterile while those producing only ovaries or both ovaries and stamens are known as fertile. Most grasses are outbreeding, only resorting to self-fertilization if all else fails, but for a small number of grasses cleistogamy or self-fertilization is a way of life, pollen being transferred to the stigma without the flower ever opening.

The sexual organs are surrounded by a number of specialized bracts, those closest to the flower being the palea and the lemma. Sometimes a stiff, feathery and often decorative bristle known as an awn is found on the back of the lemma. These, together with the reproductive organs, form the floret. The floret itself is surrounded by glumes, the whole assemblage being known as a spikelet. The spikelets are gathered together into a flowerhead known as a panicle.

THE PANICLE

The panicle is a specialized branch system that arises at the tip of a culm or stem on which the leaves have been suppressed. A typical panicle (Fig. 3) is found in *Avena sativa*, for example, but there are many variations. The panicle may be open or contracted; it may be spiciform, or spike-like, where most of the branches of the panicle

have been fused to the central axis; it may be a single raceme with spikelets on one side of the axis, on opposite sides or arranged all round the axis as in *Pennisetum alopecuroides*. The terminology employed for these floral structures is sanctioned by long usage but is technically incorrect since it proceeds on the assumption that the spikelet is analogous to a petaloid flower, which it is not.

From a gardener's point of view it is useful to classify the flowers of grasses rather more simply, and for the purposes of this book we shall be using the following seven categories (Fig. 5): open panicle (as in *Panicum virgatum*), closed panicle (as in *Paspalum glacciifolium*), oat-like (as in *Chasmanthium latifolium*), spike (as in *Panicum alopecuroides*), plume (as in *Cortaderia selloana*), whisk (as in *Miscanthus sinensis*), and digitate (as in *Eleusine indica*).

SEED

The biological cycle in grasses is completed when the fertilized flowers turn into fruits and the fruits germinate to begin the next generation. The fruits of grasses are usually called seeds or grains. The seeds are seldom scattered naked and are more usually what are known as false fruits, still with sections of the floret attached to them, which is why grain needs to be winnowed. These sections of the floret are often elaborate and are usually referred to as dispersal mechanisms, but in fact they have more to do with the way in which the seeds come to rest on or in the ground preparatory to germination. The awns are conspicuous in this respect. In some grasses they form a long, feathery, flexible tail attached to the lemmas which clasp the seed. In this case the tail acts as a parachute, ensuring that the seed touches the ground first, and then revolves in the wind or squirms as dry and wet weather alternate, gradually driving the seed into the ground.

VIVIPARY

Grasses may multiply in other ways than by sexual reproduction, one being vivipary. In true vivipary, which is rare, the seeds germinate while still attached to the plant, but the term is more commonly used of plants in which vegetative proliferation occurs in the spikelet. *Deschampsia caespitosa* 'Fairy's Joke' and *Festuca ovina* 'Vivipara' are genetically fixed examples of this, but it may also occur in other grasses when they are put under stress by cold weather in the autumn, by hormone weed-killers or by damage from pests and diseases.

Two examples of warm-season grasses, *Pennisetum alopecuroides* and *Imperata cylindrica* 'Rubra', seen against the light in early autumn.

VEGETATIVE INCREASE

A number of grasses increase vegetatively by stolons or runners, either on their own or in parallel with sexual reproduction. The common reed (*Phragmites australis*) bears purple flowers every autumn, but scarcely ever produces any seed. It spreads instead by rhizomes, and most stands of common reed are composed of but a single plant.

COOL-SEASON/WARM-SEASON GROWERS

The distinction between cool-season growers and warm-season growers is fundamental, and there can be as much as four or even five months' difference in the time that members of the two groups start into growth. The former start into growth in late winter or early spring, flower in spring or early summer, and go into a decline at the onset of high summer temperatures, though a

few may start back into growth in the cool weather of autumn, going dormant for the winter. Cool-season grasses can be planted, transplanted and divided at almost any time except in the heat of summer. Those mentioned in this book include *Arrhenatherum*, *Briza*, *Calamagrostis* × *acutiflora*, *Carex* species, *Deschampsia*, *Festuca*, *Hakonechloa*, *Helictotrichon*, *Holcus*, *Hystrix*, *Melica ciliata*, *Milium effusum*, *Phalaris arundinacea*, *Poa bulbosa*, *Stipa* and *Spodiopogon*, though some place the latter among the warm-season growers because of the lateness of its flowering. Of these, *Arrhenatherum elatius bulbosum* 'Variegatum', *Poa bulbosa*, *Holcus mollis* 'Albovariegatus', *Milium effusum* 'Aureum', *Melica ciliata* and *Hystrix patula* tend to brown out in hot weather, a tendency which can be minimized by growing them in cool woodland or other shady positions.

Warm-season grasses behave in the opposite way, waiting until the warmth of summer before starting into growth, then growing rapidly and vigorously throughout the summer. Most warm-season growers come into flower between mid- and late summer, the flowers turning quickly to seeds which then generally remain showy on the plants for many months. In cool climates it is usually disastrous to transplant or divide these grasses until they have started into vigorous growth. Warm-season grasses discussed in this book include *Schizachyrium scoparius*, *Arundo* species, *Bouteloua gracilis*, *Chasmanthium latifolium*, *Cortaderia* species, *Elymus* species, *Erianthus ravennae*, *Imperata* species, *Miscanthus* species, *Molinia caerulea* and *M. altissima*, *Panicum* species, *Pennisetum* species, *Sorghastrum nutans*, *Spartina pectinata* and *Sporobolus heterolepis*.

BAMBOOS

Bamboos differ from other grasses in their woody culms, their branching habit, their stalked leaves and in peculiarities of their flowering cycles. The culms are not woody like trees but are stiffened with silica, which gives them a flexible strength. Their culms attain their ultimate height and girth in one to three months, after which they branch and put out leaves. Each node produces only one branch, but that one branch may itself branch so close to the main culm that it looks as though several arise at the same point.

Bamboos do not flower annually like ordinary grasses but at intervals of several years. Some species seem almost always to be in flower, but with just an occasional spikelet hidden here and there among the foliage, while others burst into a profusion of flowers, producing spikelets on every twig of every branch of every culm, losing all their leaves at the same time. In some species all the individual plants across the world will flower at the same time, while other instances are known where one plant has flowered and others have not. The phenomenon is not yet well understood.

When heavy flowering has occurred, those culms that have flowered usually die. Removing flowering culms will not prevent flowering. However, in well-established plants the rhizomes usually have sufficient reserves to produce new growth sooner or later.

SEDGES

The sedge family, the *Cyperaceae*, is much smaller than the grass family, with about 115 genera as opposed to over 600 in the grasses. Unlike the true grasses, which occur worldwide, the sedges are confined to the temperate, cool temperate and arctic regions, often growing in areas that are damp or even waterlogged, though a few will tolerate extraordinarily dry conditions. Most are perennials, and many are evergreen.

Sedges differ from grasses in that their stems are solid and triangular in section, whereas those of grasses are round and hollow. Because of this they have ridges running along their length, and if the stem is rolled between finger and thumb these ridges can easily be felt. Moreover their leaf sheaths are closed, completely surrounding the stem, and are relatively difficult to pull away, whereas those of grasses are open and easily separated. The leaves of sedges are usually strongly V-shaped, with a prominent keel along the centre of the underside.

The flowerheads of sedges are also quite different from those of the true grasses. The individual flowers, like those of the grasses, lack showy petals and are arranged in spikelets, but unlike the grasses the spikelets are arranged in heads or spikes and are never paniculate. Their flowers are seldom as showy as those of the grasses, and indeed they are rarely grown for their flowers. Another difference between the two families is that the roots of sedges are always rhizomatous, while those of grasses are always fibrous.

RUSHES

The rushes, the *Juncaceae*, are a relatively small family with about 10 genera and some 325 species of annuals and perennials. All are natives of cool-temperate and sub-arctic regions. Although vaguely grass-like they are really quite distinct in their invariably basal leaves, and in that the leaves may be either flat or cylindrical. The flowers, unlike those of the true grasses, have both petals and sepals (though the two are virtually indistinguishable), and these are arranged in two distinct whorls. The individual flowers are presented in cymes, usually at the tip of the flowering stem though often appearing to be about two-thirds of the way up, due to a stem-like bract that continues the line of the stem well above the flower.

CAT-TAILS

The cat-tails, the *Typhaceae*, constitute the smallest of the grassy families with but a single genus and no more than about ten species. All are perennials with strap-like leaves in two ranks, and a strongly spreading rhizomatous root system. They are not likely to be mistaken for any other type of grassy plant on account of their unique flowers. These are borne at the tops of strong, cylindrical stems and are composed of a relatively short-lived, somewhat fluffy male inflorescence above a thickened, typically dark brown, female inflorescence which completely surrounds the stem.

Calamagrostis × *acutiflora* 'Karl Foerster' is one of the key grasses in any major grass planting.

Part Two Coloured-leaf Grasses

3 Essential Coloured-leaf Grasses

Most of the plants we grow in our gardens have relatively large, colourful flowers. Grasses by contrast have individually rather small flowers which can scarcely stand direct comparison, but their foliage, when it is coloured, is often at least as bright as the petals of garden flowers and just as attractive. It is for this reason that the first grasses many people use in their gardens are those with coloured leaves, an appreciation of the subtler charms of grasses grown for their flowers coming later. It seems reasonable therefore to look first at grasses with coloured leaves. Here they are taken colour by colour, starting with the smallest and progressing to the larger.

The basic palette is made up of those coloured-leaf grasses which are readily available from nurseries and garden centres and can be relied upon to fill a design and to perform well in the garden year after year, needing no special cultivation. Other, perhaps less reliable, coloured grasses are discussed on pp31–7.

WHITE-VARIEGATED GRASSES

White is the most luminous of colours, and it is therefore the colour to which the eye goes first. It can be used to enliven a medley of mixed colours or more deliberately to draw the eye to a particular part of a garden or, by repetition, to establish the rhythm of a garden or part of a garden. However, white is essentially a foreground colour, since in the foreground the eye can choose to look beyond it. In the distance it will draw the eye with inescapable force and, being an advancing colour, will tend to leap forward out of its context.

Most of the whites mentioned here are good, clean whites, though there is sometimes some creaminess in their colouring when the leaves first appear. The true creams, which follow, retain their creaminess right through the summer. White grasses are best planted so that they can be seen against the sun or sidelit against a dark background.

Holcus

The smallest of the essential white-variegated grasses is *Holcus mollis* 'Albovariegatus' (striped creeping soft grass), a diminutive grass growing to no more than 15cm (6in)

tall with an essentially sprawling habit. It forms tufts of no more than 23–30cm (9–12in) across, spreading slowly by throwing out runners or stolons that may be above ground or just beneath the surface of the soil. These are no menace and can easily be pulled out if the plant is exceeding its allotted space. The leaves, which are always short and close together on the culms, are no more than 20cm (8in) long, deep green at the centre and broadly margined clean, bright white. The flowers, which are borne from early to late summer, are greenish-white with a mauvish cast to them and are of little or no decorative value. It is a grass of cool, dampish places, never happy where it is hot and sunny.

Striped creeping soft grass is versatile in the garden, being at home in a shaded rock garden or used as an edging. It can even be mown provided it is growing vigorously. At York Gate, near Leeds in Yorkshire, it flourishes in the cracks between stone paving slabs. It is a typical cool-season grass in that it always looks best early and late in the season, and is inclined to look its least good in the heat of summer, even if planted in the shade.

However, there seem to be two different plants in cultivation as striped creeping soft grass. One is plainly a striped form of creeping soft grass (*Holcus mollis*), having all the characteristics of that species – the creeping rhizomes, the distinct ring of tufted hairs above each node, the habit of forming ever-increasing mats and of growing in light shade. The other has wider leaves and much wider green and white stripes and, though rhizomatous, is much less invasive. It is, moreover, happier in a sunny position. It is thus plainly not *H. mollis*, but nor is it the related species *H. lanatus*, which has more erect stems and is softly hairy all over. Possibly it is a hybrid between the two. Since it needs a varietal name to distinguish it from *H. mollis* 'Albovariegatus' I propose calling it *H.* 'Alan Cook', since it was Alan Cook, formerly in charge of the grasses beds at the Royal Botanic Gardens, Kew, who first determined the differences between these two varieties.

Arrhenatherum

Somewhat larger is *Arrhenatherum elatius bulbosum* 'Variegatum' (striped bulbous oat grass), a clumper growing to

PLATE I

Miscanthus sinensis
variegated varieties

'Dixieland'

'Morning Light'

'Variegatus'

'Cosmopolitan'

'Rigoletto'

All plants shown
approximately ½ size

'Cabaret'

about 30cm (12in) in leaf and about twice as tall in flower. It is quite the brightest of the white-variegated grasses, the rather soft, upright leaves being striped and conspicuously margined clean, pure white. It is called bulbous oat grass because the nodes and stem bases swell into bulb-like structures which, when the plant dies down in the autumn, fall to the ground and grow into new plants. This is very definitely a cool-season grass, with a tendency to fade away during the hottest days of summer. In cool climates it will grow in sun or shade, but in warm climates it should always be planted in shade. It grows best in moist soils on the acid side of neutral, and tends to languish on heavy clays.

Pennisetum

The pennisetums or fountain grasses are generally strong-growing clumpers but *Pennisetum alopecuroides* 'Little Honey' is a diminutive white-variegated sport of *P. a.* 'Little Bunny', the smallest of the current selections of *P. alopecuroides*. 'Little Honey', which at the time of writing is so new it is still under lock and key in the secure areas of the few nurseries that have it, grows into a clump about 20cm (8in) high and 41cm (16in) across, with the small, late flowers reaching about 30cm (12in) in height. Its leaves are narrow and thinly white-margined, sometimes only on one margin, so it is not as bright as either *Arrhenatherum elatius bulbosum* 'Variegatum' or *Phalaris arundinacea* 'Picta'.

Phalaris

Phalaris arundinacea 'Picta' (striped ribbon grass), which used to be known as gardener's garters in the days when gardeners tied their trouser legs up with string just below the knees, is usually the first grass gardeners are given by well-meaning friends and also usually the first they throw away, though many return to it because, in one or other of its forms, it can be relied upon to contribute good, clean white leaves over a long period year after year. The leaf mound grows to 60–100cm (2–3ft) tall, the leaves being 20–30cm (9–12in) long and up to 1cm (½in) wide, striped green and white, the white usually predominating and distributed unevenly across the leaf. The flowers are small whitish panicles, of little interest. *P. a.* 'Feesey' is vastly superior, the leaves being far whiter, tinted pink when first unfurling and somewhat less vigorous. *P. a.* 'Strawberries 'n' Cream' is even pinker, and even dwarfer. *P. a.* 'Streamlined' is taller-growing, with basically green leaves striped white. These are warm-season

grasses with a vigorous running habit which is however easily controlled. They are best planted in sun, and since the foliage tends to become drab during the summer the clumps should be cut to the ground once or twice in a season to encourage the production of pristine new leaves that are as bright as the spring foliage.

Calamagrostis

Calamagrostis × *acutiflora* 'Overdam' (striped feather reed grass) is a superb garden and landscape plant, making densely leafy upright and slightly arching clumps of strongly white-variegated foliage, the new leaves usually tinged with pink. It is a cool-season clumper, growing 60–90cm (2–3ft) tall, the narrow, purple-tinged flower plumes overtopping that. The clump tends to increase in girth quite rapidly. Like ribbon grass, the foliage becomes less showy as the season advances, and is best cut to the ground to produce a new flush once or twice during the season.

Miscanthus

The variegated miscanthus which make up the *Miscanthus sinensis* Variegated Group form superb mounds of brightly

Calamagrostis × *acutiflora* 'Overdam', after its first flush of pink, turns brightly white-striped for the rest of the summer.

white-variegated foliage that moves and rustles alluringly in the wind, and are ideal for use as specimens or to draw the eye. Like all *Miscanthus sinensis* forms they make dense tussocks. *M. s.* 'Variegatus' makes a rounded mound some 1.2–1.5m (4–5ft) tall, the foliage arching over so that the tips touch or almost touch the ground. *M. s.* 'Silberpfeil' ('Silver Arrow') is often sold in Europe as *M. s.* 'Variegatus' but is quite distinct in its upright habit, in its greater height, reaching 1.8–2.1m (6–7ft) tall, and in carrying most of its foliage at the tops of the culms, leaving the bare stems visible. The leaves, which are 1.5cm (⅝in) wide and 60–75cm (2–2½ft) long, are light green, striped creamy-white and sometimes edged with the thinnest of deep red lines. Even more striking and even larger, and probably the finest plant in the group, is *M. s.* 'Cosmopolitan', whose leaf mound can reach 2.4m (8ft) even in the relatively cool climate of the UK. The leaves are remarkably wide, as much as 5cm (2in), margined and striped a slightly creamy white. *M. s.* 'Cabaret' has similarly broad leaves and grows almost as tall, but has the reverse variegation, the centre of the leaf being white. Recently two superb dwarf forms have been introduced, 'Rigoletto' and 'Dixieland'. Both are in effect dwarf forms of *M. s.* 'Variegatus', 'Rigoletto' growing to about 90cm (3ft), 'Dixieland' to about 1.2m (4ft).

Quite different from these is *M. s.* 'Morning Light', which has quite extraordinarily narrow leaves, often no more than 4mm (⅛in) across, margined with white. The marginal variegation can really only be seen at close quarters, but the overall effect of the plant, which grows into a dense, rounded, mushroom-like mound 1.5m (5ft) high, is of greyness. It has been grown as a bonsai companion plant for centuries by the Japanese but has only recently reached the West. Like *M. s.* 'Gracillimus', of which it is a variegated form, it seldom flowers in the UK, though it does so quite freely in warmer climates.

Cortaderia

The biggest of the hardy white-variegated grasses are the variegated pampas grasses, *Cortaderia selloana* Albolineate Group, the largest of which eventually make clumps some 2.4–2.7m (8–9ft) tall and at least as much across. Several white-variegated pampas grasses have been in cultivation over the years, differing only in detail. All make arching mounds of seemingly basal leaves which are strongly white-margined and variegated, above which rise showy white plumes on usually strong, straight stems. *C. s.* 'Silver Fountain' differs from *C. s.* 'Silver Beacon' in having green

Miscanthus sinensis 'Cabaret' is one of the most striking of the striped miscanthus because the variegation is central rather than marginal and the leaves are extraordinarily wide.

flowering culms, those of *C. s.* 'Silver Beacon' being purple; both will produce leaf mounds some 2.4m (8ft) tall. *C. s.* 'Albolineata' ('Silver Stripe') is relatively dwarf, growing only 1.2m (4ft) in leaf. They are at their loveliest when the sun shines through them from the side or from behind, with a dark background of pines or laurels to emphasize their brightness. All are warm-season clumpers, and in the UK they are certainly much less frost hardy than the green-leaved forms.

CREAM-VARIEGATED GRASSES

The creams have much the same function in the garden as the whites but, being as it were adulterated whites, draw the eye less strongly. They have a warmth which the whites, being cold and passionless, lack. They can be used with the sun either falling on them or behind them.

Molinia

The smallest of the cream-variegated grasses belong to *Molinia caerulea* Variegated Group (striped purple moor grass). These cool-season clumpers are usually the last grasses to emerge in the spring and typically form dense mounds of narrow, rather limp, upright to arching cream-striped leaves 23–30cm (9–12in) tall. The flowers, which do not appear until mid or late summer, have conspicuous purple stigmas and are borne high above the foliage on stems which are variegated exactly like the leaves, which adds to their charm. *M. c.* ssp. *caerulea* 'Variegata', which is the form in general cultivation, has narrow but open panicles while *M. c.* 'Claerwen' is quite distinct in its much darker, dense, narrow panicles. These are perhaps showier but less attractive. *M. c.* 'Carmarthen' is slightly taller than either, with slightly longer, narrower leaves with a paler variegation, and the most slender and elegant of flower spikes produced on green rather than variegated stems. All turn a delectable butter-yellow as they go into winter. Natives of acid bogs, they seem to flourish on most soils as long as they are not dry.

Glyceria

Far larger than *Molinia* is *Glyceria maxima* var. *variegata* (striped mana grass). This cool-season grower is one of the most beautifully variegated of all grasses, both in detail and from a distance. The broad, blunt-tipped leaves, which

The leaves of *Glyceria maxima* var. *variegata* are pale yellow at first, tinged with pink, but become a clean white later in the summer.

can be as much as 60cm (2ft) long and some 5cm (2in) across, are strongly flushed purplish pink as they start to emerge in the spring, the colouring intensifying at the base of the leaves to almost purple before it fades. The soft leaves are upright and arching, pale or creamy yellow with thin green stripes, and the flowers, which are borne in mid and late summer, are open, much-branched, creamy-white panicles. The leaf mound grows to 60cm (2ft) with a vigorously spreading root system. Although it is a native of wet and boggy habitats and ideal at the water's edge where it attains its greatest vigour, it grows well in ordinary soils and remains quite compact. It makes a lovely companion for astilbes, candelabra primulas and waterside ferns.

YELLOW-VARIEGATED GRASSES

Yellow is the colour of spring and of the sun, and its presence in a garden seems always to gladden the heart. Though less luminous than white or cream, it is the colour to which the eye goes next, and it can be used in much the same ways. It does, however, differ from whites and creams in that while they vary but little, yellow varies over quite a wide range; it can be as soft as sulphur or as sharp as cadmium, and it can lean towards the strident tones of orange or the self-effacing tones of green. Because of this it is possible to compose garden vignettes using the differing tints and tones of yellow. It can also be used in a medley of strong colours, blues and browns, to create a focal point in a garden, with mauves or violets, with which it seems to balance, or more subtly to blend with first pale and then deeper greens. Most yellow or yellow-variegated grasses can be grown in sun or shade – though a few, for example *Milium effusum* 'Aureum' (Bowles' golden grass) do need shade – and are best positioned so that the light falls on them, though some look good when side-lit with a dark background beyond. Most yellow-foliaged plants other than grasses tend to scorch in full sun so it is often useful to be able to employ them as a background in shade with the grasses at the front of the planting in a sunnier position.

Alopecurus

The smallest of the yellow-variegated grasses is *Alopecurus pratensis* 'Aureovariegatus' (golden fox-tail grass). In spring this Eurasian grass is the brightest yellow of all grasses, though overtaken later in the season by *Hakonechloa macra* 'Alboaurea' (golden Hakone grass). The leaves are typically 10–15cm (4–6in) long, broadly margined and striped

run. *A. p.* 'Aureus' is similar but has leaves that are solid yellow without any green stripes. Both are cool-season grasses that grow best in sun in cool climates and in light shade in warm climates.

Festuca

Festuca glauca 'Golden Toupee' (golden toupee fescue) has a completely different habit to *Alopecurus* and indeed is a completely different colour, forming tight cushions some 23cm (9in) across of soft, needle-like leaves that are almost iridescent yellow in spring, later fading to the yellow side of lime green. The flowers and flower stems, which can appear from late spring until midsummer, are the same colour as the leaves, though turning beige or brown after flowering. This cool-season grass needs to be grown in full sun and in well-drained stony or sandy soils as it will not withstand winter wet on badly drained soils.

Milium

Milium effusum 'Aureum' (Bowles' golden grass) is one of the gems of spring and early summer. It is a loosely growing tufted perennial with soft, limp leaves and slender, open panicles, the leaf mound growing to some 23–30cm (9–12in). The whole plant – leaves, stems and flowers – is yellow, but in spring it is the brightest gamboge yellow, brassier in sun, a quieter greenish-yellow in shade. It is a typical cool-season grass, starting into growth in the autumn and fading away in the heat of summer. It grows best and lasts longest in shade, and will seed itself gently.

Hakonechloa

The most enchanting golden grass ever introduced is *Hakonechloa macra* 'Alboaurea' (golden Hakone grass), which gradually forms low mounds of densely overlapping leaves, each of which is about 15cm (6in) long and up to 1cm (½in) wide, a deep, rich yellow with thin stripes of green and occasional splashes of white, borne on wiry red stems. The tiny flowers are produced in early autumn in a limp, open panicle that tends to rest itself on top of the leaf mound, and at about the time the flowers appear the leaves start assuming their autumn colours, becoming first tinged with pink and then with vinous reddish-purple. The whole plant turns sere brown in winter, but the spring buds are again dark reddish-purple. The leaf mound grows 15–23cm (6–9in) tall and although slow to start will eventually makes clumps 90cm (3ft) or more across. *H. m.* 'Aureola' is similar and

Alopecurus pratensis 'Aureovariegatus' is one of the brightest yellow grasses in the spring, though it is less conspicuous later.

deep yellow, and the flowers, which are borne on slender stems, are reddish-brown cylindrical foxtails rising a little above the foliage in mid and late spring. Though it is the easiest of grasses to grow it does vary considerably in growth on differing soils; on poor soils it will make a diminutive plant no more than 5–7.5cm (2–3in) tall with leaves no more than 7.5cm (3in) long and a running habit, while on rich, loamy soils the leaves can reach 30cm (12in) but the plant then tends to form clumps rather than running. Where it adopts this clumping habit, which is most often on heavy clay soils, the clumps need to be lifted and divided every 2–3 years to maintain vigour, though on poor soils it can be left to

Miscanthus sinensis 'Zebrinus' is a vigorous plant with clearly defined leaf markings and good flowers in the autumn.

perhaps a little brighter but lacks the white splashes. The nursery trade in the UK has the two plants completely muddled. *Hakonechloa* is a warm-season grass.

Miscanthus

There is only one yellow-variegated miscanthus, and that is *Miscanthus sinensis* 'Goldfeder'. It makes an upright or upright arching clump to about 1.8m (6ft) tall, with arching leaves 75–90cm (2½–3ft) long, broadly edged and striped, a rich, slightly greenish yellow topped by rather thin, pale flowers late in the season. It is well worth growing for its colour, but as with 'Silberfeder', of which it is a sport, the culms are weak and inclined to flop, a habit which can be concealed by other plants. It is a warm-season grower.

The zebra grasses (*Miscanthus sinensis* Zebrinus Group), are so called because their variegation or banding runs transversely across the leaf rather than along it as is usual in monocots. While the leaves are interesting in themselves, a whole clump looks as though it is spotted with the lighter colour. The original zebra grass, *M. s.* 'Zebrinus', makes loose arching clumps up to 2.4m (8ft)

tall and given time will spread into large clumps or drifts several metres (yards) across. The leaves, which can be 2.5cm (1in) or so across and 75–90cm (2½–3ft) long, can develop five or six transverse bands each. The development of the banding in this and the following varieties is dependent on temperature, so it is often not present on the first leaves of spring, only becoming apparent in the heat of the summer, some varieties needing more heat to develop their stripes than others. The down side of this is that in hot summers and indeed in hot places the bands will scorch, this showing as dry brown patches on the margins or sometimes as reddish markings across the middle of the bands. It does not detract from their overall garden effectiveness, except in very warm areas such as the extreme south of the USA where the damage may be detrimental.

There are however a number of variations or even improvements on *M. s.* 'Zebrinus'. *M. s.* 'Strictus' is densely clumping rather than slowly running, a plant measuring no more than 75cm (2½ft) across at ground level after eight or ten years, the culms being so close together at ground level that you could not slip a plastic card between them. It grows to about 1.8m (6ft). Rather dwarfer are *M. s.* 'Püncktchen' and *M. s.* 'Kirk Alexander', both of which grow to about 1.5m (5ft). 'Püncktchen' is again very densely clump-forming but is slow to put on its bands, which are rather sparse even when present. It produces beautiful pinky-coppery plumes with great freedom after a long hot summer. In the USA 'Kirk Alexander' is said to have exceptionally well-marked leaves, though it also is slow to put on its bands, and to produce quite the best plumes of all the banded varieties. In the UK it is a disappointment, putting on few bands and seldom flowering. Quite the best of the dwarf varieties in British gardens is *M. s.* 'Tiger Cub', a dwarf growing to no more than 1m (3¼ft). It is the first of the varieties to show its bands, these being cream rather than buff, very freely produced on narrow, deep green leaves. It is also good in flower. *M. s.* 'Hinjo' differs in having broader, paler leaves and broader stripes, which appear a little later. It is also good in flower. *M. s.* 'Coon Tail' is the dwarfest of the group, reaching a mere 75cm (2½ft), and is the most profusely marked of the banded varieties. Sadly it is so slow-growing that it is likely to remain a collector's item.

Cortaderia

There are two gold-variegated pampas grasses. One is *Cortaderia selloana* 'Gold Band', which is a much better

Miscanthus sinensis 'Hinjo' is a relatively new dwarf zebra grass which seldom exceeds 1.2m (4ft) in flower.

garden plant than the white-variegated pampas grasses, the dark green, richly yellow-edged leaves being bright enough to give the whole plant an air of being golden. *C. s.* 'Sunstripe', a patented plant from Monrovia Nursery, differs in having a soft gold stripe down the centre of the leaf. Both form large, dense tufts of arching foliage and can reach 2.4m (8ft) tall. These warm-season growers seem reasonably frost hardy.

BLUE GRASSES

The colour of blue grasses has evolved not only to protect the leaves against damage by strong sunlight but also to reduce water loss by transpiration, such grasses being natives mainly of poor, dry soils. In the garden they should be given sharp drainage and a position in the sun, and they should never be fed, as this will make them grow out of character and may even kill them. In winter many lose their blueness, becoming drab green, this shift in colour enabling them to make the most of what little sunlight there is at that season. The blue of blue grasses is singularly pure, lacking any hint of redness. As such the blueness is cold, a coldness that can be intensified by

using it with whites, or warmed by using it with yellows, browns or reds. In the garden it can of course be used in medleys but is perhaps more effective used in drifts, among smaller quantities of other coloured-leaf plants or flowers, or as one element in the modern equivalent of a knot garden. Blue grasses should be planted where the sun falls on them, not behind them.

Festuca

The most popular of the blue grasses are the little blue fescues, of which there are several. Reputedly the bluest of all is *Festuca glauca* 'Elijah Blue'. This is a cool-season, evergreen clumper with soft needle-like leaves that are an intense silvery-blue in summer, greener in winter. It makes a rounded cushion some 30cm (12in) tall and twice as much across. There is also a smaller plant in circulation under this name, but the larger plant is the correct one. In late spring and early summer it produces slender panicles, the stems and flowers being exactly the same colour as the leaves, though both become biscuit brown as the flowers turn to seeds. Some people like the contrast in colours, though others dislike it and clip the clumps over with shears to remove them. The problem can be avoided by growing *F. ovina* ssp. *coxii*, which is broadly similar but seldom flowers. When young these fescues form dense, low, cushion-shaped tufts 15–23cm (6–9in) tall and much the same across, but as the years go by they increase in girth with the result that the centre dies, leaving a blue ring of fescue which continues to grow outwards, ultimately breaking up into tufts, each one just like the original plant. To avoid this it is usual to lift and split the plants every two or three years, a procedure which also helps to keep the colouring intense, since the best colour is to be found on young, vigorous plants. *Festuca glauca* and its forms should be grown fully exposed to the sun, in well-drained soils: they will tend to die of winter wet if the drainage is poor.

There are several similar species and varieties differing mainly in intensity of colouring, though *F. g. minima* is notable in growing to no more than 10cm (4in). *F. g.* 'Caesia' is similar to 'Elijah Blue', growing to 30cm (12in), but has narrower leaves; *F. g.* 'Azurit' is also 30cm (12in) tall, bluer and less silvery; *F. g.* 'Harz' is a darker, duller blue but useful as a contrast; *F. g.* 'Meerblau' is a strong grower with blue-green leaves. *F. dalmatica* and *F. valesiaca* 'Silbersee' ('Silver Sea' or 'Seven Seas') are similar. On soils that suit them, all these varieties are lovely with spring bulbs.

Elymus

Elymus hispidus (blue wheatgrass) is far more relaxed in its habit than *Festuca*. It is the most intensely blue of all grasses, indeed one of the bluest of all garden plants. It is a loosely tufted evergreen perennial to about 60cm (2ft), the narrow blue leaves, which are deeply ridged beneath, held erect at first but becoming more spreading later in the season. The panicle is a dense, narrow, wheat-like spike, the same intense silvery-blue as the leaves at first but quickly fading through pale straw yellow to beige. Several forms seem to be in cultivation, some larger, some smaller, but they are not distinguished by name. Quite distinct is *E. magellanicus* which, while having leaves of a similar colour, has a lax, spreading habit, and though perennial in its native habitat, the cold southern tip of South America, cannot be considered soundly perennial in the UK, often behaving as an annual or biennial. Both are cool-season growers, and will grow in most soils though they are not happy on heavy clays. They should be planted in sun.

Helictotrichon

Helictotrichon sempervirens (blue oat grass) is less intensely blue than the two *Elymus* species mentioned above, but it makes a more shapely plant, the narrow, tapering

Elymus hispidus is the most intensely blue of all hardy grasses. It needs full sun and good drainage to flourish.

grey-blue leaves radiating outwards from the centre. Some forms have narrower leaves, some wider. It is an evergreen, clumping cool-season perennial that is easily raised from seed and grows to about 60cm (2ft) in leaf but about 1m (3¼ft) when in flower. The oat-like flowers are borne in early and midsummer in an open, one-sided panicle, grey-blue at first then quickly becoming a pale straw colour and gradually bleaching to almost white. The stems and chaffy, empty seed cases remain attractive until late summer. It is a cool-season plant and will not flower reliably in warm climates. The variety *H. s. pendulum* has arching flower stems and is not so showy; *H. s.* 'Saphirsprudel' has leaves of a stronger blue. These grasses need a sunny position in well-drained soil and suffer the peculiarity that ants like to make their nests right in the middle. Proprietary ant remedies are usually effective.

Panicum

The switch grasses (*Panicum virgatum*) are natives of the tallgrass prairies that once covered endless acres of the American interior. Not surprisingly some variation occurs and switch grass can vary from green-leaved to quite grey or blue. Wild forms, whether green or grey, often have floppy stems but cultivated forms usually remain erect. The switch grasses are warm-season growers that form upright clumps varying in height from 90cm to 2.1m (3–7ft), overtopped by huge open panicles of tiny purplish spikelets that create a haze of colour above the foliage. *P. v.* 'Heavy Metal' was the first of the blue forms to be selected and named, and there is considerable variation in height and in the intensity of the blueness within the Heavy Metal group. 'Heavy Metal' itself forms tight, upright, rather stiff clumps reaching about 90cm (3ft) tall, the leaves and culms being soft blue-grey under pale British skies but a richer blue in warmer climes, turning purple in the hottest parts of the USA. The foliage turns butter yellow in the autumn. *P. v.* 'Pathfinder' is similar, but has a more relaxed habit and looser panicles; *P. v.* 'Cloud Nine' and 'Blue Tower' are relative giants and both much more definitely blue. 'Cloud Nine' grows to 1.8m (6ft) with broad, arching leaves making a rounded mound of steely blue foliage, while 'Blue Tower', which is even bluer and more upright in habit, will reach 2.4–2.7m (8–9ft) in warm American gardens. Bluest of all is *P. v.* 'Prairie Sky', almost as intensely blue as *Leymus arenarius* (blue lyme grass). It grows to about 90cm (3ft) tall and makes a rounded mound of foliage. *P. v.* 'Shenandoah' is also a good blue but is mostly remarkable for the tones of violet and purple the whole plant assumes in the autumn. It reaches a height and spread of 90cm (3ft). *Panicum virgatum* and its forms will tolerate most soils, but they do prefer a moist and fertile one. These blue forms are rather fussier as to their growing conditions than the green-leaved forms, needing full sun and perfect drainage; if the drainage is not good enough they develop what is known as yellow tip death, the tips of the leaves turning yellow and then decaying.

Leymus

Leymus arenarius (blue lyme grass) was Gertrude Jekyll's favourite grass. She must have had more energy or more gardeners than we do today, for it runs in all directions and takes real work to control. The reward is that it is almost as blue as *Elymus hispidus* (blue wheatgrass), but much bigger. It is a loosely tufted grass growing to 1m (3¼ft) in leaf with a vigorously running root system: in the wild it binds sand dunes. The flowers are borne from early summer until early autumn in a long, dense, wheat-like spike 30cm (12in) or more above the leaf mound. They and their stems start as blue as the leaves but quickly fade to a pale shade of ripe wheat. In cold climates the whole plant turns yellow as winter approaches but in warmer areas it is virtually evergreen. It is a warm-season grower and should always be planted in sun. It tolerates most soils, but is slow to increase in heavy clays. Like the majority of blue grasses it looks remarkably well in terracotta pots, or against terracotta bricks or paving, and is lovely as an underplanting to pale pink roses. If it is cut down just as the flowering stems emerge a flush of fresh blue foliage will be produced. *L. racemosus* is similar but marginally smaller and less spreading, as is *L. secalinus*. *L. elongatus* is altogether more manageable but has narrower leaves and panicles and is tightly clump-forming.

Arundo

The largest of the blue grasses, and indeed the largest of the hardy grasses, is *Arundo donax* (Provençal reed), which can grow as much as 4.5m (15ft) tall with culms over 2.5cm (1in) across and leaves as much as 10 cm (4in) wide and 60cm (2ft) long, the whole plant being greyish-blue-green. It attains its fullest development in a sunny position in warm, sheltered gardens on rich, moist soils. A warm-season grower from southern Europe, it tends to be a clumper in cool gardens though it will spread persistently in warm gardens. It is a most architectural plant, the leaves being produced at right angles to the culms in opposite pairs and evenly spaced about 15cm (6in) apart up the culms, which are stiffly vertical in the spring and early summer, though inclined to splay outwards later in the year. It can be used as a stunning specimen, or simply as a hedge or background, or to create a subtropical ambience in association with *Miscanthus sacchariflorus*, for example. At the end of the season the culms start to branch and the leaves develop split ends and start to look untidy, so the usual practice is to cut the culms to the ground every winter, though if flowers are wanted the culms should be left for a second year. The flowers are as spectacular as the plant, being huge fluffy panicles as much as 60cm (2ft) long and 25cm (10in) across. Sadly they are seldom produced in cold climates.

RED GRASSES

There is only one grass with truly red leaves, other so-called red grasses being sedges or hook sedges with foxy-red foliage. These are discussed under Brown Sedges (see page 43).

Imperata

The most brilliantly coloured of all grasses is *Imperata cylindrica* 'Rubra' (Japanese blood grass). The leaves, which begin to emerge in early spring, are held erect and are at first a yellowish-green with the tip just touched with red, but as the season advances the blood drains downwards, staining the whole leaf blood red, the colour attaining its greatest intensity in midsummer to early autumn. The most remarkable effects are achieved when it is planted so that the sun shines through it from behind and the leaves glow with borrowed effulgence like a glass of red wine held to the light. It grows 30–45cm (12–15in) tall, spreading all too slowly from shallow rhizomes, and it rarely flowers. It is a warm-season grower that needs to be planted in sun and tolerates most soils: it will even endure droughts but the tips of the leaves may scorch. There is no record of it ever flowering in Europe or North America, but it very occasionally reverts to the more vigorous green-leaved form which may flower, especially in the continental climates of Europe and North America. There is a form of the green-leaved plant with a white-striped variegation (see page 32). It originated in Japan.

4 Lesser Coloured-leaf Grasses

The coloured and variegated grasses discussed in the previous pages are not only first-rate in their own right but also reliable in their performance. They are the plants around which one builds a scheme or design, but to fill out that design one may need a supporting cast of lesser grasses. The grasses discussed below are not quite in the first rank because they are not so showy, or not so dependable, or need special care and attention, or because their use in gardens is confined to a particular soil or situation. No doubt some of them would be considered, on their performance in some gardens, good enough to join the main players. So be it.

WHITE-VARIEGATED GRASSES

The whites listed here are in no way inferior in their whiteness to those listed as essential coloured grasses, but they are on the whole less often encountered and more demanding in their cultural requirements.

Phragmites

Phragmites are not often grown in gardens because of their need for wet ground and their reputation for running at the root. However, the two mentioned here will grow in ordinary garden soil and when they are so grown are not unduly invasive. *Phragmites karka* 'Variegatus' is the most brightly white-variegated of these lesser grasses, the tapering leaves being margined and striped white. It is a slender-stemmed, refined plant growing to about 2.1m (7ft), the culms being freely branched, especially on the lower half of the culm, thus presenting a clump of dense and leafy appearance. *P. australis* 'Candy Stripe' is a selection of *P. australis* remarkable for its minty green, white-striped foliage and for its culms, which are brightly striped with white and peppermint pink. It reaches the same height as *P. karka* 'Variegatus' and in late summer both carry loose, one-sided plumes of dusky purple high above the foliage. Both are best contained, only to be let loose in the very largest of gardens. They do best in wet, rich soil in sun.

Leymus racemosus is neither so intensely blue nor so vigorously running as *L. arenarius*, but is nevertheless probably the better garden plant.

Dactylis

Dactylis glomeratus 'Variegatus' (striped cock's foot grass) forms dense tussocks 30cm (12in) or so high and at its best is brilliantly white variegated. Its problem in life is that the clump tends to become clogged with its own dead leaves, and so declines and disappears. To keep it vigorous it needs regular grooming, spring and autumn. The flowers are carried in a dense, one-sided panicle, and have little decorative charm.

Melica

Melica uniflora 'Variegata' (striped wood melic) is not showy like the phragmites but rather is treasured for the subtlety of its colouring and the fact that it flourishes in shaded and woodland gardens, its quiet colouring being appropriate to the quieter mood of such places. It forms loose tufts to about 15cm (6in) high of seemingly basal, thin-textured leaves which are delicately white-margined and striped. The tiny, dark spikelets are borne on thread-like stems in an open panicle in late spring and early summer, but are no more showy than the leaves. This cool-season grass is slow to increase and is usually best planted in drifts of several to many.

Muhlenbergia

The muhly grasses are little-known in the UK but *Muhlenbergia japonica* 'Variegata' (striped Japanese muhly grass) is particularly useful as a groundcover plant on account of its prostrate habit. The culms are erect to start with, reaching no more than 15–20cm (6–8in), but later become trailing, extending to 60cm (2ft) or more in a season, sometimes rooting at the nodes. The leaves are narrow and tapering, seldom more than 7.5cm (3in) long, margined white with thin, pencil-like stripes down the centre of the blade. The culms terminate in small panicles of whitish flowers with a purplish cast which are in keeping with the colour and tone of the plant, but not showy. This warm-season grower needs good soil in sun or semi-shade.

Panicum

The strangest, and perhaps also the whitest, of these less essential grasses is *Panicum virgatum* 'Forest Snow', whose leaves and culms emerge white and gradually become suffused with green, turning ever greener as the temperature rises, each new leaf emerging white against the prevailing greens so that a mature clump appears to be white on the outside, where the new culms arise, and green in the centre. It reaches a height of 1.2m (4ft).

Imperata

A white-variegated *Imperata cylindrica* was found recently in Japan by Dr Yukoi, a well-known collector of variegated plants. It grows taller than the red form, to about 70cm (2⅛ft) in leaf. The tips of the new leaves in spring are flushed white, and as this fades to green the thin white stripes on the leaves become more apparent. This plant is as yet unnamed.

Spartina

Even newer than the former plant and if anything more startling is a form of *Spartina pectinata* whose new leaves emerge bright white, later turning green. It is, not surprisingly, named 'Spring Snow'. In the USA the leaves stay white until the temperature reaches 24°C (75°F), usually in late spring. In the cooler climate of the UK they may be white until well into summer. The whole plant forms a mound of arching, ribbon-like leaves about 1.5m (5ft) high. It grows best in moist soil, and runs slowly at the root.

Hakonechloa

Hakonechloa macra 'Alboaurea' (golden Hakone grass) is so bright, so good and so well known that less familiar varieties such as *H. m.* 'Albostriata' (white-striped Hakone grass) tend to be overlooked. This variety is broadly similar to 'Alboaurea', forming rounded mounds of densely overlapping leaves, but differs in its greater vigour, the leaf mound growing 30–38cm (12–15in) tall, in the greater amount of green striping on the leaves and in the colour of the variegation. This is certainly not a bright white variegation: the striping in the spring is definitely yellowish-cream and it is not until about late summer that it has faded sufficiently to be called white. This paler variegation makes a pleasant change from the more familiar form.

CREAM-VARIEGATED GRASSES

The cream-variegated grasses differ from the white-variegated grasses in retaining their creamy colouring throughout the season, whereas many white-variegated grasses, though creamy-coloured at first, later turn a pristine white.

Hakonechloa

Hakonechloa macra 'Mediovariegata' is not nearly so brightly coloured as the better known *H. m.* 'Alboaurea' but it is considerably more vigorous, growing to a height of 38–45cm (15–18in), with relatively larger leaves and panicles. The leaves are narrowly margined pale yellow, one margin usually being a little wider than the other but never wide, and striped with two or three thin pale yellow pencil lines down the centre of the leaf. This variety is well worth growing and is an excellent foil to brighter grasses.

Miscanthus

Most of the variegated miscanthus are very showy, but *Miscanthus tinctoria* 'Nanus Variegatus' (dwarf striped miscanthus) is only quietly variegated. It is the smallest of the miscanthus grasses, growing to no more than 30cm (12in) in leaf, the small, elegant, copper-coloured plumes being produced in late summer and early autumn on culms no more than 18in (45cm) tall. The short, tapering leaves are asymmetrically striped creamy-yellow, the amount of variegation differing from leaf to leaf. This warm-season grower is one of the best miscanthus for small spaces or for using in drifts in larger areas. It has a shallow, slowly spreading rootstock but is never a problem to control. The leaves turn a bright but ochrous yellow in autumn.

YELLOW-VARIEGATED GRASSES

The yellow-variegated grasses discussed below are a mixed bag as regards brightness of colouring and cultural requirements, but they contribute greatly to the variation of texture among the yellows.

Deschampsia

Deschampsia flexuosa (fairy grass) varieties are usually noted for their dark green leaves, but in *D. f.* 'Tatra Gold' (golden fairy grass) the leaves are a singularly vibrant acid yellow through the whole season, disappearing in winter. This plant forms dense tufts some 15cm (6in) tall and about the same across, the abundant open, airy panicles being produced in mid to late summer on 30cm (12in) stems. It is a cool-season grower best in humus-rich acid soils and definitely unhappy on chalk, although it will

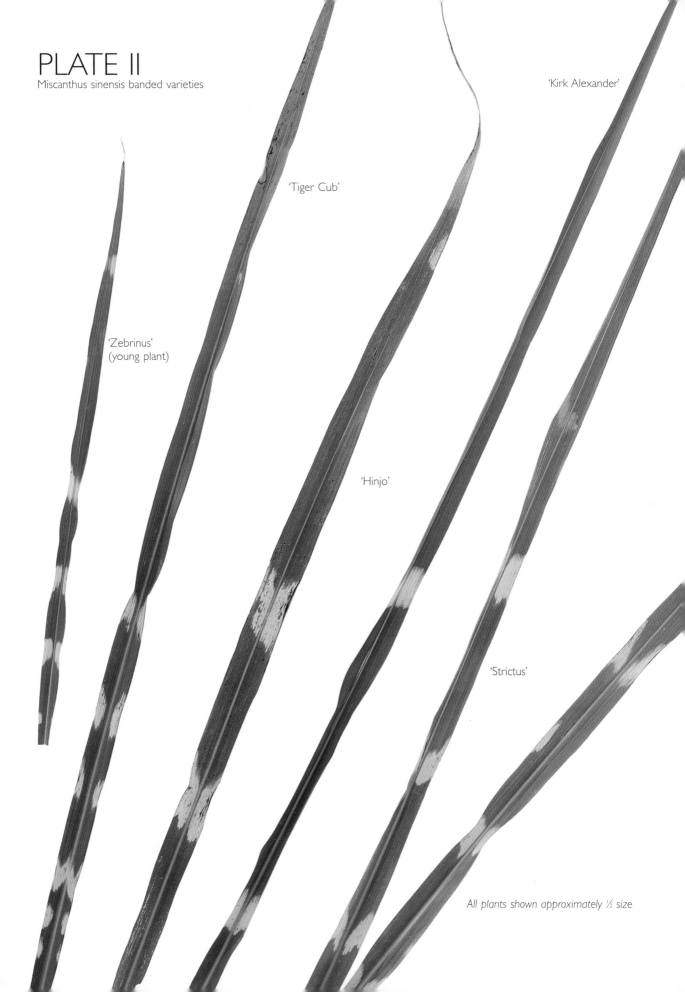

PLATE II
Miscanthus sinensis banded varieties

'Kirk Alexander'

'Tiger Cub'

'Zebrinus'
(young plant)

'Hinjo'

'Strictus'

All plants shown approximately ½ size

tolerate dry shade. *D. caespitosa* 'Ladywood Gold' is a selection of *D. c.* 'Goldtau' (see page 55), with golden-yellow foliage in spring. It grows to about 90cm (3ft) in height and spread.

Bromus

Bromus inermis 'Skinner's Gold' is a relatively new grass with leaves that are strikingly but assymetrically striped gold and green, above which are borne, from early summer until about early autumn, elegant, open panicles composed of relatively large, drooping, corn-gold spikelets. It spreads at the root, though not fast enough to cause alarm, and, since it tends to make an untidy clump, especially on rich soils, is not suitable for the more manicured parts of the garden. It is a native of dry sandy or stony soils, and differs from all other brome grasses in lacking awns.

Spartina

Spartina pectinata 'Aureomarginata' (variegated prairie cord grass), makes large mounds 1.2m (4ft) tall of arching, dark green, ribbon-like foliage that is thinly margined rich gold and sways and sighs with the movement of the wind. It is a variegation that is better in detail than at a distance. The panicles are borne high above the foliage from late summer onwards, and are composed of curious green comb-like spikelets from which hang conspicuous purple anthers, the spikelets later turning reddish-brown. The whole plant turns a glorious yellow in autumn and then settles into a pale biscuit winter colouring. It holds its form through the winter rather

Spartina pectinata 'Aureomarginata' (variegated prairie cord grass) grows best in damp ground near water.

better than many grasses. While it is at its most vigorous in wet ground where it will run (though not uncontrollably), it will grow perfectly well in any fertile soil that is not actually dry.

Phragmites

It is one of the oddities of the plant world that whereas the wild, green-leaved form of *Phragmites australis* will only grow in wet ground, the gold-variegated form (*P. a.* 'Variegatus') is perfectly happy in ordinary garden soil where it does not grow so tall nor run so vigorously, though it still needs controlling. The slender culms and tapering leaves of this warm-season grass form a loose upright clump and are variegated rich, bright yellow, though the colouring gradually loses its intensity after midsummer. The large, open, purple panicles are produced late in the season.

Arundo

Arundo formosana is a clumper, and makes a fountain-shaped bush of bamboo-like culms and leaves about 2.1m (7ft) tall. It is unusual among true grasses in that the culms branch in the first year, and this adds to the bamboo-like effect. The flowers, confusingly, resemble those of *Phragmites*. The leaves of the typical species are grey-green but there is a variegated selection, 'Golden Showers', with softly-spoken golden stripes and also one with wholly gold leaves, as yet not named.

BLUE GRASSES

Grasses with blue foliage may be used as a neutral colour to separate other colours that might clash, as an equal partner with, for example, bronzes and yellows, or simply to emphasize the greenness of greens.

Festuca

Festuca punctoria is known variously as the hedgehog fescue and as porcupine grass, both names no doubt denoting its extraordinary prickliness, for unlike other blue fescues the leaves of this one are rigid and have tips that are sharp enough to pierce the skin. They are curved, and are presented like clusters of upturned claws. The panicles are small and dense, of no particular ornamental value, though they do occasionally produce viviparous plantlets, which are quaint. It is a plant of sun-baked stony hillsides in Greece, and needs perfect drainage in full sun in the garden. It grows 10–12cm (4–5in) tall and makes a good companion for *Sedum lidakense*.

There are two larger fescues that are worth considering for dry gardens: *Festuca longifolia*, which has needle-fine leaves that are blue with a whitish cast and grows 30cm (12in) tall, and *F. californica*, a grass that is attracting a great deal of attention at present in the USA. It produces tight clumps of long, arching, silvery blue leaves about 60cm (2ft) tall, above which are produced abundant showy, airy, open panicles that can reach 90cm (3ft) or more in height. These panicles are green at first, becoming purplish and maturing to a ripe corn colour. In the wild, forms with green or blue leaves can be found, and every shade in between. The excitement is that forms with ever bluer leaves are being found and introduced to cultivation, and many of these forms have leaves that turn purple once touched by frost. Though rated for zones 8–10, it seems to be hardy in the south of England in well-drained soil.

Koeleria

There are two small *Koeleria* (blue hair grasses) in cultivation, *K. glauca* and *K. vallesiana*, which resemble each

Koeleria vallesiana is sometimes mistaken for a blue fescue in leaf but it has far showier flowers.

Though the creamy flowers only bloom for about two months, the narrow blue leaves of *Koeleria nitidula* last nearly all year.

other and to confuse things still further look rather like some of the little blue fescues. The leaves differ, those of the fescues being usually rolled so that they appear round and very narrow while those of the koelerias are broader and flatter, but the only infallible guide is the panicle. In the fescues this is a weedy little one-sided affair at the tip of the stem, while in the blue hair grasses it is a dense spike some 10cm (4in) long, produced in early and midsummer and good enough to pick. It is at first green, silvery or purplish, becoming buff and remaining conspicuous well into the autumn. The leaf mound resembles a blue hedgehog, but is soft to the touch. It grows about 23cm (9in) tall and twice as much across. *K. nitidula* is similar to *K. vallesiana* but has larger, showier panicles. These cool-season growers are natives of chalklands and hard limestone, and need well-drained soil in sun: they are not happy in damp, very acid soils.

Sesleria

Sesleria caerulea (blue moor grass) is as curious as it is useful; the leaves are matt blue on one surface and deep shiny green on the other. It forms low, somewhat untidy tufts of blunt-tipped leaves some 15cm (6in) high and 30cm (12in) or more across. The panicles are dense little pom-poms borne on the tips of short stems in spring and early summer. Its habit of growth is singularly dense and weed-proof, making it a good ground cover. *S. nitida* is altogether bigger and bluer, making a dense, upright-divergent clump of leaves that are blue on both surfaces. The leaf mound grows to about 60cm (2ft) with the

panicles, which are again dense little pom-poms on the ends of slender stems, reaching 90cm (3ft). It too flowers in spring or early summer. Both are cold-season growers.

Helictotrichon

Helictotrichon pratense could easily be confused with *Sesleria caerulea* since both have a similar habit of growth when young, the upper surface of the leaves being blue, the lower surface deep green. But the similarities end there, for the leaf mound of the sesleria is twice as tall as that of the helictotrichon, and the panicles of the former are miserable little beige knobs while those of the latter are open and composed of long-awned spikelets some 60cm (2ft) tall, produced in early summer. *H. filifolius* is another grass with leaves that are dark green on one surface and blue on the other. It makes an upright tussock about 30cm (12in) tall, its stiff leaves being rather broader than those of *H. sempervirens* and also rather stiffer. The tips taper to points that are sharp enough to pierce the skin. The panicles are unremarkable and tend to break early.

Alopecurus

Quite the bluest of these lesser blues is *Alopecurus alpinus* ssp. *glaucus* (alpine fox-tail grass), a cool-season grower from the Arctic regions of both Europe and North America. It forms loose clumps of straight, intensely blue leaves growing no more than 10cm (4in) in leaf, with small, purplish knob-like flowerheads held aloft on 20cm (8in) stems, often as soon as early spring. In cultivation it needs the sunniest possible site and really sharp drainage. It spreads slowly but is never a problem to control.

Poa

In addition there are two cool-season grasses from the Antipodes, both of which can bring a good quality of blueness to a garden. *Poa colensoi* (New Zealand blue meadow grass) is most simply described as New Zealand's equivalent of the northern hemisphere's blue cushion-shaped fescues, but it differs in several ways. The round or rolled leaves are limp, and have a curious rubbery texture; they are more blue than silver; and, which makes them particularly useful, they stay blue throughout the winter, even in light shade, which the blue fescues do not, even in sun. The clumps are looser and larger than those of the blue fescues and the flowers of little interest. It needs a moisture-retentive soil. The other *Poa*, *P. labillardieri*, is endemic to Australia as well as New Zealand.

It is quite different from *P. colensoi* in that it forms dense clumps some 60cm (2ft) tall and 90cm (3ft) across, with the culms packed very closely together. The narrow blue leaves rise upwards and arch stiffly outwards, like a well-worn shaving brush. The flowers are of little beauty. It needs a sunny position in well-drained soil.

Sorghastrum

Sorghastrum nutans (Indian grass) was one of the major ingredients of North America's now fast-disappearing tallgrass prairie, and in the wild may be green, grey or blue. *S. n.* 'Sioux Blue' (blue-leaved Indian grass) was selected not only for its remarkable blueness, which gradually becomes stained rich purple as the nights cool after midsummer, but also for its stiff, upright habit. It is a warm-season clumper that will grow 75cm (2½ft) tall in leaf, with quite dense branching panicles of a rich reddish-tan bespangled with golden anthers reaching up to 90cm (3ft). *S. n.* 'Indian Steel' is similar, with foliage that is more grey-blue than blue.

Schizachyrium

Schizachyrium scoparium (little bluestem) is a clumping warm-season grass from the prairies of eastern North America that is grown not only for its blueness but for the way it changes colour through the seasons, the whole plant emerging pale grey-green in spring, gradually becoming intensely blue towards midsummer after which the leaves and stems gradually become flushed with rich,

The grey-green leaves of *Schizachyrium scoparium* take on rich tones of violet and purple as summer advances.

deep purples, later touched with tints of red and flaming orange. By winter the entire plant is a burnished coppery brown or tan. The narrow leaves are about 36cm (14in) long, and the slender culms bear curious wispy flowers from mid to late summer on stems some 1m (3¼ft) tall. The panicles are small and open and are composed of small, hairy, violet spikelets which have an amazing ability to catch and hold the luminosity of the sky. They remain in good heart right through the winter. *S. s.* 'Blaze' is a seed cultivar that was originally developed for forage but is said to have the brightest autumn colouring, while *S. s.* 'Aldous', another seed cultivar, is said to be the most intense blue. American literature cites as one merit of these grasses that they remain upright all through the winter. In the UK, presumably because of the lack of summer heat, they are inclined to flop, the slender culms which stay erect for much of the summer usually keeling over once flowering begins. For this reason they are usually best grown in bold groups or drifts, rather than as a single plant. They flourish in poor soils, becoming lax on richer ground. They benefit from being clipped or mown down to about 10cm (4in) in spring.

BROWN GRASSES

Chionochloa

Although there are a number of brown carices there is only one true grass that is brown and that is *Chionochloa rubra* (red tussock grass), the dominant plant of the Alpine Desert in New Zealand's North Island. In the wild it grows to as much as 1.5m (5ft), making upright-divergent clumps with little clemisias and silvery raoulias at their feet. In cultivation in the UK it is usually about half that height. The stiff evergreen leaves are narrow, almost rolled, and of a bright, foxy red, while the panicles, being small and much the same colour, tend to pass unnoticed.

MULTI-COLOURED GRASSES

Deschampsia

Multi-coloured plants usually draw the eye very strongly when growing in pots in a nursery, only to prove difficult to place in the garden when one gets them home – some of the many colours in them are bound to clash with the established planting. *D. caespitosa* 'Northern Lights', which is variegated red, pink and gold, is so striking it may be best grown on its own as a specimen or in a pot. It forms dense clumps about 90cm (3ft) high in flower.

5 Bamboos

Bamboos are the evergreen trees and shrubs of the grasses world and when they are used to give height or substance in grass plantings they look wholly at home and in harmony. There are only a comparatively small number of variegated or coloured-leaf bamboos that can be relied on to perform well in most soils and situations; the others are too temperamental to bother with.

The best of the white-variegated bamboos for general planting is *Pleioblastus variegatus*, whose short leaves, borne on slender erect canes, are boldly marked with both broad and narrow white stripes. It will grow some 1.2m (4ft) tall in time and in moist, fertile soil, but is more usually seen at about half that height. It runs steadily and persistently at the root but not particularly fast and is easy enough to control. *P. chino* f. *elegantissimus* has more slender canes and smaller leaves and never creates such as dense a plant as *P. variegatus*.

Pleioblastus shibuyanus 'Tsuboi' is again variegated with both broad and narrow stripes, a little on the creamy side of white, but is quite different from the two previous species in its pendulous habit of growth, though like them it does run at the root. The young, leafless canes stand erect and will reach 1.2m (4ft) but then become very leafy, the sheer weight of the leaves causing the canes to bend under their weight. This lovely bamboo is best grown where it is in shade for at least part of the day.

Phyllostachys aurea 'Albovariegata' is not so heavily variegated as those already mentioned, the leaves having only thin white stripes on them, but is useful for its greater height and for its interesting canes, which are dark green with the lower internodes conspicuously shortened or compressed. It forms an upright-divergent clump and will grow to some 3.6m (12ft) in the UK, but is much taller in warmer climates.

Pseudosasa japonica 'Akebonosuji' is a clumping bamboo growing 2.4–3m (8–10ft) tall and increasing in girth only slowly. It has larger leaves than all of the above, 30cm (12in) long and 2.5cm (1in) wide, boldly variegated creamy-yellow. Some branches produce leaves that are entirely cream, others leaves that are entirely green. Overall it is a most colourful bamboo, having everything except elegance.

× *Hibanobambusa tranquillans* 'Shiroshima' has leaves that are strikingly variegated green and white, with alternating stripes of each colour in about equal amounts. It has relatively thin culms, and in the UK grows to about 1.8m (6ft), but will reach as much as 4m (13ft) in warm climates.

The best yellow-variegated bamboo is *Pleioblastus auricomis*, which, like *P. variegatus*, forms dense, leafy clumps growing to about 1.2m (4ft) high and spreads slowly and persistently. The leaves, which are the richest imaginable golden-yellow with thin green stripes, are about 20cm (8in) long and about 2.5cm (1in) wide, borne in great abundance. It needs to be grown in sun to achieve the brightest colouring, though some prefer the subtler lime-green colouring that can be obtained in shade. The very brightest colouring is on the new leaves produced in the spring, especially if the old canes have been cut down. By midsummer the leaves turn gradually greener, but if the canes are cut down a new flush of bright yellow leaves will be produced. *P. a.* f. *chrysophyllus* is a variant that has solid yellow leaves without any green stripes: it needs to be grown in shade and is not so vigorous as *P. auricomis*.

For those who find plants such as these too garish and prefer their colouring to be more subtle there is the further possibility of those bamboos whose canes are brightly coloured. *Phyllostachys vivax* 'Aureocaulis', a tall bamboo to some 3.6m (12ft) with thick canes of a rich golden yellow, could be used to echo the yellow of *Pleioblastus auricomis* or *P. a.* f. *chrysophyllus*, for example. There are a number of other bamboos with coloured culms, and they are discussed on pages 140–1, 156 and 159.

The bamboos mentioned here are all easy to grow in normal garden conditions, but those with cream or yellow variegation generally look best when the light falls on them, those with white variegation when seen with the sun beside or beyond them. White-variegated bamboos may scorch if grown in full sun unless there is adequate moisture at the roots.

Like all bamboos grown for their showy canes, *Phyllostachys vivax* 'Aureocaulis' benefits from having the lower branches trimmed away to reveal the cane colour.

6 Sedges

The sedges are not nearly such a diverse group as the grasses either in leaf or in flower, the leaves gradually tapering from the base to the tip, the flowers very often being an unremarkable green or dull brown. Most make dense arching tufts of seemingly basal leaves and are quite low plants, the majority no more than ankle high, with just a few reaching knee height or more. Most will, and indeed need to, grow in shade and in rather damper conditions than the grasses, thereby providing a diversity of forms and colours to fill a type of garden habitat where the true grasses would not be happy, carrying on their essentially linear contribution.

WHITE-VARIEGATED SEDGES

Of the white-variegated sedges those with a central variegation on the whole contribute a greater effect of whiteness to the garden than those that are marginally variegated. The largest and brightest of these is the evergreen *Carex oshimensis* 'Variegata', which makes a dense, rounded mound to about 25cm (10in) with a spread of some 45cm (18in), the evergreen leaves thinly margined dark green with a broad white stripe down the centre.

Carex comans pulls together this composition of *Cerinthe major* 'Purpurascens', *Origanum, Kniphofia* 'Little Maid' and *Agapanthus*.

It produces little brown flowers in spring. *C. ornithopoda* 'Variegata' is so similar in general appearance to *C. oshimensis* 'Variegata' that it could be mistaken for it, but it is smaller, only reaching some 15cm (6in) tall and about 30cm (12in) across, and is completely deciduous. *C. saxatilis* 'Ski Run' is quite different in style, growing to no more than some 7.5cm (3in) tall and producing a slowly increasing carpet of leaves that twist and squirm on or just above the ground. The leaves again have a bright white central variegation, and disappear completely in winter. It needs damp, humus-rich acid soil and shade. These three all hold their variegation right through the summer.

C. siderosticha 'Variegata' forms a low, slowly spreading tuft of 2cm (¾in) wide, densely overlapping, thinly textured leaves which are richly flushed with pink when they first emerge in the spring, but which then turn pale green and are margined and striped with a good clean white that lasts the whole season. It is deciduous, and grows best in dampish soil in shade. Two new selections from Japan will soon be available: *C. s.* 'Shima Nishiki' is similar to the above, but with gold instead of white variegation, while *C. s.* 'Kisokaido' produces new leaves that are tipped with white in spring and early summer and are later thinly striped with white.

C. morrowii (Morrow's sedge) has several variegated forms, of which *C. m.* 'Variegata' is the best known. It is a porcupine of a plant, having 60cm (2ft) long, thick, straight, tapering evergreen leaves that form dense tufts with all the leaves pointing upwards and outwards from the centre of the plant, the leaves being dark green thinly margined and striped white, and wholly green below. The flowers, which are beige and cream and quite showy in season, are borne in spring just above or among the leaves. It is tolerant of both damp and dry conditions, and will take shade or some sun. *C.* 'Silver Sceptre' is not a *morrowii* at all, though it was introduced as one. It is generally similar in the colouring of the leaves, but instead of being straight they tend to twist, and are slightly more heavily variegated. It is also completely different in its flowers, which are pale and wispy and not remotely like those of *C. morrowii*, and in its root system, which, without being far-reaching, spreads persistently at a steady pace. *C.* 'Ice Dance' is similar but more dramatically variegated, having darker leaves with more conspicuous white stripes on them. It is similar in habit to 'Silver Sceptre', and both, together with the real *C. morrowii*, make excellent ground cover among shrubs or bamboos

in shaded places. *C.* 'Silk Tassel' probably belongs here, though it is more usually assigned to *C. morrowii temnolepsis* var. *temnolepsis*. Under whatever name it makes 60cm (2ft) clumps of thread-like foliage, each incredibly narrow leaf having a white stripe down the centre. From a distance it creates a silvery effect. It is a plant for woodland or for damp soil beside a pond.

C. conica 'Snowline' is a particularly neat and pleasing little sedge, with narrow, arching, dark green leaves with narrow white margins and spikes of whitish flowers that stand just above the leaf mound, which grows into dense, tight clumps about 15cm (6in) tall by 30cm (12in) wide. It is deciduous.

C. comans (New Zealand hair sedge) is different again in having evergreen leaves that are so thin (no more than 1mm wide) that they appear hair-like, hence its popular name, but they are distinct too in their colouring, being evenly light whitish-green without any variegation. The leaves on young seed-raised plants are held upright in a tight, narrow clump about 60cm (2ft) tall, but as the clump grows the leaves tend to diverge increasingly so that in mature clumps they arch upwards and outwards, their somewhat curly tips trailing on the ground. The flowers, which are not remarkable, are the same colour as the leaves and are borne on stems again the same colour that often trail out well beyond the main leaf mound. A selection named *C. c.* 'Frosted Curls' differs in its more compact habit, in its more curly, more tangled leaves and in having a hint of bronze in its colouring. *C. albida* is similar but smaller and whiter.

CREAM-VARIEGATED SEDGES

Carex pilulifera 'Tinney's Princess' (variegated pill-sedge) is an enchanting little semi-evergreen sedge and is most simply described as a miniature version of *C. oshimensis* 'Variegata', though the variegation is cream rather than white. It grows to no more than 10cm (4in) tall and 15cm (6in) across and produces pale flowers in spring or early summer. It is happy in most moisture-retentive, lime-free soils and in sun or shade, and is small enough for sinks or troughs, or for the front of a border. It is quite distinct from all other sedges in that the leaves when crushed smell of turpentine.

C. morrowii 'Fisher's Form' is just like *C. m.* 'Variegata' and flowers at the same time but is larger in all its parts and with a cream, not white, variegation. In the USA the same plant is called 'Gold Band'. *C. m.* 'Gilt' may be the same.

Carex pendula 'Moonraker', one of the most exciting finds of recent years, was discovered growing in a field by a farmer.

YELLOW-VARIEGATED SEDGES

Quite the most popular yellow-variegated sedge is *Carex* 'Evergold' which, with a yellow band running longitudinally between deep green margins, looks exactly like a yellow-variegated version of *C. oshimensis* 'Variegata'. There is much debate as to whether 'Evergold' belongs to *C. oshimensis* or *C. hachijoensis*, but if both species are grown side by side in their green-leaved forms it will be seen that *C. hachijoensis* has a more loosely tufted habit, is different in flower and moreover flowers at a different time. It is probably best to call 'Evergold' *C.* 'Evergold' without assigning it to a species. The colouring of the centrally variegated portion of the leaf varies from cream to yellow. *C.* 'Everbright' is a cultivar that was around before 'Evergold' and indeed may still be around. It was, or is, of a deeper, richer yellow, but it seems to have been superseded and subsumed by 'Evergold'.

Far larger and altogether different is *C. pendula* 'Moonraker' (evergreen golden weeping sedge), whose young leaves in spring are palest cream, almost white when they emerge, becoming rich creamy yellow with a few thin green stripes, gradually acquiring more green stripes as the summer wears on and slowly fading to an overall green by the end of the summer. In cool summers it will keep its pale colouring until late summer. It forms rounded mounds of strongly keeled arching foliage to about 75cm (2½ft) tall but more across, and in spring and early summer it produces tall wands bearing the pendulous, catkin-like flowers from which it derives its specific name. It is a relatively new plant and young plants from division are hard to come by. However, seedlings usually come variegated, though it is too early to say whether the variegation will be as well-defined as in the original.

As with the white-variegated sedges, those sedges with golden margins to their leaves do not contribute nearly so much colour to the garden as those with a central variegation. Quite the most striking of the gold-edged varieties is *C. muskingumensis* 'Oehme' (golden palm-leaf sedge), which carries its leaves aloft on slender stems, the leaves being narrow and slightly recurved and borne all the way up the stems. The flowers are carried just above the leaves on long slender stalks that arise from leaf axils near the bottom of the stem. It is a deciduous plant growing to about 75cm (2½ft) tall and spreading slowly at the root, eventually making quite large clumps.

The evergreen *C. dolichostachya* 'Kaga-nishiki' (golden fountain sedge) is a much more typical sedge with long, narrow, gold-edged leaves that make dense arching mounds about 25cm (10in) tall and 30–38cm (12–15in) across. In a rather quieter idiom is the deciduous *C. nigra* 'Variegata' (striped black-flowered sedge), whose narrow, arching leaves are light green margined with gold, though the colour takes time to gather strength, being merely pale cream at first. It grows about 30cm (12in) tall and spreads slowly but persistently, making it a lovely ground cover for woodland.

Carex flava (yellow sedge) is a solid colour of soft, subtle, greenish-yellow and makes an excellent yellow highlight in a shade garden or in woodland. It grows only about 38cm (15in) high and has curiously spiky fruits in the autumn. It is deciduous.

BLUE SEDGES

The great thing about the little blue sedges is that they can be used to carry over into shade the colours and tones created by the blue grasses, fescues and lyme grasses which themselves would not be happy in such a position. Quite the bluest is the evergreen North American *Carex glauca*, whose broad, somewhat pleated leaves are much the same electric blue as the leaves of *Hosta* 'Halcyon' all year round. It is a clumping sedge, making tufts about 23cm (9in) tall, and producing blue flowers on blue stems in early summer. *C. flaccosperma* is similar in its wide pleated leaves but taller, growing to about 30cm (12in) and about the same across, and its leaves are at their best in the summer, when for sheer colour they can scarcely be distinguished from those of *C. glauca*. In winter they tend to fade to a dull bluish-green. Again, the flowers and flower stems are the same colour as the leaves.

Quite different in appearance are the carnation grasses, two narrow-leaved blue sedges. The better known of these is *C. flacca*, which to confuse things is sometimes sold as *C. glauca*. It forms carpets some 30cm (12in) high of narrow blue arching leaves about 8mm ($^1/_4$in) wide and 45cm (18in) long and runs in all directions fast enough to need some controlling in all but the very largest of gardens, but is a lovely blue. Because of its running habit it may be worth confining to a low, wide pot, preferably of terracotta since it is the perfect complementary colour for the blue. *C. f.* 'Bias' is a selection with a white margin on one side of the leaf. Similar to *C. flacca* but altogether smaller and scarcely running at all is *C. panicea*, which is virtually the same colour, with leaves of virtually the same width but much shorter, forming little tussocks no more than 23cm (9in) tall. It is probably the better of the two. Both produce slender arching stems with chocolate-brown flowerheads in early summer and are happy in ordinary garden soil, in sun or shade.

C. spissa (San Diego or tall blue sedge) is extremely useful on account of its height, for unlike other blue sedges it will grow to some 71cm (2⅓ft) tall and about the same across. Its leaves are blue-green in spring becoming bluer in summer, though never so intensely blue as those of *C. glauca*, and are about 1cm (½in) wide and held rather upright. The flowers, which are much the same colour as the foliage, are produced in late spring. They have little ornamental merit, and both they and the leaves should be cut down straight after flowering to produce the best and bluest foliage.

C. trifida var. *chatamica* (New Zealand blue sedge) is a strong-growing sedge with broad, strongly keeled leaves that are as intensely blue as *Elymus hispidus*. It forms dense tussocks about 60cm (2ft) high and rather more across and produces compact, three-fingered spikes of chestnut-brown flowers in early summer. Its hardiness is as yet not tested, but the typical green-leaved *C. trifida* is hardy enough.

BROWN SEDGES

Most of the bronze or brown sedges are natives of New Zealand where, it is said by those who are supposed to know about these things, they have developed their curious colouring as a protection against the high levels of ultra-violet to which they have been exposed over the long, slow aeons of evolutionary time. They may be considered more curious than beautiful, but they certainly do have their uses in the garden, providing a colour that few other plants can supply. They often look good in combination with blues, silvers, reds or blacks (such as *Ophiopogon planiscapus* 'Nigrescens', which is not unlike a grass).

The problem with most of these New Zealand sedges is that they all look broadly alike and are difficult to distinguish even with a botanical key. Moreover, they are often seen in nurseries and gardens under the wrong name. A further problem is that young plants in pots may have an upright habit even though they may sprawl at maturity. *Carex buchananii* (New Zealand everbrown sedge) is distinct in that it has an upright habit of growth, both in its youth and at maturity, the narrow, rolled, reddish-brown leaves, with little curly pig-tails at their tips, growing to about 60cm (2ft). It needs well-drained soil and will withstand drought quite well once established. *C. petriei* (Petrie's brown sedge) at little more than 30cm (12in) is the smallest of the group and has a less upright habit than *C. buchananii*, though it is not a weeper like the rest of the bunch. Like *C. buchananii* its leaves seem to be rolled and to bear little pig-tails at the tips.

Carex spissa (San Diego or tall blue sedge) is particularly useful for the height it contributes to a planting scheme.

Carex buchananii is relatively hardy and easy to grow. It has a much more upright habit when young than in maturity.

C. flagellifera, which still sometimes passes as *C. lucida*, is totally different in habit at maturity, the leaves seeming to arch upwards and outwards from the centre of the clump, then bending downwards to trail along the ground. The leaves are a darker brown than those of *C. buchananii*, and tend to bleach and tatter at the tips in winter. It is not too fussy as to soils and will grow well in sun or shade. Its weeping habit can be used to advantage in pots or tubs, where it can trail over the side, or on slopes where the foliage will spill downhill. *C. comans* bronze form is similar but has thinner, more thread-like leaves, and a more compact habit of growth, though as a proportion of seedlings from the typical *C. comans* come bronze there are several different plants in circulation

under this name. *C.* 'Small Red', with reddish-brown rather than bronze foliage and a relatively compact habit, resembles them. Both *C. comans* 'Bronze Form' and *C.* 'Small Red' need good drainage, but will flourish in sun or shade. All the above produce dark brown or blackish flowerheads on long, trailing stems that extend far beyond the leaf mound. The leaves of *C. secta* var. *tenuiculmis* are a rather lighter brown, with an arching habit but not recurving enough to touch the ground. It will reach 45cm (18in) tall, and has a more open habit than the other brown New Zealand sedges. It is also quite different in its flowers, which are borne in midsummer on the last quarter of stems that ascend and then arch.

Completely different is *C. berggrenii*, which has short, rather blunt-tipped leaves, about 9cm (3½in) long and 4mm (⅛in) across, the colour of creamed coffee above but much darker beneath. It makes stubby little tufts which spread slowly into a dense mat, but it never travels to any great extent. The flowers are much the same colour and are borne just above the leaves.

Uncinia rubra (red New Zealand hook-sedge) has leaves that are more red than brown, and really should not be confused with the preceding sedges because not only are the leaves quite broad and strongly keeled, but the floral parts are distinct in that there is a little hook attached to each seed, whose purpose, no doubt, is to aid dissemination. These hooks will tweak the hairs on one's arm or leg if the inflorescence is dragged across them, a discomfort one does not suffer with the inflorescences of the carices. *U. rubra* will grow to about 30cm (12in) tall and about 90cm (3ft) across, and does best in rich, dampish soil in light shade. *Carex uncinifolia* is almost the same colour and indeed looks very much like a dwarf, narrow-leaved version of *Uncinia rubra*, hence its name. It grows slowly, ultimately forming a clump about 23cm (9in) high and 30cm (12in) across. Its flowers are much the same colour as the foliage and are seldom noticed.

Schoenus pauciflorus, a rush-like sedge from the North Island of New Zealand, is even redder. There are no leaves as such, these having been reduced to cylindrical leaf sheaths, and it is these which are red. Small flowers are borne at the tips, but their flowering usually passes unnoticed. It will grow in most soils so long as they are not too dry, in sun or shade, though it colours best in sun and only attains its maximum development in boggy ground, when it can reach 90cm (3ft) in height.

Curiouser still are two New Zealand sedges which depart somewhat from the brown theme. The brownest of these is *C. dipsacea*, whose leaves are a rich dark olive green, assuming in winter reddish, yellowish and brownish streaks and patches. By contrast the leaves of *C. testacea* are of a most unusual ochrous olive bronzy-yellow, turning almost orange in sun and almost green in shade. Both are evergreen and grow into rounded mounds of arching foliage some 45cm (18in) tall, both will tolerate sun or shade but grow best in good, slightly moist soil, but *C. testacea* has longer, narrower leaves than *C. dipsacea* and paler brown flowers, those of *C. dipsacea* being almost black.

GREEN SEDGES

There are several green-leaved sedges that are every bit as worth growing in the garden as those possessing blue, brown or variegated leaves. The largest of these is *Carex forsteri*, which makes large, architectural clumps about 90cm (3ft) tall of broad, pleated leaves and pro-

duces good spikes of white flowers in early and midsummer. *C. trifida* makes bold clumps of about the same size, with broad, keeled and pleated leaves that are dark green above, silvery beneath. Without its flowers it could easily be mistaken for *C. pendula* but in flower there is no mistaking them, for in *C. trifida* the flowers are produced in short, upright spikes in groups of threes, scarcely peeping over the top of the foliage. *C. hispida* makes clumps of much the same size, but the leaves are relatively narrow and are bright green. *Uncinia clavata*, which is a hook sedge rather than a true sedge, makes tussocks that are wider than high, and grows to about half the height of the other three. It differs in having particularly dark leaves and in producing black clavate (club-shaped) flower spikes in midsummer. Both *C. texensis* and *C. caryophyllea* 'The Beatles' make low-growing mounds of dark green narrow leaves but whereas 'The Beatles' makes a mophead of foliage, *C. texensis* runs slowly and in warm climates might even make a lawn substitute.

C. secta is distinct in that as it grows it builds up a trunk of dead roots and leaf-bases which eventually raise the living tussock to some 90cm (3ft) above the ground. The leaves are bright green and about 30cm (12in) long, deeply grooved and strongly keeled. The flowers are borne in clusters at the tips of slender stems, but are not showy. This species, which often grows in wet ground in its native habitat in New Zealand, is useful in tussock gardens for growing beside water.

The cascading foliage of *Carex petriei* makes it ideal for use in pots and larger containers.

7 Painting the Picture

The grasses described in the preceding pages may be regarded as the colours from which garden pictures may be made. Where the grasses differ from the colours on a painter's palette is that they cannot be mixed to produce a new colour as painters might use blue and yellow to produce green. However, when one colour is placed beside another each is modified.

Coloured-leaf grasses can be grown simply for themselves or used in the garden in much the same way as any other source of colour. However, because of their linear qualities they tend to draw the eye more strongly than other plants, and for this reason are particularly useful when grown in groups and repeated along a border or round a garden to create a reassuring sense of rhythm.

In a border, grasses can be planted to echo the colours of flowers or foliage or to contrast with them. The yellow spring leaves of *Hakonechloa macra* 'Alboaurea' go particularly well with the flowerheads of *Euphorbia chariacas* ssp. *wulfenii* 'John Tomlinson' and with those of *E. myrsinites*, while their summer foliage is an excellent foil to the silvery-blue of *Hosta* 'Halcyon' and larger blue hostas such as *H.* 'Big Daddy', *H.* 'Snowden' and *H. sieboldiana* 'Elegans'. It also works well with the blues of *Myosotis*, *Brunnera*, *Omphalodes cappadocica* and, later, *Camassia*.

Many grasses can be used to create a continuity of colour

Left to right, *Hakonechloa macra* 'Alboaurea', *Imperata cylindrica* 'Rubra' with *Panicum virgatum* 'Warrior' behind, *Festuca glauca* 'Elijah Blue' with *Hakonechloa macra* 'Mediovariegata', and *Festuca glauca* 'Golden Toupee' with *Molinia caerulea ssp. caerulea* 'Variegata' behind.

among broad-leaved plants whose flowering lasts for but a brief time. In our white garden we grow in the space between *Aralia elata* 'Variegata' and the rose 'Winchester Cathedral' a group of *Miscanthus sinensis* 'Morning Light', on the other side of which is a clump of *Phalaris arundinacea* 'Feesey'. Beside 'Morning Light' we have planted *Hosta* 'Snowden', whose huge silver-grey leaves afford a pleasing contrast with the linearity of the grasses. In other parts of the white garden we grow *Cortaderia selloana* 'Silver Fountain' and the smaller *C. s.* 'Silver Stripe' as well as *Miscanthus sinensis* 'Variegatus' and the shorter-growing *M. s.* 'Dixieland' and *M. s.* 'Rigoletto'. Together these grasses ensure a continuity of whiteness from snowdrop time until the last of the tall autumnal anemones.

PLANTING IN DRIFTS

There is another way of using grasses with coloured or variegated leaves, and it is something that can really only be done with grasses, though it has much in common with heather gardens. It is to plant the grasses in drifts or bands, with taller grasses standing up singly here or there to draw the eye, or planted in drifts as a background. The organizing principles are first that the grasses be planted closely enough to suppress weeds, and secondly that they be in sequences of colours to please the eye. When used on a large scale the biggest drifts should be nearest the house or the place from which the planting is intended to be seen, becoming progressively smaller as they move further away, creating a false perspective. If the strongest colours, the reds and yellows for instance, are used nearest the house and the paler colours, the blues and greys, further away, this will also enhance the sense of the planting moving into the distance. It is important in such a scheme to exploit the variations in the colour green, using the strong, dark green of *Deschampsia caespitosa* (tufted hair grass) or *Ophiopogon intermedius* (mondo grass) in the foreground, the lighter green of *Hakonechloa macra* further away.

In our own garden we have made a planting of coloured grasses, but because it runs across the front of the house rather than away from it no attempt has been made to add perspective. The grasses are set out in coloured bands, like segments of concentric rings, through the midst of which runs a brick path curving in the opposite direction and thus creating a dynamic tension. The scheme is held together by the repetition of the colour blue, though it is contributed by different plants in different places. It starts with *Carex dolichostachya* 'Kaga-nishiki', whose narrow, mid-green leaves are edged with gold, and next to this we have perhaps the brightest blue of all the sedges, the broad-leaved *C. glauca*, and beyond that *Luzula sylvatica* 'Aurea', whose leaves are brightest yellow in midwinter, with *Carex flaccosperma* next to it. Adjacent to this is the red *Uncinia rubra*, and beyond that the blue of *Poa colensoi*, in the midst of which is the taller tussock of *Miscanthus sinensis* 'Adagio'. This part of the planting is at its most effective during the winter, which is why it was planted close to the house.

Across the path, tucked away in the curve of the brick path and then extending across it again on the far side, the scheme moves into grasses that are showier in summer, the two schemes linked together by the continuing band of *Poa colensoi*, which on this side is punctuated by the single tussock of *Miscanthus sinensis* 'Sarabande'. In this scheme *Imperata cylindrica* 'Rubra' is placed next to *Hakonechloa macra* 'Alboaurea', and is separated from the intensely blue *Elymus hispidus* by a narrow band of black

Ophiopogon planiscapus 'Nigrescens'. Beyond this the planting runs into our winter garden, but fingers of other grasses, *Hakonechloa macra* 'Mediovariegata', *Festuca glauca* 'Elijah Blue' and *F. g.* 'Golden Toupee', extend into that scheme, mingling with variegated hollies and winter irises, variegated euonymous and fragrant Christmas box (*Sarcococca*).

While my own predeliction is for such schemes to be composed wholly of grasses, other effects can be achieved by mixing the grasses with broad-leaved plants grown either for the colours of their foliage or for their flowers. Such effects might be rather Burle-Marxian.

Kurt Bluemel, America's leading grasses nurseryman, made a most interesting planting of grasses in the garden of his house in Maryland. Against a background of dark conifers he created a large bed of a freehand, amoebic shape which he filled with one of the bluer selections of *Festuca glauca* with, in one place, a ribbon of *Imperata cylindrica* 'Rubra' (Japanese blood grass) separating the blue from the green of the lawn. Into this matrix of blue fescue he planted single specimens of such grasses as miscanthus and *Molinia caerulea* ssp. *arundinacea* (tall moor grass), groups of *Spodiopogon sibiricus* and a few dwarf conifers. Many variations could be played upon this theme, and certainly in the cooler climate of the UK one might use one of the blue sedges, *Carex panicea* for example, rather than the fescue to make the underplanting.

Another possibility would be to vary the blueness by using different varieties of fescues, possibly mixed with blue sedges, to avoid having too vast an expanse of a single tone. One might use the rather heavy blue-green of *Festuca glauca* 'Harz', then the distinctly blue *F. dalmatica* and finally the silvery blue of *F. longifolia*. These might be set out in clearly defined patterns, as in a knot or parterre or in drifts, with one tone merging into another, perhaps in gradations from darker to lighter.

Although the use of coloured grasses in gardens is increasing in popularity, the real potential for what can be achieved with them has as yet hardly been explored. While their colours can plainly be used in much the same way as the colours of flowers, being foliage they have a different texture, and may need to be handled differently. They can certainly be used to great effect in Jekyllian schemes, and indeed Gertrude Jekyll herself often employed them – but people are making grass plantings in other ways in the late 20th century, and these will be discussed in Part Four.

Part Three The Flowering Grasses

8 Essential Flowering Grasses

The most important point to grasp when using flowering grasses is that their decorative qualities lie first and foremost in their form and structure and only secondarily in their colour, whereas with the more familiar broad-leaved plants it is flower colour that contributes most, form and structure being secondary. It follows from this that effects are achieved by setting panicles of differing forms in juxtaposition with one another, much as they would be in a single colour garden, in harmony or counterpoint. In a white garden, for example, where all the flowers are white or whitish, interest is created by varying the form, with large flowers next to tiny ones, daisy flowers next to bell-shaped ones, spikes counterbalanced with pendulous heads, and so on. So it is with grasses.

In any such planting the design needs to be held together by grasses that may be depended upon to perform well season after season, on most soils and in most situations. It is these that I regard as the essential flowering grasses. Lesser flowering grasses may be used to supplement the effects created with these.

Calamagrostis

The key grass in any such scheme is *Calamagrostis × acutiflora* 'Stricta' (feather reed grass), and the reason it is so important is because, from the time of its coming up to its dying down, it is the very paradigm of verticality and, like anything vertical, it draws the eye very strongly, thereby not only asserting its own presence but also drawing attention to other plants grouped around it. Feather reed grass is a clumping, cool-season grower with rather nondescript narrow dark green leaves that form a tuft about 75cm (2½ft) tall. It is the panicles that are arresting. These start to emerge in late spring, slender as a pipe-cleaner atop shiny green stems that are straight as a ramrod, ultimately reaching some 1.5m (5ft) in height. In early summer the panicles relax, becoming loose and open and subtly purplish-tinted. Then, once flowering is over, the branches of the panicle close up against the main axis and the panicle again becomes as narrow as a pipe cleaner, gradually changing in colour to a rich beige, which it remains all through the summer and autumn and into the winter, the stiff stems bending under the weight of

rain or before the force of the wind, but never breaking and always resuming their vertical stance. Grown in shade it loses its stiffness. It is a sterile hybrid and so produces no unwanted seedlings but is easily increased by division in spring or autumn. *C. × a.* 'Karl Foerster' is similar but more showy in flower and less emphatically vertical in its overall appearance. It is some 25cm (10in) taller than *C. × a.* 'Stricta', with broader, more open and fluffier panicles which it produces some 10–14 days earlier. In early summer, when the panicles of 'Karl Foerster' are fully expanded, those of 'Stricta' are still folded against the central axis and are as narrow as rat's tails; moreover, 'Karl Foerster' goes on producing new panicles throughout the summer, which 'Stricta' does not. Overall, 'Karl Foerster' is the more desirable plant unless the verticality of 'Stricta' is required. The feather reed grasses can be used as single specimens or in drifts: when they are planted *en masse* a very strong horizontal line appears because all the flowers are produced at the same time and at the same height.

Pennisetum

Having established a visual centre of gravity with one of the feather reed grasses it is useful to plant a grass with a strongly rounded shape to afford a contrast, and in the front rank of grasses that can perform this function are the fountain grasses, *Pennisetum*. The archetypal fountain grass is *P. alopecuroides*, a warm-season clumper that forms a rounded mound of good green foliage some 75cm (2½ft) tall and perhaps as much as 90cm (3ft) across. The flowers, which look like pink-brown fox-tails, are borne in late summer on slender arching stems all over the clumps, and it is these that create the fountain effect whence comes the common name. When in flower, fountain grass can stand as much as 1m (3¼ft) tall in the UK, more in warmer climates. Its only problem is that in cold British gardens the summers may not be long enough nor hot enough to produce a good show of flowers, but there are several selections which are more reliable in flower, the best of these being *P. a.* 'Woodside', which grows marginally smaller. *P. a.* 'Weserbergland' is similar but with greenish-white flowers and slightly smaller again. *P. a.* 'Hameln' is a dwarf selection, growing to some 45cm

(18in), while *P. a.* 'Little Bunny', as one might expect, is a mere midget, growing 23–30cm (9–12in) in flower. These last two are both reliably free-flowering, but the stems are rather stiff and consequently do not produce the famous fountain effect. At the other extreme is *P. a.* 'Paul's Giant', an outstanding selection introduced by Longwood Gardens that reaches 1.8m (6ft) high in flower and has bigger, fatter flowers than the others. The whole plant is green to start with but around midsummer the tips of the leaves turn purple, the purple gradually bleeding down the leaves. *P. a.* 'Cassian' is a selection noted for its autumn foliage colours; it reaches a height of 60cm (2ft) and spread of 1m (3¼ft).

There are two other fountain grasses which are every bit as decorative as *P. alopecuroides*, but not so useful in the structuring of a garden because of a suspicion of tenderness. These are *P. villosum* (Ethiopian fountain grass) and *P. orientale* (oriental fountain grass). Both are perennials in the wild and in warm gardens but are often grown as annuals in colder gardens. As annuals they both flower in their first year from seed. *P. villosum* makes a sprawling tussock about 30cm (12in) high and 90cm (3ft) across and produces all summer and into the autumn fluffy white rabbit's tails of panicles that are extraordinarily eye-catching. The panicles are shorter and wider than those of *P. alopecuroides*. In my own garden on the rare occasions it is killed by frost seedlings appear as soon as the ground warms up and are in flower by midsummer. *P. orientale* makes tufts of soft, arching, grey-green leaves 30–45cm (12–18in) tall and across, above which are borne the soft panicles which resemble long, thin bottle-brushes in a subtle shade of mauvish-pink – a shade that goes beautifully with the wispy flower spikes of *Aloysia chamaedrifolia* and with the various shades of *Perovskia*. In southern England and the cooler zones of the USA

Pennisetum orientale (Oriental fountain grass) at first light, its flowers still wet with dew.

P. orientale will start to flower at midsummer and continue until the frosts, but in warmer zones it may start to flower as early as Easter and still go on until the frosts. I am told there is a white form called *P. o.* 'Pakistan' which sounds delectable, though I have not seen it.

There are two other fountain grasses which are perfectly hardy and pleasingly showy, but are all too seldom seen. The first is *P. incomptum* (meadow fountain grass), whose strong, arching, grey-green leaves grow to about 45cm (18in) while the erect panicles, which are like long, thin bottle-brushes, much more slender than those of the common fountain grass, are white and chaffy and borne at the tops of 1.2m (4ft) stiff, straight stems. The flowers are produced in midsummer. It sounds enchanting and so it is, but it is not called meadow fountain grass for nothing. It runs – not slowly or moderately but vigorously. It is not a grass to admit into any but the largest of gardens but where space abounds it can be one of the loveliest of grasses, particularly fine in meadows mixed with the flowers of the field. It is also suitable for pots, but because of its height looks most at home in wide, shallow ones. It is both frost-hardy and drought-tolerant. There is a form with delicious dusky purple panicles called *P. i.* 'Purple Form', purple, of course, meaning brown, for in the days when the Romans coined the word *purpureum* the colour intended was that of the Emperor's toga, which to our eyes was the colour of dried blood.

P. macrourum is sufficiently similar for the two to be sometimes confused, but differs profoundly in its clumping rather than running habit, and in flowering in late summer rather than at midsummer. The leaf mound is

PLATE III
Pennisetum

P. orientale

P. setaceum
'Rubrum'

P. macrourum

P. alopecuroides
'Weserbergland'

*All plants shown
approximately ½ size*

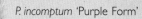

P. incomptum 'Purple Form'

P. alopecuroides
'Woodside'

P. incomptum

P. villosum

much lower, making the flowers look as though they are on taller stems, though in fact they are the same height as those of *P. incomptum*. The panicles are white or nearly so, and sway most elegantly with even the slightest of breezes. It is a native of South Africa and may be tender in cold gardens. It should always be planted in early summer, rather than autumn.

Panicum

The perfect grass with which to blend *Calamagrostis* and *Pennisetum* is *Panicum virgatum* (switch grass), another warm-season clumper but one whose whole growth is so open and airy that it readily links any two more solid clumps. The stems on the cultivated forms are slender and stiff, with well-spaced ascending or arching leaves, and the culms are topped from midsummer onwards with huge, open, airy panicles of tiny mauve or purplish spikelets which create a cloud-like effect, rather as though a swarm of tiny midges were hovering in the humid air on a warm summer evening.

A native of the fast-vanishing tallgrass prairies of North America, the switch grass has a vast natural range from Florida to Canada and almost from coast to coast and so not surprisingly varies considerably. Most of the forms in cultivation grow to 90–120cm (3–4ft) in flower. *P. v.* 'Strictum' has a narrower, more upright habit than most and turns evenly yellow rather than purple in the autumn, gradually mellowing to tan for the winter. The name *P. v.* 'Rubrum' is applied to varieties whose leaves become tinted with vinous reddish-purple in the autumn; *P. v.* 'Rehbraun' grows to 1m (3¼ft) and has foliage that turns

Panicum virgatum 'Warrior', one of the new selections that produces richly coloured flowers in great profusion.

a brilliant orange-red in the autumn; *P. v.* 'Hänse Herms' is similar but a little shorter, while *P. v.* 'Rotstrahlbusch' is similar but a little taller. *P. v.* 'Red Cloud' is smaller-growing and has notably reddish spikelets. Two superb varieties just becoming available are *P. v.* 'Warrior' and *P. v.* 'Squaw'. Both are vigorous varieties growing 1.2–1.5m (4–5ft) tall with huge heads of purplish spikelets, but differ in that whereas 'Warrior' has autumn colour in shades of yellow, 'Squaw' takes on hues of red and purple almost as intense as *Imperata cylindrica* 'Rubra' and is rather floppier than 'Warrior'.

Deschampsia

Deschampsia species (hair grasses) have panicles which are just as light and airy as those of *Panicum virgatum*. They are particularly useful not only because they flower earlier than most other grasses, in late spring and early summer, but also because although they will grow well enough in the sun they are one of the relatively few genera that will perform brilliantly in the shade, making them the ideal foil for ferns, hostas and *Helleborus orientalis* (Lenten rose). The best among them for flower is *D. caespitosa* (tufted hair grass), several named cultivars of which are grown on both sides of the Atlantic. However the majority are European cultivars and in North America, especially in warmer Mediterranean climates, it may be found that they perform poorly, homegrown American selections being freer flowering. In the USA *D. caespitosa* is native from southern California to Alaska and from Virginia to Greenland. With such an extensive range considerable variation can be expected.

D. caespitosa forms dense tussocks of dark green leaves up to about 30–60cm (1–2ft) tall, with the flowering culms, which are upright-divergent and sometimes pendulous, reaching 75–90cm (2½–3ft). In the UK the leaves are more or less evergreen, as they are in zones 8 and 9. The loose, airy panicles, which start silvery green and produce yellow or bronze spikelets, are borne from late spring until the end of summer in such profusion that they may obscure the leaves. *D. c.* 'Bronzeschleier' ('Bronze Veil') is the best-known selection, with bronzy spikelets on 90cm (3ft) culms and pendulous branches to the panicles, and is one of the better cultivars for warmer climates. Of the selections with golden spikelets both *D. c.* 'Goldgehänge' ('Golden Showers') and *D. c.* 'Goldschleier' ('Golden Veil') grow to 90–120cm (3–4ft), but the latter flowers earlier, from early summer until late summer, while 'Goldgehänge' does not come into flower

Deschampsia caespitosa 'Goldtau' with *Achillea* 'Lachsschönheit'. The flowers of the deschampsias are effective in the garden from midsummer until well into the winter.

until midsummer. Of the two 'Goldschleier' is the better known, with silvery green panicles quickly assuming golden-yellow tints. 'Goldgehänge' has rather more pendulous branches to the panicles, giving the flowerheads a more weeping appearance. Both *D. c.* 'Goldstaub' ('Golden Dust') and *D. c.* 'Goldtau' ('Golden Dew') are smaller growing. 'Goldstaub' has golden-yellow spikelets on stems which are a contrasting green, while those of 'Goldtau' start silvery green and do not really turn golden until they are fully open. 'Goldschleier' and 'Goldtau' are particularly good when grown together, for the first is at its prime, flaunting its tall gold panicles, while the latter is only at its knees, its panicles still closely furled and verdant green.

D. c. 'Schottland' ('Scotland') is a vigorous, robust variety with extra-dark green leaves and flowering culms that reach 90cm (3ft), while both *D. c.* 'Tardiflora' and *D. c.* 'Tautraeger' ('Dew Bearer') are late flowering, 'Tardiflora' reaching 90cm (3ft) in bloom, 'Tautraeger' only 30–60cm (1–2ft), its panicles almost blue when they first open, but ripening to a rich golden colour. *D. c.* 'Waldschatt' ('Forest Shade') has dark brown panicles, quite unlike the others, reaching 60–90cm (2–3ft). *D. c.* var. *parviflora* is a smallish variety growing to less than 90cm (3ft), but quite distinct in that it holds its remarkably beautiful spikelets horizontal, rather than drooping as in most other varieties. *D. c.* 'Fairy's Joke' is a viviparous form, producing plantlets where there ought to be flowers. It is a curiosity only.

Very similar to the cultivars of *D. caespitosa* is *D. media*, with leaves narrower and paler than those of *D. caespitosa* itself. It grows to about 90cm (3ft) and flowers in mid and late summer, producing shimmering masses of exceptionally delicate bronzy-green flowers that age to tawny gold. It performs better in sun than in shade. *D. m.* bronze form is perhaps even lovelier, its spikelets bronzy-brown. *D. wibeliana* is similar in being sun-loving, but is smaller, growing to a mere 30cm (12in), and earlier in flower, the panicles being silvery-green with a purplish iridescence.

D. flexuosa (wavy hair grass) is a grass of exceptional beauty forming low tufts of dark, more or less evergreen leaves of thread-like fineness about 15–23cm (6–9in) long, overtopped by airy panicles of shimmering silvery-brown spikelets that grow to about 75cm (2½ft) tall. It is native to sandy or peaty soils, usually occurring in woodland clearings in dry soils, though it is occasionally found in damp or even wet habitats. Though it is usually tuft-forming it does sometimes run, and while I have read that this is a habitat-induced phenomenon I have never managed to ascertain which habitats induce it. There is a form with acid yellow-green leaves, *D. f.* 'Tatra Gold', which produces shimmering reddish-brown flowers in early summer. In my garden it seems to grow best in well-drained peaty soil in a little shade. It is just the right shade of yellow to look good with mauves and purples, particularly mauve and purple violas, which are just right for scale, and can enjoy the same conditions.

D. setacea, sometimes known as bog hair grass, is similar in general appearance to *D. flexuosa* and is sometimes confused with it, especially as it too will grow in damp or wet conditons. A native of the margins of acid bogs and wet heathlands, it is a lovely grass for damp, preferably acid woodlands. Like other hair grasses, it is very beautiful in flower, in general resembling forms of *D. caespitosa*, but rather smaller, growing to no more than 45cm (18in) in flower. It is distinct from *D. flexuosa* in its very thin, bristle-like leaves, and in its narrower panicles, those of *D. flexuosa* being broadly pyramidal.

There are two problems one needs to be aware of when growing tufted hair grasses. One is that they tend to seed themselves back into the fringes of the parent clump and, the leaves being identical in colour and texture with those of the parent, these seedlings pass unnoticed until it is realized that some of the flowers are not quite the same as one started with, at which point the clump needs to

Stipa calamagrostis goes on producing new green panicles among the fading biscuit ones from early summer until the frosts.

be dug up and divided, the errant seedlings being discarded, or a new plant bought true to name. The other is that they are regarded by rabbits as a particular delicacy.

Stipa

The genus *Stipa* contains many of the most beautiful of all ornamental grasses and yet is so varied that it is sometimes difficult to see why the various species belong together in the same genus, a sentiment with which some botanists evidently agree. There are moves in some quarters to split the genus, which at present contains over 300 species, into smaller and more homogenous groupings. Thus some botanists would like to see the familiar *S. gigantea* become *Macrochloa arenaria* and both *Stipa splendens* and *S. extremiorientalis* move to *Achnatherum* along with *Stipa brachytricha*. There is however no general consensus that these changes should be made and for the purposes of this book I shall stay with the established naming. The stipas are best divided into feather grasses – those with long, trailing, feather-like awns such as *S. barbata*, *S. pennata* and *S. tirsa* – and needle grasses which have long, needle-like awns, such as *S. capillata* and *S. turkestanica*. This still leaves a few anomalies, such as *S. gigantea*, *S. (Calamagrostis) brachytricha* and *S. robusta*, which do not seem to belong to either group.

All these grasses are natives of the wide open grasslands of the world, steppes, prairies, meadows, even tundras, and so in the garden they need to be planted in full sun, in well-drained soil. Most come from dry areas and have evolved a considerable economy both of form and lifestyle. The leaves are very fine, often hair-like, usually

rather sparse, and often amount to no more than a quarter of the total plant, thus minimizing the transpiring surface, while the panicles and their supporting stems often make up the greater part, the showy awns aiding photosynthesis where it can best help the reproductive process. The down side of this is that the panicles perform their biological function all too quickly, the flowers soon turning to seeds, with the result that though the panicles may be exceptionally beautiful, the whole plant declines rapidly thereafter. Many defend themselves against the long, sun-baked and wind-blown summers by going dormant until the winter rains: if stressed, they simply die, leaving the seeds to secure the future. There are problems in the garden too: a number of them are difficult to propagate by division and are better grown from seed, and many deteriorate in pots.

To blend grasses such as *Calamagrostis*, *Panicum* and *Deschampsia* together one needs a soft, feathery, almost fluffy grass, and there are two feather grasses which can play this role to perfection. The first of these is *Stipa calamagrostis* (still sometimes seen in older gardens as *Lasiogrostis splendens*), which forms rounded mounds of narrow, arching green foliage about 90cm (3ft) tall above which are borne in abundance, from early summer until the frosts, soft, feathery, greeny-white plumes that gradually change to beige, so that for much of the summer the plant has both fresh green flowers and the beige maturing seedheads on it. If it is cut down after its first flush of flowers it will flower a second time, rather than flowering continuously. *S. c.* 'Lemperg' is a compact selection popular in continental Europe.

Stipa tenuissima, an indispensable grass that contributes grace and elegance to the garden from spring until the depths of winter.

Across the pond, the panicles of *Stipa gigantea* are touched by the sun's last rays at the head of a grassery in Wiltshire (see page 92).

Another feather grass that can fill much the same role is *S. tenuissima*, which has a completely different habit of growth. It springs out of the ground with its stems bunched together at the base and splayed out above like the bristles of a shaving brush, the resemblance further enhanced by the way in which the flowers, which are produced in narrow but open and airy panicles, are borne all over the top of the plant, the panicles starting jade green and soon turning beige. It grows best in poor soil in sun: when grown in rich soil it loses its upright habit and flops from the centre. The flowers are produced continuously from late spring until the first hard frosts, and these two feather grasses must be among the most free-flowering of all grasses. *S. ambigua* is similar to *S. tenuissima* but taller, to 90cm (3ft), with rather less open panicles. *S. tenuissima* should never be confused with *S. tenacissima*, a coarse grass rarely met with in gardens.

Calamagrostis brachytricha (Korean feather reed grass) is still widely known as *Stipa brachytricha* and as *Achnatherum brachytricha*. It is rather more of a star in its own right and perhaps not quite so good in a supporting role. It

forms a mound of upright-divergent but later almost weeping foliage with a height and spread of about 60cm (2ft), the young leaves being tinted with bronze at first, becoming light green later. In late summer it produces at the tops of 1.2m (4ft) culms, high above the leaves, almost ovoid, feathery panicles of pinkish grey which are most attractive, freely borne and long-lasting. In the warmth of American summers the habit is stiffly upright but in the UK the habit is inclined to be floppy, though this does not detract from its overall performance.

Perhaps the most popular grass for a specimen position is Spanish oat grass – *S. gigantea*. This cool-season clumper is not merely one of the most spectacular of all grasses but one of the most spectacular of garden plants, making dense, low mounds of dark, evergreen leaves about 75cm (2½ft) tall. In late spring, huge open panicles rise above them on 1.8m (6ft) stems, the tips of the panicle branches bedecked with large golden spikelets that shimmer in the wind and from which hang, in season, large yellow anthers. After flowering the panicles gradually turn golden brown, then old straw yellow, a colour they retain right through into the winter. The spikelets break up increasingly rapidly once the hard frosts start, and the stems usually need cutting before the new year. It is a

The large flowers of *Melica macra* fit in well with other grasses, particularly *Stipa gigantea,* and with the bolder flowers of broad-leaved perennials.

relatively drought-resistant grass and will take all the sun it can be given. Though it is usually used as a specimen, it is even more brilliant when used in drifts of several to many, which is how it grows in its native haunts on dry rocky hillsides in Spain. It is easily raised from imported seed but home-grown British seed often seems to be infertile. *S. g.* 'Gold Fontane' is a selection with larger, showier panicles.

A superb companion for *Stipa gigantea*, and also for *Ampelodesmos mauritanicus*, is *Melica macra*, all three of which are in flower at the same time, making a veritable triumvirate for early summer effect. The melic makes rounded mounds of narrow dark green leaves to about 45cm (18in) which set off to startling effect the cream-coloured filaments of the flowers, borne in great abundance. None of the other melics can match it for sheer showiness. If to these three one were to add the trio of *Miscanthus, Panicum* and *Pennisetum* for late summer and autumn display, and to link these two groups together through the season with a few *Deschampsia*, one would have a superlative display of grasses from early spring until midwinter.

Molinia

Equally good either as specimens or in drifts is *Molinia caerulea* ssp. *arundinacea* (tall moor grass), which can grow

1.8–2.1m (6-7ft) tall but which is not spectacular in the same way as the Spanish oat grass: rather it is grown for its grace and elegance, for the way it sways with the wind and arches down to the ground when wet or laden with dew, springing up straight again when dry. The tall moor grasses are essentially grasses of cooler climates, and though they flourish in gardens in Pennsylvania and Maryland, they are not happy in the heat of North Carolina and of states further south. There are several of them, all of them beautiful, but to my mind the very best is *M. c.* ssp. *a.* 'Zuneigung', because it has the most elegant habit. From a dense mound of narrow, light green leaves arise in midsummer tall slender stems some 1.8m (6ft) high, at the tips of which are relatively dense, heavy panicles of light green flowers which cause the upper part of the stem to arch outwards, and then, as though in perfect balance, to sway with the slightest breath of air. In stronger winds the stems twist and entwine like lovers in the night, resuming an air of serenity at dawn. When sodden with rain or wet with heavy dew the stems will curve downwards, almost touching the ground, but gradually resume their former stance as they dry out. The flowers change gradually to golden brown, but in early autumn the whole plant turns first yellow and then a luminous cinnamon, slowly fading through the winter to a wan beige.

There are several similar selections. *M. c.* ssp. *a.* 'Fontäne' has much the same habit but, having thinner panicles, is less showy. *M. c.* ssp. *a.* 'Windspiel' is said to do in American gardens everything 'Zuneigung' does in Europe, and perhaps it does in the warmer American summers, but in my own garden in southern England it stands stiffly to attention all summer long. These arching varieties of tall moor grass are generally best grown as single specimens so that one can enjoy the architecture of their stance and the rhythms of their movement: when planted in drifts the stems of one plant tend to get tangled in the stems of the next, and much of the movement is lost.

This is not the case with the more erect varieties of tall moor grass which, while lovely as single specimens, are even lovelier when grown in groups. *M. c.* ssp. *a.* 'Karl Foerster' is an old variety but still one of the best, making good mounds of arching green foliage and growing some 1.5m (5ft) tall in flower with quite broad panicles of flowers produced in early or midsummer, just a little earlier than those of other varieties: *M. c.* ssp. *a.* 'Skyracer', an American selection, is reputed to be the tallest at 2.4m (8ft): *M. c.* ssp. *a.* 'Transparent' grows to about 1.8m (6ft) and has tiny spikelets produced on a panicle that is so diffuse you can look right through it: *M. c.* ssp. *a.* 'Bergfreund' by contrast has large, showy heads of tiny greenish-purple spikelets but grows to much the same height.

There are several other moor grasses grown for the beauty of their flowers and for their autumn colour, but they belong to the smaller-growing group *M. c.* ssp. *caerulea* (purple moor grasses). Of these *M. c.* ssp. *c.* 'Strahlenquelle' ('Fountain Spray') and *M. c.* ssp. *c.* 'Dauerstrahl' ('Ramsey') grow to about 90cm (3ft) and have an arching habit; *M. c.* ssp. *c.* 'Heidebraut' ('Heatherbride') has an upright-divergent habit and is the tallest of the purple moor grasses, growing to 1.5m (5ft). It has the bonus of some yellow in the spikelets which causes them to glisten in the sun and it also has richer yellow autumn colour than other purple moor grasses. *M. c.* ssp. *c.* 'Moorhexe' ('Bogwitch') is the dwarfest of the moor grasses at 60cm (2ft), and is especially useful for that very reason. *M. c.* ssp. *c.* 'Moorflamme' is a little taller at 75cm (2½ft), develops rich purple hues in the leaves in autumn and has singularly dark showy panicles. *M. c.* ssp. *c.* 'Edith Dudszus' has dark, red-purple stems and dense spikes of very dark spikelets of a rich purple; it grows to about 90cm (3ft).

The moor grasses have a couple of eccentricities. The first is that, unlike most ornamental grasses, they are totally deciduous, the leaves falling away completely in the winter while with most other ornamental grasses the foliage, though it goes dormant, remains attached to the plant. The other peculiarity is that, whereas other grasses normally grow away strongly once planted, the moor grasses can be slow to establish, often taking two or three seasons to settle down. For this reason it pays to obtain larger, rather than smaller, plants. While they all are quite splendid in ordinary garden soil, they attain their optimum development in soil that is rather damper.

Miscanthus

No modern garden is complete without one or more miscanthus, or eulalia grasses, as they are also known (*Miscanthus sinensis* was once *Eulalia japonica*). The modern hybrids, which account for the miscanthus now mostly grown in gardens, are primarily the work of Ernst Pagels of Leer in East Friesia in Northern Germany, a former pupil of that pioneer of grass gardening Karl Foerster. Pagels was already world-famous as a breeder of perennial plants before he turned his attentions to miscanthus in the late 1970s. The problem he set out to solve was that miscanthus would not flower in the relatively short, cool summers of northern Europe. His starting point was *Miscanthus sinensis* 'Gracillimus' (maiden grass), which is not only known to flower regularly but also to exhibit considerable variation. Among his first batch of seedlings was one that was particularly free-flowering. It was the seedlings from this plant, the F_2 generation, that exhibited the hoped-for diversity, and from these were bred or selected the new generation of miscanthus, the so-called new hybrids.

These new hybrid miscanthus have exactly the qualities Pagels was looking for. They are floriferous and early flowering, and vary considerably in the poise of the panicles, the width of the leaves and also in stature, some being dwarf, some tall. All form dense rounded mounds of good green foliage, usually with a distinct white or silvery mid-rib, and have panicles which are usually described as whisk-like, but they might also be considered to bear a resemblance to attenuated Prince of Wales feathers. Most modern varieties begin to flower in mid-summer, the folded flowers emerging a rich, vinous, reddish-purple, fluffing out to silvery plumes and then gradually turning white and slowly becoming pale beige as the seeds disperse, leaving the empty husks, which will usually remain looking beautiful until well after mid-winter. In most gardens they are used as specimens but many varieties are even more attractive when planted in drifts. There are now well over a hundred named varieties, and it is easier to compare their merits if they are broken down into groups.

The Maiden Grass Group
This group is based on *Miscanthus sinensis* 'Gracillimus', which forms very dense, rounded, rather mushroom-shaped mounds that in time can reach as much as 1.8m (6ft) tall, and rather more in width, though it is usually seen rather smaller than this. The leaves should be dark green and very narrow, and they should not all be the same, some being wider, some narrower. It is really treasured for the fine texture of its leaves and for its overall form, which is particularly useful in large landscapes. In the UK it seldom flowers but in the warmer climate of the USA the copper-coloured flowers may be produced in late autumn. *M. s.* 'Sarabande' is a considerable improvement and in the USA it has now largely ousted *M. s.* 'Gracillimus' as the trade standard. It has

PLATE IV

Molinia caerulea ssp. arundinacea
(tall moor grass)

'Karl Foerster'

'Bergfreund'

All plants shown approximately ½ size

'Zuneigung'

'Windspiel'

'Fontäne'

narrower leaves that give it a finer overall texture and also flowers more freely, the fingers of the flowers being much more slender than those those of most miscanthus.

The Early Flowering Group

The Early Flowering Group contains hybrids of *Miscanthus sinensis* 'Gracillimus' that were specifically bred to flower early in the cool summers of northern Europe. The only pre-Pagels selection to flower at all freely was *M. s.* 'Silberfeder', which is still sometimes grown though by modern standards it is not reliably good in flower and is inclined to flop. The first to flower in northern Germany is *M. s.* 'Nishidake', which grows to some 2.4m (8ft) and is remarkable for the sheer quantity of bloom it produces. The first to flower in my own garden in Hampshire in southern England, usually within two or three weeks of midsummer's day, are *M. s.* 'Malepartus' and *M. s.* 'Ferne Osten'. The former is the classic among the modern hybrids, the yardstick by which the others are measured. It grows some 1.5m (5ft) tall in flower, with a strongly upright habit and quite broad leaves that are rather darker than usual borne all the way up the stem. The flowers unfurl an exceptionally rich vinous reddish-purple, fluff out to a silky whiteness when in flower and then turn a curiously dark, dusky café-au-lait while the leaves assume autumnal tints of reds and yellows and purples, after which the whole plant fades through yellows to a sere beige for the winter. Even darker in flower is *M. s.* 'Gewitterwolke' ('Thundercloud') whose sultry plumes are a singularly deep, vinous purple. It has an upright habit of growth.

Miscanthus sinensis 'Ferne Osten' ('Far East') is similar but smaller, growing to about 1.5m (5ft), and altogether more delicate in its build: the flowers, which open at the same time, are exceptionally rich in the reddishness of the early purple colouring. *M. s.* 'Rotsilber' is notable for the silvery stripe down the centre of the leaves, which are narrower than those of 'Malepartus'. It grows to 1.5m (5ft), and has flowers that are particularly deep red at first but then turn white and fluffy. *M. s.* 'Vorläufer' is similar but smaller, growing no more than 75cm (2½ft) tall. *M. s.* 'Gearmella', lacking the conspicuous reddish-purple colouring in the opening flowers, affords a useful contrast to these varieties: it grows to about 1m (3¼ft) and has quite broad leaves and large heads of silvery flowers.

All these varieties hold their panicles upright: more attractive if anything are those varieties whose panicles are somewhat pendulous. The three following varieties are all so good that there is little to choose between them, though *M. s.* 'Sirene' is my own favourite. It grows some 1.2m (4ft) tall in flower with proportionately large flowers that fluff out to a silvery white and are pendulous, moving with the slightest breath of air. *M. s.* 'Flamingo', one of the best, is marginally taller, up to 1.5m (5ft), and has more red in its plumes. The fingers of the flowers arch upwards and then droop gracefully. *M. s.* 'Haiku' is similar but smaller, while *M. s.* 'Kleine Fontäne' is again similar but with thinner fingers to the flowers. *M. s.* 'Kaskade' has broader leaves than either of the two preceding varieties, with a white central midrib, and stouter flower stems which bear flowers that are reddish at first and positively fountainous in their form. It grows to about 1.8m (6ft).

The Graziella Group

The Graziella Group flower two weeks to a month later than those in the Early Flowering Group, but are just as lovely. *Miscanthus sinensis* 'Graziella' itself is said to be in many ways fairly typical of the wild species but is in fact vastly superior, with narrow leaves, long stems and large panicles held well above the foliage, silvery at first gradually turning pure white, then fading to beige, the flower form somewhat resembling ostrich plumes. At maturity it can reach as much as 1.8m (6ft) tall. *M. s.* 'Undine' is similar but built on altogether lighter lines. It grows to about 1.4m (4½ft) tall and has bright green leaves and coppery-pink panicles.

Contrasting miscanthus flowers: on the left the typical wild form of *Miscanthus sinensis* with open plumes and on the right *M. s.* 'Rotsilber' with narrower but more richly coloured plumes. In the foreground is *Hystrix patula*, the bottlebrush grass.

M. s. 'Kleine Silberspinne' ('Little Silver Spider') grows to scarcely 90cm (3ft) in flower and has very narrow, horizontally held leaves and relatively large plumes of silvery-grey flowers. *M. s.* 'Nippon' is distinct among the smaller miscanthus in having very narrow, very upright plumes that never seem to relax or fluff out, making it a singularly neat, tidy plant. It grows to about 1.2m (4ft) in flower. *M. s.* 'Blutenwonder' ('Wonderful Blooms') is a little taller, growing to 1.5m (5ft), and is notable for producing its white plumes at staggered heights, creating quite a different effect from other miscanthus. *M. s.* 'China' is considered by Ernst Pagels to be the most refined of his hybrids. It has narrow, small, olive green leaves and is remarkable both for its long-stemmed, large plumes and for the brilliance of its autumn colouring. It is relatively dwarf, reaching some 1.2m (4ft). *M. trans-morrisonensis* is similar but has narrower, dark green leaves and plumes with more slender fingers.

The Emerald Giant Group

This group contains a number of varieties that will grow as tall as the upper limit of the wild species, that is to around 3m (10ft). It is based on *Miscanthus sinensis* 'Emerald Giant', which is a green-leaved reversion from *M. s.* 'Cosmopolitan', selected and named by Greg Speichert. It has the same broad leaves as 'Cosmopolitan', and the same or greater vigour, growing if anything a little taller and producing, late on in the summer, sumptuous silvery plumes. The plumes are exceeded in size only by those of *M. s.* 'Poseidon' which, however, only grows to some 2.1m (7ft). Two of Ernst Pagels' hybrids, *M. s.* 'Roland' and *M. s.* 'Silberturm' ('Silver Tower'), reach much the same proportions, but each has different qualities. 'Silberturm' has silvery plumes and is stiffly upright, while 'Roland' has richer-coloured plumes but tends to flop while in flower, becoming upright for the winter. 'Roland' is the better plant where space permits.

The Silberspinne Group

Miscanthus sinensis 'Grosse Fontäne' ('Big Fountain') has broad green leaves with a silver midrib and large panicles of weeping flowers that contain more silver than red. It grows to some 1.8m (6ft). *M. s.* 'Silberspinne' ('Silver Spider') is smaller at 1.2m (4ft), and is distinct in that the narrow leaves instead of arching or curving stand out at right angles to the stems: the panicles are made up of long spidery fingers, reddish at first, becoming silvery.

The Adagio Group

There are a number of dwarf miscanthus that are a boon to those with small gardens for which the larger miscanthus would be too gross. Most are excellent in pots, and for massing. The group is based on *Miscanthus sinensis* 'Adagio', which grows to no more than 90cm (3ft) in flower and is early-flowering. It is generally considered the most elegant of all the small miscanthus. The members of this group are not all forms of *Miscanthus sinensis*, though one which has been circulating in Europe for many years under the name *M. yakushimensis* may in fact turn out to be just that. It was collected on Yakushima Island, Japan, and is fairly typical of the miscanthus found there. It makes a very dense clump, much in the manner of *M. sinensis* 'Gracillimus', but grows only to some 1.2m (4ft) in flower, the narrow foliage becoming suffused with unassuming tints of orange and yellow in autumn, the oatmeal plumes being held well above the foliage mound. It is notably free-flowering. The name *M. sinensis* 'Yaku Jima' has in the past been applied both to this plant and to an even dwarfer strain endemic to Yakushima Island, where many of the plants are smaller than their counterparts on the mainland. This diminutive plant grows to little more than 30cm (12in) in flower, and should now

Cortaderia selloana 'Pumila' produces its short, plump plumes with greater freedom than any other pampas grass.

be called *M. s.* 'Little Kitten' to avoid confusion. It has extraordinarily narrow leaves, and looks much like a miniature version of M. s. 'Gracillimus', but is not free-flowering. *M. tinctorius* 'Nanus Variegatus' is rather larger, growing to about 75cm (2½ft) in flower, but is quite different in that it has a running habit, and is somewhat variegated with creamy stripes on most of the leaves. It is a pretty plant, with plumes that are rust-coloured at first. Similar to these in stature is *M. nepalensis*, which produces rich tawny-gold plumes; sadly it is more tender than the *M. sinensis* varieties.

The Purpurascens Group

This group is based on what has been grown for years as *Miscanthus sinensis* 'Purpurascens', although it differs in a number of important respects from *M. sinensis*. It is a smaller plant, growing to 1.2m (4ft) at most rather than the 2.1m (7ft) typical of *M. sinensis* in the wild, has a more open habit and thinner leaves which give good autumn colour. The panicles are also more upright and are produced earlier in the season. Modern thinking is that this and the other miscanthus grown for their autumn colour belong to *M. oligostachyus*, a closely related Japanese species, a suggestion which is further borne out by the rather different cultural conditions they require, for these flame grasses, as they are known, are not happy in dry heat, preferring moister atmospheric conditions and needing a touch of cold to initiate the final flames of autumnal colouring.

Flame grass itself, *M. oligostachyus* 'Purpurascens', is a compact plant with mid-green leaves that have a distinct reddish tinge to them, even in the spring, the colour intensifying as the year goes by until in the early autumn the whole plant becomes incandescent with reds and oranges, while at the same time the panicles billow out startlingly white in contrast; later the leaves fade to a smouldering reddish ochre while the panicles turn a fluffy oatmeal. *M. o.* 'Herbstfeuer' ('Autumn Fire') is slightly shorter and has brighter autumn colour, while *M. o.* 'Africa', which only grows to some 90cm (3ft), has the brightest autumn colour of all. All three will grow in shade or semi-shade, where their autumn colouring will be in pastel tints. *M. o.* 'Roterpfeil' is rather taller and happier in sun. It produces the typical narrow, upright plumes of the group. These are marvellous plants to use as seasonal highlights among other grasses or in mixed schemes, the very essence of grass gardening being to keep wave after wave of interest arising as the season waxes and wanes.

Miscanthus × oligonensis

The miscanthus in this hybrid group are the results of crosses between *Miscanthus sinensis* and *M. oligostachyus*, and look in effect like medium-sized forms of *M. sinensis* but with bright, light green leaves. All have much pinker, rather chunkier plumes than those of *M. sinensis*. They are better known in continental Europe than they are in the UK, and may not be hardy enough for the USA. *Miscanthus × oligonensis* 'Juli' is so named because characteristically it is in full flower in July. *M. × o.* 'Wetterfahne' is similar but with the bonus that the leaves turn reddish in early winter. Both grow to about 1.2m (4ft). *M. × o.* 'Zwergelefant' ('Little Elephant') reaches about 1.8m (6ft) and produces rosy-pink plumes on top of the foliage. It is notably free-flowering. The name is derived from the way the plume emerges from the flag-leaf, looking somewhat like an elephant's snout.

The Tall Group

There are three miscanthus that grow far taller than any of these, and are primarily grown for the sub-tropical luxuriance of their foliage, which is very broad for a grass. These are *Miscanthus floridulus*, *M. sacchariflorus* and *M.* 'Giganteus', all of which are useful as accent plants to draw the eye to the middle of broad plantings of grasses or of broad-leaved plants and to give height to such plantings. In the UK there is some confusion among nurserymen as to which is which, but *M. floridulus* as at present understood is a smooth plant growing to 2.4m (8ft) with an upright, clumping habit, *M. sacchariflorus* has stems covered with short, fine hairs and reaches 3m (10ft) tall with a robust upright but spreading habit, while *M.* 'Giganteus' is the tallest of the three at 3.3m (11ft) and is hairy like *M. sacchariflorus* but does not run. Moreover it flowers in most seasons in the UK, which the other two do not. All three are winter dormant, leaving tall, bleached, leafy skeletons that shiver in the pale winter sunshine.

Cortaderia

Cortaderia species (pampas grasses) have the largest and showiest panicles of any of the hardy grasses and they also make the largest mounds of foliage and so are not suitable for all gardens. Having said that, they can look absolutely stunning planted right at the back of a deep border, in a corner with sufficient plants in front of them to hide most of the foliage, so that all that is seen is the flower plumes towering above everything else. All the pampas grasses form large rounded tussocks of arching, evergreen foliage, the leaves being edged with retrorse teeth so that one can plunge one's hand into the heart of the clump without harm, but be literally cut to the bone trying to draw it out: always wear tough leather gloves when handling pampas grasses. The plumes are silken to begin with, but gradually fill out and become fluffy. They are produced in mid and late summer in the USA, but usually not until early or mid-autumn in the UK.

Although the pampas grasses are generally considered hardy in the UK they are only rated as hardy to zone 5 in the USA. However, for those who live in cold winter areas two new species may bring hope. These are *C. patagonica* and *C. uspellata*, both of which are strong-growing varieties from parts of South America where they have to endure extremely cold winters. They are reported to have blue foliage and to be free-flowering.

Plants of *C. selloana* are either male or female, and the female's flowers are the showiest. Most named selections are female. Where both sexes are grown together seedlings may occur, and some of these may be variegated. Of the many varieties of *C. selloana*, 'Pumila' is one of the smallest and probably the freest of all in flower, the white plumes rising to 1.5m (5ft), which is about twice the height of the leaf mound. *C. s.* 'Monstrosa' on the other hand is probably the tallest of the cultivated clones, with

Cortaderia selloana 'Sunningdale Silver', one of the tallest and showiest pampas grasses.

plumes which are perhaps the whitest in the group reaching 3m (10ft), though the leaf mound is only 1.2m (4ft) tall. *C. s.* 'Sunningdale Silver' is an old variety that has stood the test of time. It grows to about the same height in flower as 'Monstrosa' but has fuller plumes on stouter stems that are notably sturdy and wind resistant, and a much taller leaf mound.

There are also several varieties with pink or purplish plumes, though these are not so often seen. *C. s.* 'Carminea Rendatleri' is a tall variety, to 3m (10ft), with plumes that are pink flushed purple. The colour of the plumes is most attractive but the flower stems are weak and easily broken in the wind. *C. s.* 'Carnea' produces shorter stems with paler pink plumes and is generally more satisfactory. *C. s.* 'Rosea' and *C. s.* 'Roi des Roses' are not really pink but have plumes that are basically white with a pink flush, while *C. s.* 'Violacea' has plumes that are tinted violet.

All the pampas grasses are best planted where they can be seen against a dark background such as pines or laurels with the sun either beside or behind them. so that they appear to possess their own luminescence. They should all be grown in sun in well-drained but moisture-retentive soils.

Many other varieties of pampas grass used to be grown in bygone days and they may still lurk in private gardens, to emerge in the trade again in due course. While most are good garden plants, those mentioned above have stood the test of time, and in any case would be hard to better.

9 Lesser Flowering Grasses

While there is a broad consensus as to which grasses are ornamentally the most important, there is no such general agreement when it comes to those that are perhaps just a little less ornamental, or less easy to come by, or less easy to grow. This is partly because there are so many grasses to chose from, about 1000 species worldwide, and partly because ideas of what is decorative and what is not are highly personal. But there is a defining factor, and this is that not all grasses grow equally well in all gardens or all climates. Our first grass in this section is a prime example of this.

Saccharum

Saccharum ravennae (*Erianthus ravennae*), Ravenna grass, is often described by American nurserymen as a giant

Cortaderia fulvida is one of the largest of all ornamental grasses and one of the most richly coloured.

among ornamental grasses. And so it is – in the USA. Its multitudes of slender, silvery, feathery plumes, like stretched pampas grass panicles, rising from dense clumps of arching, dark green leaves in late summer and lasting through until midwinter, can be 60cm (2ft) long and reach as much as 3.6m (12ft) tall, the whole plant metamorphosing through shades of orange, tan and purple to subtler tones of beige and brown. In southern England it is a miserable thing, making a leaf mound no more than 90cm (3ft) tall and producing, if at all, an occasional bedraggled flower spike only 1.5m (5ft) tall that usually breaks in the first wind, while further north, lacking the summer baking it gets in the USA, it is not even hardy. Perhaps it would flower better if it were to be given a good baking at the foot of a south wall: certainly it is showy enough in flower to justify the effort.

Another saccharum, *S. arundinaceum*, which is scarcely known even in its native USA, grows even larger, making a mound of grey-green leaves as much as 3m (10ft) tall and as much across, with the plumes borne up to 90cm (3ft) above that, but it may suffer from lack of summer heat in the UK, just as Ravenna grass does.

Cortaderia

Nearly as large and just as showy is *Cortaderia fulvida*, the toe-toe (pronounced 'toy-toy'), often known as New Zealand pampas grass, which has broad, smooth, upward-arching leaves that can form a mound 1.5m (5ft) tall and more across. In midsummer, high above the leaf mound on tall, arching stems, it bears large, somewhat drooping, one-sided plumes that are white or an eye-catching flamingo pink. In British gardens it generally suffers the defect that every year, as summer advances, whole bundles of leaves die off in the midst of the otherwise flourishing clump. This does not seem to be caused by any pestilence but may simply be a problem of soil condition, for all the plants I know of in the UK are growing in ordinary earth while in its native New Zealand it grows at the edge of lakes and rivers, not merely with its roots in water but with as much as a third of the clump at least seasonally submerged. Perhaps it would do better in conditions more nearly approaching its wild habitat.

The showy South African grass *Merxmuellera macowanii* is hardy in zone 7.

Ampelodesmos

A generally more reliable plant for anyone in the UK wanting a specimen that is a little out of the ordinary is *Ampelodesmos mauritanicus* (rope grass), a surprisingly hardy Mauritian endemic now naturalized in parts of South Africa, where it is used for rope-making. It forms large clumps of dark, lustrous evergreen leaves, much in the manner of the pampas grasses, the leaves retaining their lustre through the winter. The buff flowers, which appear in early summer, could scarcely be more different from those of the pampas grasses, the 45cm (18in) panicles consisting of bundles of big spikelets borne on the tips of slender, pendulous branches at the tops of tall outward-arching stems, the panicles having a one-sided appearance. To give of its best it needs a sunny, well-drained position, and it is not reliably hardy in the colder parts of the UK.

Merxmuellera

In terms of sheer beauty *Merxmuellera macowanii* really belongs among the grasses of the first order and it is placed among the lesser grasses only because at present it is virtually unobtainable, though that may soon change. It forms a rounded mound of thin, reed-like leaves, about knee high, and from late spring to midsummer bears well-filled plump panicles of an extraordinarily showy foxy reddish-brown colour. The only reason I can imagine for a plant of such outstanding beauty being so little known is that it hails from southern Africa and so may initially have been suspected of tenderness, though plants have been grown outside at the Royal Botanic Gardens, Kew, for many years now.

Graminea sp. Nepal

Superbly showy is a grass species that has only recently been introduced from Nepal, where it is known as cat grass. It produces impressive, rather pampas-like one-sided panicles which look good from midsummer until late winter, and grows to about 1m (3¼ft) in flower.

Panicum

The switch grasses and fountain grasses are generally in the front rank of flowering plants but there are a couple of species in each genus which though generally useful are not so well known, presumably because they are not quite so good. Of the switch grasses, *Panicum bulbosum* is only a little inferior in flower to the more widely cultivated *P. virgatum* forms. It grows to some 1.2m (4ft) and has green leaves with a greyish surface sheen, produced a little earlier than those of *P. virgatum*, the leaves gradually becoming suffused with red in late summer, again a little earlier. The green flowers are also borne earlier in the season.

The second of the lesser switch grasses is *P. clandestinum*, known as deer tongue grass. This is grown more for its foliage than for its flowers, the leaves being, as the common name suggests, very broad for a grass and bearing a fancied resemblance to the tongue of a deer. They are soft and a rich, lustrous green, gradually turning glowing yellows and russets with unusual purple tints as autumn approaches, but are borne on surprisingly thin stems that often become almost prostrate under the weight of late summer and autumn rains. It is to the tiny, bead-like flowers that the specific epithet refers, and what is clandestine about them is that they never open, so that the sexual processes occur in secret. In the UK the flowers are borne among the leaves and are scarcely seen, but in the USA they are borne above the leaves in a diffuse panicle typical of the switch grasses, at first silvery but later becoming brown. Plants differ considerably in stature between the UK and USA, making arching mounds of foliage as much as 1.2m (4ft) tall in the USA but scarcely reaching 90cm (3ft) in the UK.

Pennisetum

Pennisetum alopecuroides 'Moudry' and *P. a.* 'National Arboretum', the late-flowering or black-seeded fountain grasses, may be a mixed blessing. They form much lusher clumps than the ordinary fountain grass, but it is the flowers that are so dramatically different – they are like thick, broad bottle-brushes opening a dark chestnut brown and maturing black. In the USA the flowers emerge at the very end of summer, while in the UK the summers are seldom long enough to tempt them into flower at all. In the USA 'Moudry' can become a pest because it produces fertile seed in abundance. The name *P. a.* 'Viridescens' is sometimes incorrectly applied to 'Moudry', but this plant differs in having pale green panicles. It too needs long hot summers to induce flowering.

Melica

Melica altissima (Siberian melic) and its white and purple forms, 'Alba' and 'Atropurpurea', have long been beloved of flower arrangers and have traditionally been grown in flower borders: having tried them in a planting of pure grasses I can see why, for they lean on their neighbours for support. They form loose tufts of soft leaves rising to about 60cm (2ft) with the flowers held another 60cm (2ft) above the foliage. Typically the panicles are held erect and consist of loose spikes of showy florets which can be white, as in 'Alba', or mauvey-purple, as in 'Atropurpurea', the florets being followed by rice-like grains which in 'Atropurpurea' are jet black. In the wild these cool-season grasses grow in woodland margins or glades, often leaning for support on woody plants or on perennials with a firmer skeleton, or else sprawling their way up through hedgerows. They will tolerate light shade, though they will also grow in hot, drying sun. *M. a.* 'Atropurpurea' is the form most often grown, and its sumptuously dark flowers, which tend to hang to one side of the spike, go well with dark-leaved plants such as the purple orach, purple plantain or purple-leaved cannas, though, like most purple-flowered plants, they also look good among silver plants and harmonize well with the nacreous flowers of *Salvia turkestanica*, which seem to combine both silver and purple. *Melica transsilvanica* is similar but smaller, with grey-green leaves and fluffy, purplish-pink flowers. *M. t.* 'Atropurpurea' has delicious, deeper-coloured flowers.

Bouteloua

The side-oats grama and the blue grama or mosquito grass are warm-season clumpers from the North American shortgrass prairies, both notable for their one-sided panicles borne on wire-thin stems. The better-known of the two is *Bouteloua gracilis*, the mosquito grass, so-called because of the way in which the spikelets hang down beneath the horizontally held axis like the larvae of mosquitoes hanging from the surface of a sheet of water. The finely textured foliage is a light grey-green and makes dense mounds about 15cm (6in) tall, with the flowers rising some 30cm (12in) above the foliage. These are produced in summer and are silvery-grey at first gradually growing darker to reach almost purple at maturity, the whole plant assuming purplish autumnal colour before bleaching for the winter.

B. curtipendula, the side-oats grama, is an altogether larger and coarser grass, and perhaps all the showier for that. It differs most fundamentally from mosquito grass in that the panicles are held erect, in line with the stem, instead of being set at an odd angle. The large spikelets, which are borne on one side of the stem from mid-summer onwards, are reddish-purple at first gradually becoming golden-beige and then bleaching out once the frosts start. The tufts of grey-green leaves grow to about 45cm (18in), while the flowers may reach as much as 75cm (2½ft). Both are grasses that need well-drained soil, especially in winter, and because of this need for good drainage they are often recommended for rock gardens, though a lone plant surrounded by rocks can look desolate. They are really better grown in drifts, as they grow in the wild, or as the matrix for meadows. Once established they will survive the driest of summers.

Briza

Quaint rather than beautiful, fascinating rather than showy, is perennial quaking grass. It forms loose, slowly increasing tufts of rather thin, mid-green leaves and in early summer produces branching panicles bearing at the tips of the branches small, locket-like spikelets, the whole reaching about 60cm (2ft). The plant is green to start with but gradually take on shades of biscuit, becoming dormant in the middle of summer. By the time the autumn leaves turn new leaves have started into growth for the following season and the old flowering culms break loose soon after that. *B. m.* 'Limouzi' is a slightly taller selection with bluer leaves and larger spikelets.

Eragrostis

Eragrostis curvula (African love grass) has an ethereal beauty. Its dark green leaves, almost hair-like in texture, can grow to as much as 90cm (3ft), making large, low, arching clumps from the midst of which arise, from midsummer to early autumn, slim, arching, 90cm (3ft) stems bearing large, delicate, diffuse grey-green panicles which are lovely both in detail and from a distance, and which are so delicate and borne on such fine stems they sway with every suspiration of the air. In winter the leaves bleach out, but the airy panicles remain, greenish-grey. The flowers emit a peculiar odour, only noticeable at close quarters, as though some animal had left its scent.

E. chloromelas (Boer love grass) is broadly similar but larger, growing to 1.2m (4ft), and differing most notably in its overall colouring which is greyish in some forms but a blue almost as intense as *Elymus arenarius* in the best forms. The panicles are generally similar and borne on similarly long slender stems, but greyish rather than grey-green. Of the two, *Eragrostis chloromelas* is slightly the hardier. Both of these warm-season grasses take up a lot of space on the ground relative to their height, covering a diameter of some 1m (3¼ft). Although both are usually grown as single specimens, making first-rate foils to more virile plants, they are also effective used in large drifts and planted thus are remarkably good weed suppressors. Their arching habits make them ideal for growing at the edge of a raised bed, or in large pots, where their foliage and flowers can droop over the sides.

Eragrostis trichodes (sand love grass) is more spectacular, producing large, diffuse panicles some 90cm (3ft) long bearing myriad tiny shimmering amethyst spikelets, the panicles being unusual in that they are narrowest at the bottom and widest at the top, the flowers being borne so freely that they obscure the foliage. *E. t.* 'Bend', known as Bend love grass, is a selection with larger panicles of reddish-bronze spikelets that can measure as much as 20cm (8in) across. The panicles are so large they tend to splay outwards under their own weight. *E. spectabilis* is similar but has smaller panicles and bright, almost iridescent violet spikelets. Both are cool-season clumpers that grow vigorously until the flowers begin to emerge in midsummer, the mid-green leaves making tufts to about 60cm (2ft). They are marvellous grasses for a specimen position, but, like most grasses with diffuse panicles, equally lovely massed, especially where they can be seen with the sun shining through the flowers.

Andropogon

The North American bluestems are so called because of the silvery blueness of their stems, though these are often suffused with purple, and are grown more for this colouring than for their flowers, though their Latin name is derived from *aner*, man, and *pogon*, beard, referring to the silky white hairs found on the spikelets of most species. The bluestems all used to be *Andropogon*, but have now been split, to the confusion of gardeners, between *Andropogon* and *Schizachyrium*. In older books and catalogues the one name is often used incorrectly for the other. The bluestems used to be a major constituent of both the tallgrass and shortgrass prairies, but are becoming scarce in the wild just as growers and nurserymen are begining to take a real interest in them. As they have such a vast native range there is often considerable variation within the species, and forms will soon be on the market that have been selected as having even bluer stems, even brighter autumn colour or greater or lesser stature.

The best known of the bluestems in Europe is the big bluestem, *A. gerardii*, a species that varies greatly in stature in its native haunts, which stretch from Oklahoma to Canada and from Ohio in the west to Colorado in the east. It grows as much as 3m (10ft) in flower under optimum conditions at the eastern end of its range, where it is known as the king of grasses, though it grows to little more than 90cm (3ft) at its southern limit. The forms grown in Europe are at the shorter end of the range, seldom more than 1.2m (4ft) tall in flower. They form tight clumps of strongly upright, silvery-blue stems with arching bluish leaves, usually tipped and stained with purple, the purplish colouring intensifying and spreading over larger areas of the leaves and into the stems once mid-summer is past, the whole plant turning rich purple in late summer and then, as the nights turn colder, a castaneous brown, a colour they hold well into the winter. The flowers, borne in late summer and early autumn, are rich, reddish-purple with soft white hairs protruding from the tips, and are carried on long, slender stems. Because of its elegant upright habit, big bluestem is often used as a single plant in a specimen position, and as such it goes well with greys and silvers, and with many of those plants of the Michaelmas season that have flowers in shades of mournful mauves, for example the *Aster novi-belgii* varieties such as 'Chequers', 'Coombe Rosemary' and 'Royal Velvet' or the lighter tones of the long-flowering *A.* × *frikartii* 'Mönch' or 'Flora's Delight'.

A. saccharoides is sometimes known as silver bluestem but more often as silver beardgrass, which rather reflects the fact that it is grown more for its flowers than for its foliage. It forms dense clumps of glossy green leaves about 30cm (12in) high and produces slender erect stems topped with spike-like flowers some 90cm (3ft) tall from midsummer onwards, the flowers expanding at maturity to allow silky white hairs to emerge, and it is these which give this grass its particular appeal. Once the nights start

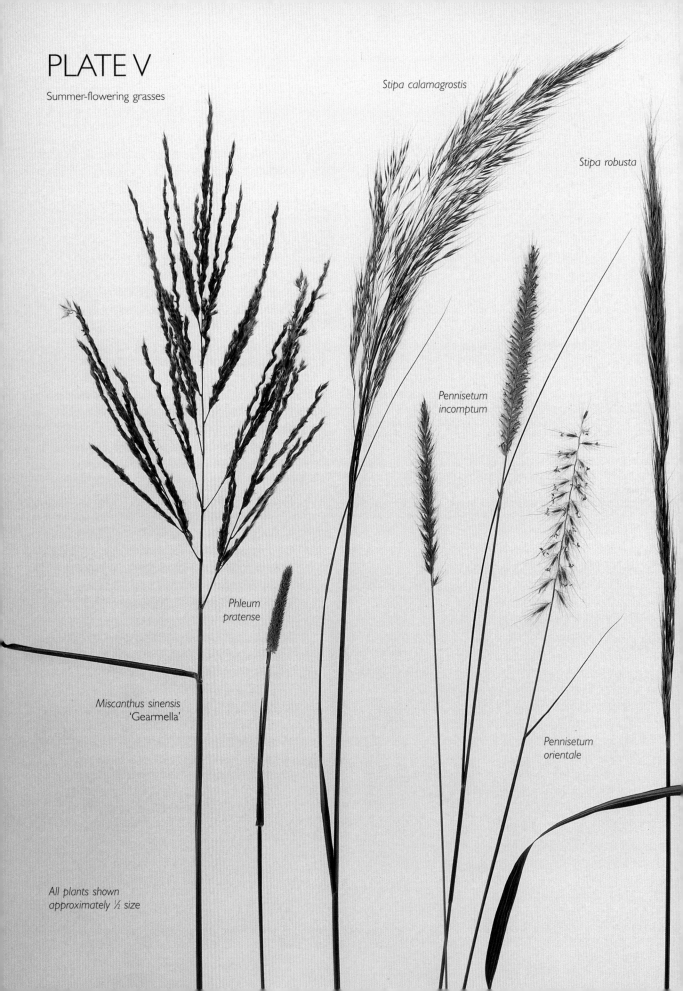

PLATE V

Summer-flowering grasses

Stipa calamagrostis

Stipa robusta

Pennisetum incomptum

Phleum pratense

Miscanthus sinensis 'Gearmella'

Pennisetum orientale

All plants shown approximately ½ size

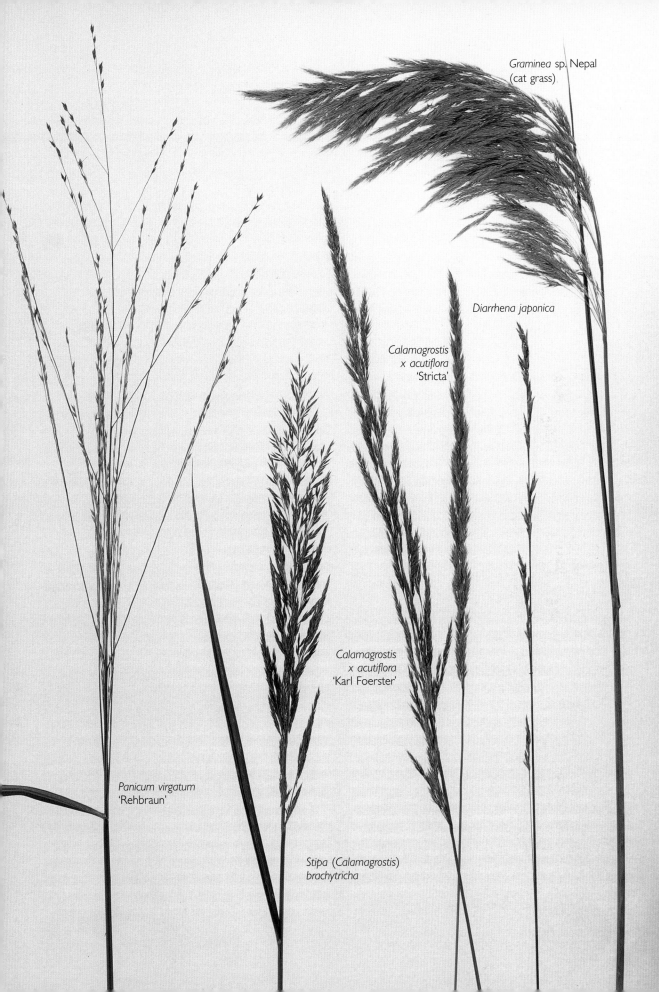

Graminea sp. Nepal
(cat grass).

Diarrhena japonica

Calamagrostis
x acutiflora
'Stricta'

Calamagrostis
x acutiflora
'Karl Foerster'

Panicum virgatum
'Rehbraun'

Stipa (Calamagrostis)
brachytricha

to turn cold the whole plant becomes flushed with purple and orange, colouring which lasts for several weeks into the winter before being succeeded by bleached beige. Both of these bluestems need light, well-drained soil and a position in the sun.

Imperata

The satintail and Japanese blood grass belong in the same genus, *Imperata*, but whereas the blood grass (*I. cylindrica* 'Rubra') is grown for its foliage and has never been known to flower in the West, the satintail (*I. brevifolia*) is grown for its flowers, its curious reddish or brownish foliage being of merely secondary interest. They are borne in a cylindrical, spike-like panicle, satiny and pinkish or light brown when they first appear in midsummer, later covered with long, silky, cotton-white hairs, creating a fluffy effect. Satintail is a slowly spreading warm-season grass producing more or less vertical leaves, much in the manner of the blood grass, some 30–45cm (12–18in) long, at first translucent light green gradually becoming flushed with red, though never so brightly as in the blood grass, the whole plant becoming in the autumn a glowing purplish-red. It is not a sufficiently arresting plant for a prime position in the garden, and, with its liking for damp or even waterside conditions, is better in a background role. It is ideal for naturalizing or for mixing in meadows where the soil is damp, or even for planting by the waterside, on the banks of streams or ponds.

Tridens

Tridens flavus (purple top) is a native of the eastern states of the USA where it is generally loathed by farmers who consider it a pestilential weed, but loved by everyone else for the haze of purple it spreads over meadows in the late summer and autumn. It is a warm-season clumper with 1cm (½in) wide leaves forming upright tufts some 45cm (18in) tall that take on purple tints in the autumn before turning a golden straw colour. Large, open panicles of rich, reddish-purple spikelets are produced on pendulous branches at the tops of 1.2m (4ft) stems that sway elegantly in the gentlest of breezes. It is an adaptable grass, reaching its finest development in moist, fertile soils in sun but also growing in shade, though it will not flower so freely and will tend to flop. Once established, it is surprisingly drought-tolerant. It makes a most interesting specimen, but is also ideal for naturalizing in meadows.

Muhlenbergia

Muhlenbergia filipes (purple muhly), a native of the southeastern states of the USA from North Carolina down to Florida, is even more striking in its colouring, producing what look like clouds of violet purple floating above the foliage, the clouds being made up of huge open panicles with incredibly fine, thread-like branches. It is a clumping, warm-season grass, thought by some botanists to be merely a form of *M. capillaris* (hairy awn muhly), from which it differs most remarkably from a gardener's point of view in its richer purple colouring and in flowering later, often as late as mid and late autumn, even in its native states. The panicles rise some 90cm (3ft) above the rather unremarkable foliage, which forms a mound about 30cm (12in) high. Like most muhlys, it needs perfect drainage in full sun, preferably on a light, sandy or stony soil.

M. rigens (deer grass) could hardly be more different in flower, the panicle, being merely thin and whip-like, as much as 60cm (2ft) long. They are grey at first becoming buff and are carried on stems up to 1.2m (4ft) tall, vertical at first but becoming arching, moving with every wind and affording a total contrast to almost any other grass panicle. The grey-green leaves of this cool-season clumper are evergreen, and build up into a mound some 75cm (2½ft) tall. This Californian native is surprisingly frost-hardy and, while it grows best in moist but well-drained soils, is extraordinarily tolerant of drought conditions, making it an ideal specimen for a large pot or tub, especially for those who seldom have time to water. While it is excellent as a specimen, affording a strongly vertical accent, it is also perfect for massing, in which capacity it creates a strongly horizontal accent because, like *Calamagrostis* × *acutiflora* 'Karl Foerster', it produces all its flowers at the same height.

Sesleria

Sesleria autumnalis and *S. heufleriana* (autumn moor grass and green moor grass) also have spike-like panicles but are not nearly so showy in flower as *Muhlenbergia rigens*. Nevertheless they are among the best of grasses for general planting and for massing in the open or in light shade because they are easy to grow, adaptable to a variety of soils and conditions, and little troubled by pests and diseases. *S. autumnalis* has a remarkably long season of flower because although its main flowering season is midsummer until the autumn it can begin flowering as early as late spring or early summer, the panicles, which can bè

Nassella trichotoma continues to produce new panicles from spring until the first frosts of winter.

as much as 15cm (6in) long, being fat spikes, purplish-black at first becoming silvery grey and covered with silky white stamens. This is a clumping, cool-season grass with greeny yellow, almost chartreuse, V-shaped ever-green leaves that make an upright divergent tuft to about 45cm (18in). It is excellent for massing.

S. heufleriana is by contrast a spring-flowering species, the first flowers appearing among the crocuses, late snow-drops and early daffodils, the panicles being long spikes of dark brown almost hidden by a mass of showy white stamens. It is valuable as being among the first grasses to flower, but the disadvantage is that in flowering so early the flowers have finished long before the summer is over. The foliage, however, is interesting, being evergreen, mid-green above and silvery beneath, held in an upright-divergent tuft so that one sees the backs of some of the leaves as well as the tops of others. This plant grows into

a mound some 30cm (12in) in height and spread, with the flowers reaching about 75cm (2½ft). Like *S. autumnalis*, it is best massed.

Sporobolus

The American native *Sporobolus* (dropseed) is little known in the UK, which is a pity, for this genus is floriferous in the extreme, rather in the manner of *Panicum virgatum* (see page 54), but more so. The only one currently offered in the UK is *Sporobolus fertilis*, which oddly enough does not seem to be much grown in the USA. It makes elegant, evergreen tufts of thin olive-green leaves, the colour being so distinct that it is almost worth growing for that alone. The showy panicles of tiny spikelets are borne on long stems in the autumn and reach some 1m (3¼ft).

S. airoides (alkali dropseed), a warm-season clumper from the great grass valleys of California, forms humble, upright-arching clumps of fine grey-green leaves up to 90cm (3ft) tall, above which are carried in midsummer great pink cloud-like pyramidal panicles, often produced so densely that the foliage almost disappears, the whole plant turning corn-yellow later in the season.

All the dropseeds need well-drained soil in full sun and, once established (which may take two or three years), are reasonably drought-tolerant. They are seen to best advantage grown where the sun can shine through them from behind or from the side, preferably with a dark background.

Nassella

Nassella trichotoma used to be *Stipa trichotoma* and one can readily see the similarities with, for example, *S. arundinacea*. It is one of the few Andean grasses in cultivation in Europe and is most refined, with extremely fine, bright green leaves, at first upright but becoming arching and eventually making a small mound of greenery with almost trailing leaves, no more than 30cm (12in) tall and half as much again across. The panicles, like those of the dropseeds, are broadly pyramidal, delicate and extraordinarily diffuse, and are borne in early summer in such profusion that they create above and around the shining green foliage mound a pinky-mauve haze so dense it almost hides the leaves. In the midst of this cloud the

The fine, feathery awns and slender leaves of *Stipa tirsa* give an ethereal effect in the garden.

little dark dots of incipent seeds hover, like the heads of dragonflies among their shimmering wings. The flowering culms are weak, so that many of the panicles rest on the ground, creating an insubstantial skirt around the plant.

Phaenosperma

Phaenosperma globosa by contrast is grown for the broadness of its leaves, these being some 30cm (12in) long and over 2.5cm (1in) wide. They are light green with darker ribs, appearing pleated. It forms low clumps above which the thin, straight flower stems appear almost absurdly tall, rising to some 1.5m (5ft), the pyramidal panicles composed of widely spaced whorls of branches bearing tiny spikelets which produce almost round seeds, though the whole affair is too insubstantial to be of much decorative worth. It is evergreen in mild winters, and needs a sunny site.

Stipa

Of the true feather grasses, as opposed to the needle grasses, *Stipa barbata* is the finest in flower, with long, white, wispy, feathery awns measuring some 25cm (10in) long. *S. b.* 'Ecume d'Argent' ('Silver Feather') is said to have even longer awns. It makes an upright-divergent leaf mound about 45cm (18in) tall and the same across of rather undistinguished leaves, from the midst of which the flower stems arise in midsummer. The long-awned panicles are aligned along the same axis to start with, the awns looking like well-greased feathers lying flat against the mid-rib, but then they become angular and the feathers fluff out into feathery, light-trapping luminescence, so seemingly weightless that they appear to float on the currents of air. But this moment of beauty is too good to last and, at the first rough winds, the panicles begin to shatter – the feathery awns, which are no doubt in part a dispersal mechanism, carrying the seeds no further than 90cm–1.2m (3–4ft) from the parent plant. The awns themselves are attached to large heavy seeds by means of a spirally twisted 7.5cm (3in) limb and act as a parachute, ensuring that the seed always lands tip first on the ground; the action of the wind then causes the awn to gyrate, thus drilling the seed into the ground. Having shed its seed the plant, with typical stipa economy, collapses, often going into summer dormancy, at which stage it may look quite unattractive and is best cut down. Sometimes it will recover, growing new leaves in the cool rains of autumn, but not invariably, which is why it is always worth saving some of the seed and sowing it. *S. tirsa* is similar, with even finer, feathery awns and more slender leaves. It is also more soundly perennial. *S. pennata* is smaller, growing to about 75cm (2½ft), with blue-grey leaves which form tight clumps, the feathery plumes not quite so long nor so wide.

S. capillata, though sometimes known as a feather grass, is in fact a needle grass with spikelets that are formed very much in the fashion of *S. gigantea* (see page 57) but are very much longer, drawn out to thin points, and silvery, not golden, carried on stiff stems as much as 90cm (3ft) tall. The leaves are thin and make an insubstantial but dense clump, with the panicles and their stems making up most of the plant. *S. cernua* (nodding feather grass) is similar, as are *S. pulchra* (purple needle grass), *S. offneri* and *S. lepida* (foothill feather grass), though this last is only for warm climates. All of these are best planted in fertile soil in sun, and are most effective grown in drifts rather than as specimens.

There are two stipas to which the name needle grass is highly appropriate. These are *S. extremiorientalis* and *S. turkestanica*, both of which it is now suggested should be translated to the genus *Achnatherum*. The whole appearance of the spikelets is of slender lobster claws attenuated to needle-like extremities, rather than of spikelets subtended by feather-like awns. *S. turkestanica* grows to about 90cm (3ft) and bears its elegant green panicles from early to late summer; it is so showy it makes an excellent substitute for *S. gigantea* in smaller gardens. *S. extremiorientalis* grows to much the same size but has broader, yellowish-green leaves and produces its panicles of green flowers in late summer and early autumn, the leaves turning yellow in autumn and then foxy beige for the winter, contrasting with the panicles which unexpectedly turn black. It reaches its finest flowering just as *S. gigantea* is beginning to fade and, since the two are very similar in the structure of their panicles, *S. extremiorientalis* is useful for filling the same visual space later in the season.

S. arundinacea (which was once *Oryzopsis lessoniana* and which some now call *Anamethele lessoniana*) is a New Zealand native and quite different in appearance from the other species mentioned here. The new leaves are chocolate brown becoming olive green overlaid with a rusty colour which intensifies as autumn approaches to the point where the leaves become splashed and blotched with yellows, reds and oranges. It flowers in the autumn, the panicles being lax and extremely open, bearing few

spikelets and only just appearing beyond the foliage. The panicles, and their manner of presentation, are very similar to those of *Nassella trichotoma*, which was also once *Stipa*. The whole plant is quite ravishing from a little after midsummer until almost midwinter, the foliage rippling in waves like a cornfield when the wind crosses it.

Quite the strangest of the stipas is *S. filiculmis*, whose flowering culms and panicles are so attenuated that, rather than standing up and shaking their flowers in the wind, they flow like tresses of hair, first gathering themselves into waves and then trailing gracefully along the ground. It is not a plant to everyone's taste, nor would it be easy to accommodate in a small garden, but in the right place it could certainly be used to draw the eye.

S. robusta is called sleepy grass because it is reputed to have a narcotic effect on cattle and even more so on horses. It is quite different to any of the species described above, the panicles being tan-coloured, pencil-thin spikes borne at the tops of 1.8m (6ft) stems. The leaves are grey-green and make arching mounds about 90cm (3ft) tall and as much across. It is a good grass for a specimen position, but because of its height it needs a taller background, otherwise the panicles are lost against the sky.

Oryzopsis

Oryzopsis miliacea (rice grass) gains its common name from its general similarity to rice. It is a fast-growing, drought-tolerant, cool-season clumper from the Mediterranean and is grown in gardens for its highly decorative panicles which emerge from early summer through until the frosts. The panicles arch upwards and outwards from the mound of bright, shiny green leaves, and then droop, the silky green spikelets swaying at the tips of slender branches, each panicle being as much as 20–30cm (8–12in) long. The panicles mature to a golden-brown, and remain showy well into the winter. In California, where it has naturalized, it is known as smilo grass.

Sorghastrum

Sorghastrum nutans (Indian grass) is one of the loveliest of the North American natives and was once a major constituent of the tallgrass prairie. It is a warm-season clumper whose leaves can vary from grey-green to almost blue, becoming bright yellow or orange in the autumn, though the form in cultivation in the UK has decidedly green leaves, which may be a matter of lack of summer heat. It also varies greatly in stature, reaching as much as 2.4–3m (8–10ft) in rich, moist fertile soils in the American

Stipa filiculmis produces its slender flowering panicles in such profusion that they hide the foliage. Here they have been gathered by the wind into curious tresses.

Mid-west, but only 60–90cm (2–3ft) in the drier soils of California. In Europe it usually reaches about 90cm (3ft) in flower. The large, dense panicles, which can be 15cm (6in) long and 3in (7.5cm) across, are produced in late summer on stout, stiff, yellow stems, and are coppery tan with long, protruding, rather bristly awns and highly conspicuous golden-yellow pollen sacs. In the autumn the whole plant turns yellow, and then dries to a warm shade of umber. It is equally good grown as a specimen or in drifts, or even naturalized in meadows, in which situation it can stand, and indeed even benefit from, a high mow in the spring. It is adaptable to a wide range of soils but needs sun, becoming lax and shy-flowering in shade.

Chrysopogon

Chrysopogon gryllus, which is closely related to *Sorghastrum nutans* and is sometimes known as *Chrysopogon nutans*, forms large rounded tussocks of strongly two-ranked arching green leaves and produces in midsummer large, showy, pyramidal panicles 15cm (6in) long of gold and purple long-awned spikelets. The branches of these panicles are produced in well-spaced whorls, creating an open and elegant head 1.2m (4ft) tall.

Themeda

Themeda triandra var. *japonica* (Japanese triandra) is a warm-season clumping grass with relatively wide, almost trans-lucent green leaves that seem to have a way of catching and holding the sunlight. They make an upright arching mound some 60cm (2ft) tall. The flowers are little more than small green knobs strung out along the tops of the culms, which radiate stiffly from the leaf mound. In autumn the whole plant turns blazing yellows and oranges before desiccating to a light beige for the winter. It grows best in sun, in good fertile soils, failing to produce its autumn colours in shade.

Bothriochloa

Bothriochloa bladhii gives the appearance of being a soft grass, the pale green leaves being soft to the touch and somewhat limp, but making good, substantial mounds up to 60cm (2ft) high. From midsummer until the first of the severe winter frosts there arise a succession of thin stems tipped with branched panicles which somewhat resemble a rather coarse bottle brush, of an arresting, iridescent maroon, beset with creamy pollen sacs. In autumn the whole plant assumes intense tones of red and purple. Though hailing from Malaysia and Indochina it is surprisingly hardy, but is best in sun and on soils that are not too wet.

Poa

Poa imbecilla (lunatic grass) is a diminutive gem that seems to be scarcely known. It makes dense tufts of needle-thin, dark green leaves to about 10cm (4in) tall and rather more across above which are borne from midsummer until the frosts a long succession of very broad, wide-open green panicles with tiny white spikelets. It is a real treasure for the very front of a border, where it will seed itself about, making pleasing little patches of dark greenery. It seems happiest in moist, fertile soil, with a little shade during the heat of the day.

Lygeum

Lygeum spartum (albardine) is so different from other grasses as to be worth a place on well-drained soils. One of the esparto or paper-making grasses, it makes dense mounds of narrow, bluish-green, rush-like leaves to about 75cm (2½ft) tall and bears its small panicles in late spring and early summer. These panicles are small and softly hairy, like rabbits' tails: what makes them conspicuous is that there is a small, parchment-coloured hood-like bract above each panicle, making the plant look as though a flight of moths has alighted.

FRAGRANT GRASSES

Anthoxanthum

Anthoxanthum odoratum (sweet vernal grass) is grown mainly for the fragrance of its leaves, which is particularly strong through late spring and early summer when it is in flower. It is a small, clumping, evergreen grass with soft, mid-green leaves that make tufts about 18cm (7in) tall, the cylindrical, spike-like panicles, which are silky green at first becoming whitish, rising to about 38cm (15in). It is not showy in flower, but the leaves smell strongly of coumarin when crushed. It is a useful edging to borders, especially where it spills over on to paths, emitting its fragrance when crushed underfoot, or it may be used in meadows, again in positions where it is likely to be walked on. It can also be mown, lightly and occasionally. Its fragrance is strongest when dried and crushed.

Hierochloë

Hierochloë odorata (vanilla or holy grass) has a fragrance like that of vanilla, and was much used in bygone days as one of several aromatic herbs that used to be scattered on floors to make life smell a little sweeter, it being perhaps the most fragrant of all grasses. It is not, however, a grass to be planted in haste or wantonly for it has a root system that resembles that of common couch or twitch grass and a similar capacity to run in all directions with great speed and vigour. It forms loose clumps of indeterminate diameter, the fragrant leaves being narrow, the open panicles, composed of tiny, locket-like spikelets, being among the first to open, in southern England usually before mid-spring. Though really not sufficiently beautiful to justify such favoured treatment, it is probably best grown in a large pot or container where the leaves can be plucked or crushed as one walks by. The lack of visual interest in leaf or flower can easily be compensated for by planting spring and summer bulbs around it.

Sporobolus

Sporobolus heterolepis (prairie dropseed), one of the most refined and elegant of American grasses, has large, delicate, diffuse panicles, borne on slender stems and almost hair-like branches, in great clouds high above the foliage, sometimes reaching as much as 1.2m (4ft). Unusually for a grass the panicles are strongly scented, though there seems to be no agreement on the nature of the smell: some say it smells of coriander, others that it is sweet. The foliage is just as refined as the panicle, very narrow and bright green, making upright-arching mounds about 60cm (2ft) tall which in the autumn assume yellow and orange tones before the whole plant turns light camel in winter.

Milium

Milium effusum var. *esthonicum* is grown for the coumarin fragrance of its broad, arching, pale green leaves, which is most apparent when they are crushed. The flowers are produced in loose, open panicles and are followed by showers of tiny dark seeds. It is clump-forming, and needs some shade.

The plants discussed above are but a selection of lesser flowering grasses and many others could be added, were there space enough. Which of them one grows depends very much upon one's perception of the beautiful, on one's style of gardening and on the habitat in which one is gardening. Several other species and varieties with specialized requirements appear in Part Four.

10 Annual Grasses

The most floriferous of all grasses are annuals, which flower as though their sole purpose in life were to populate the world with their progeny or flower themselves to death in the attempt. They can be used as underplantings to drifts of perennial grasses, in perennial borders where their visual delicacy and movement complements the more rigid shapes of broadleaved perennials, in pots, tubs or containers or among other annuals. In any context they exercise a subtle enchantment.

Being natives of disturbed ground, they are easy to grow. They need to be in sun for most of the day but are generally not fussy as to soil, though they dislike ill-drained soils. The best results are obtained if they are sown where they are to grow in spring, and lightly covered with sand or soil. If they are sown in drills rather than broadcast it is easier to distinguish the seedlings from weed grasses. Most will germinate within two or three weeks, and once the seedlings are 5–7.5cm (2–3in) they should be thinned, usually to 15–23cm (6–9in) apart. In areas with short summers some species are better started under glass and then planted out once they are about 7.5cm (3in) high. If only small quantities are wanted it is best to sow the seed in pots under glass and to thin the seedlings once they are large enough to handle, leaving three seedlings in each pot, the most vigorous seedling eventually suppressing the others. Alternatively, seed can be sown in cell trays, though no more than two or three seeds should be put in each cell. The seedlings can then be set out in the garden, and will be most effective if planted in groups of threes or fives. Growing seedlings in pots under glass is essential if they are wanted for use in larger pots and containers, or for hanging baskets, and of course for tender annuals.

Most of the annual grasses are botanical species rather than varieties and so will come true from seed, which can be collected annually, if desired. A few genera will often germinate in the autumn from seeds that have been allowed to lie where they fell. The seed collected in autumn should be stored in a dry tin in a cool but not frosty place over winter. Seed sown the following spring will germinate very readily.

If a particular grass tends to seed too freely the remedy is to remove the flowerheads before the seeds are shed. To avoid annual grasses getting themselves mixed up, grow each species in a patch of its own, well away from the next patch of annual grasses.

The foliage of annual grasses is for the most part inordinately unremarkable, and it usually dies off long before the effectiveness of the flowers is over. This means that annual grasses tend to be grown where the flowers can be seen to advantage, with the foliage hidden.

The smallest annuals, such as *Lagurus ovatus* 'Nanus' (dwarf hare's tail grass), *Lamarckia aurea* (goldentop) and *Agrostis nebulosa* (cloud grass), are suitable for the front of the border or even as edgings. They often look well grown in association with low perennial grasses such as *Helictotrichon sempervirens* (blue oat grass), or one of the hair grasses such as *Deschampsia caespitosa* 'Bronzeschleier', the strong lines of whose foliage afford a pleasing contrast with the fluffy heads of the annual grasses. Taller annual grasses such as *Panicum miliaceum* 'Violaceum' (purple millet), *Sorghum nigrum* (great or black millet) and the ornamental varieties of *Zea mays* are best grown towards the back of a border, among taller perennials.

Many annual grasses are grown specifically to provide material for picking and drying. Since the main objective of an annual's life is to scatter seed, many shatter relatively quickly once flowering is over. The way to avoid this is to pick the grasses before the flowers are fully open. Dry them in a light, airy place such as a garage or a garden shed, always ensuring that there is plenty of fresh air circulating.

Briza

By far the most popular of the annual grasses is *Briza maxima* (larger quaking grass), which has curious locket-shaped heads composed of overlapping scales, somewhat reminiscent of the tip of a rattlesnake's tail, produced between late spring and midsummer on a loosely tufted plant that grows about 30cm (12in) tall. *B. m.* 'Rhodes Form' is shorter and has substantially larger spikelets. The rather similar *B. minor* (lesser quaking grass) grows to

Hordeum jubatum in the daylily garden at Apple Court. It is an annual or short-lived perennial

Briza maxima 'Rhodes Form' has larger spikelets and is shorter-growing than the typical form

about 23cm (9in) and has much smaller spikelets than *B. major*, but they are even more freely produced and each is a little jewel in itself. Several other species are grown in collections, and have their lesser charms.

Hordeum

Hordeum jubatum (squirrel-tail barley) has long-awned heads like barley, which belongs in the same genus, but it is a much more refined plant. The heads are finely wrought, with long, thin, straight, silky awns that are often tinted shimmering crimson or pink, nodding on the tops of erect or oblique stems. As the flowers fade and turn into seeds the whole head becomes light brown and develops a spiral twist along the floral axis, but it soon shatters. If the heads are wanted for drying they should be picked at the shimmering pink stage. Though usually grown as an annual, the plant will make a loosely tufted, short-lived perennial about 23cm (9in) high. *H. hystrix* is similar but smaller, with shorter panicles.

Lagurus

Lagurus ovatus (rabbit-tail grass) has neat tails, these being flame-shaped 5cm (2in) pom-poms seemingly made of soft beige hairs with well-groomed long awns protruding from the shorter hairs, all pointing in the same direction. It makes a loosely tufted plant with short, hairy leaves and grows to about 45cm (18in). There is a delightful dwarf form, *L. o.* 'Nanus', which grows to 15cm (6in) and is suitable for the very front of a border. *L. o.* 'Bunny Tails' is the same.

Setaria

Setaria macrostachya is the showiest of several annual species of so-called fox-tail millet. It is tall for an annual grass, growing to about 90cm (3ft), with coarse leaves, the stems topped by what look like huge, vivid green, very hairy caterpillars whose long bristles often have a purplish tinge. The sheer weight of the inflorescence causes the culms to lean over and droop in a characteristic way. This is usually lost in the drying, since it is usually most satisfactory to tie grasses together round the bottoms of the stems and hang them upside-down in a bundle, which effectively straightens the caterpillar. Other fox-tail millets worth mentioning are *S. pumila*, which has much smaller, narrower, straight caterpillars, and *S. glauca*, which is similar but has bluish leaves and red-tinged awns.

Aira

Aira elegantissima is another of those grasses that are known as hair grass, or occasionally as cloud grass, which is much more appropriate, so diffuse is the panicle. It is low growing, to about 25cm (10in), with open, pyramidal panicles composed of purple-tinted, hair-fine branches tipped with tiny, silvery-grey spikelets. It is decorative both in the garden and when picked, but can be a problem to dry if tied together in bunches since the spikelets and branches become entangled and break when the bunch is pulled apart. It may be better dried flat.

Briza minor has the tiniest spikelets in the genus and is not reliably self-seeding in most gardens.

Lamarckia

Lamarckia aurea (goldentop) is both beautiful and distinct. It forms loosely tufted clumps about 30cm (12in) tall, or sometimes rather less, the inflorescence being spike-like but quite distinct from other grasses in that the awns and spikelets, instead of pointing towards the tip, point backwards, the whole head being silky and yellow, sometimes becoming flushed with purple. In southern England it will flower in early summer from seed sown out of doors in the spring, but earlier flowering can be achieved by starting plants under glass.

Catapodium

Of similar stature, and similarly variable as to flowering time, is *Catapodium rigidum* (fern grass), which produces panicles that look like much-divided fern fronds. Its real peculiarity, however, is that the whole plant is rigid, as though it has been carved out of wood. Though it is green to start with, the whole plant gradually takes on testaceous tints, eventually turning a burnished bronzy-brown. It is almost too small for the open border, being perhaps more noticeable given a place in a raised bed or sink garden.

Pennisetum

Pennisetum setaceum (tender fountain grass) differs from the other grasses mentioned here in that it is perennial in nature, though in cooler climates it is treated as a tender annual. It is also rather later flowering than the others, so that in areas where summers are cool it needs to be started under glass to ensure a long enough growing season. However, it is worth the extra trouble, for it grows to some 90cm (3ft) in flower, has rather better foliage than most annuals, the leaves being broad and of a good green, and the panicles are superb, resembling those of *P. alopecuroides* in their bottle-brush structure, but narrower, silkier and altogether much more refined, often as much as 30cm (12in) long and over 2.5cm (1in) wide, slightly curved and decidedly pink. There are several highly desirable cultivars, but unlike the typical species, they will not come true from seed. Seemingly the best way to handle these is to cut them down to a mere 5cm (2in) in the autumn before any danger of frosts, and then split the clumps, putting small, rooted divisions into cellular trays in a sandy, free-draining mix and over-wintering them in a heated greenhouse. The plants will grow away vigorously in the spring and be strong enough to set out once danger of frosts is past.

The most intriguing cultivars of *Pennisetum setaceum* are those with red leaves and red flowers, if indeed they are forms of *P. setaceum*, which some question. *P. s.* 'Rubrum' ('Atrosanguineum', 'Cupreum') has an upright habit, 1.5cm (¾in) wide leaves of a deep, glowing maroon and 30cm (12in) long flower spikes, again in deep maroon. *P. s.* 'Burgundy Blaze' ('Rubrum Dwarf') differs only in its shorter stature, growing to some 60cm (2ft). For those who like sharp contrasts, these red-leaved grasses can look vibrantly exciting planted with the bright blue *Elymus hispidus*, *Mertensia maritima* or *Cerinthe glabra* 'Kiwi Blue'; for those who prefer subtler tones and harmonies they mix well with other dark-leaved plants such as *Ricinus communis* 'Gibsonii', *Atriplex hortensis* var. *rubra* (purple orach) or *Lysimachia ciliata* 'Firecracker' and of course with *Imperata cylindrica* 'Rubra'. They will also look good with dark-leaved plants with sultry flowers such as *Lobelia cardinalis* and with *Dahlia* 'Bishop of Llandaff' or the sumptuous *D.* 'Blaisdon Red' or simply with plants with strongly red flowers in season such as *Monarda* 'Mrs Perry' or *Crocosmia* 'Lucifer', perhaps gingered up with the slender soft orange pokers of the small, late-flowering *Kniphofia triangularis*.

Avena

Avena sterilis is known as the animated oat because the long awns twist and writhe whenever the atmospheric humidity changes, especially when the panicles have been dried. It forms a loosely tufted plant as much as 90cm (3ft) tall with particularly light, open, widely branched, arching heads with nodding spikelets, green at first, becoming straw-coloured. It is one of the few annual grasses that seems to do better on heavy soils.

Bromus

Bromus madritensis (compact brome) forms a loosely tufted plant about 60cm (2ft) tall, producing showy panicles about 15cm (6in) long in early summer, these being composed of coarse-bristled spikelets that look like bundles of small whisks. It is one of the few annual grasses that will do well in some shade, but it is also one of the few that cannot be relied upon to dry well, even if picked before the flowers open.

Coix

Quite distinct from any of these is *Coix lachryma-jobi*. It is known as Job's tears because of the size of the seeds or grains it produces, which once were used to make

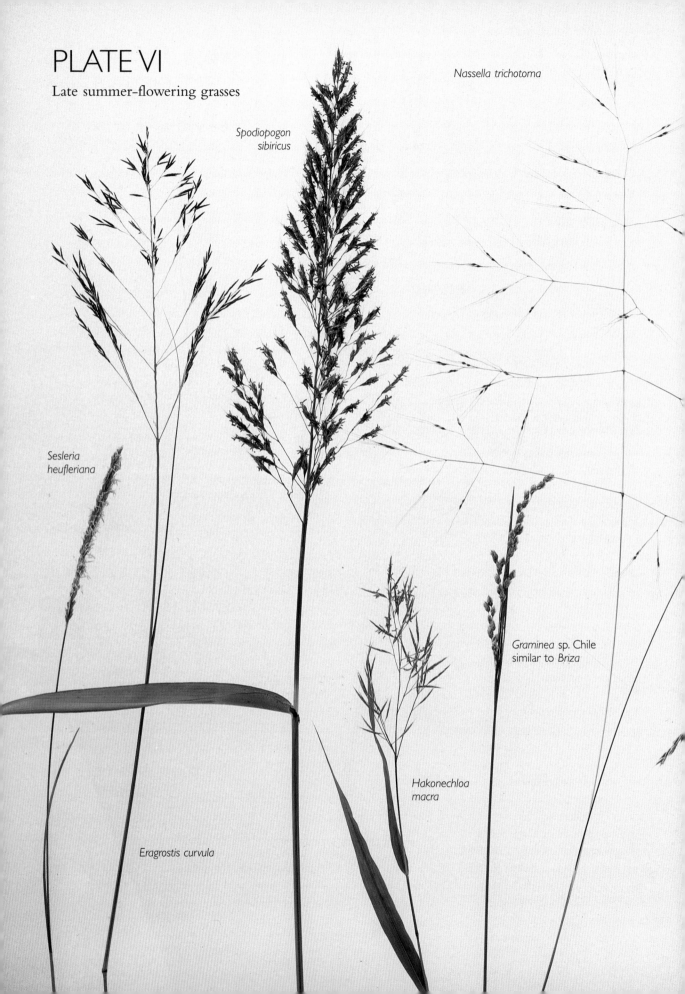

PLATE VI
Late summer–flowering grasses

Spodiopogon sibiricus

Nassella trichotoma

Sesleria heufleriana

Graminea sp. Chile similar to *Briza*

Hakonechloa macra

Eragrostis curvula

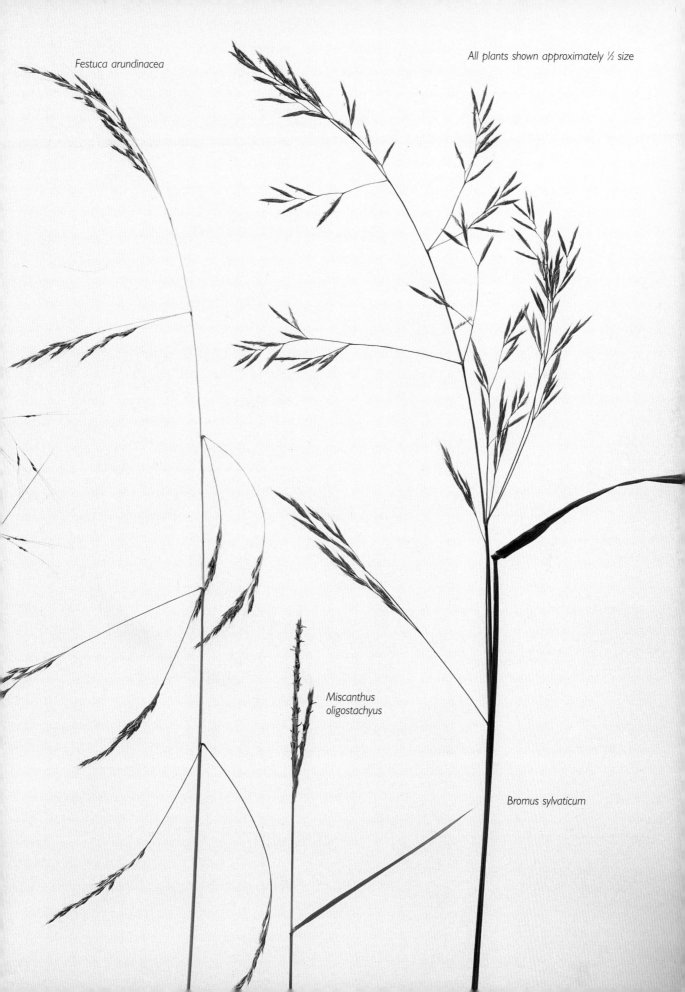

Festuca arundinacea

Miscanthus
oligostachyus

Bromus sylvaticum

necklaces and rosaries. It is really a warm-climate plant, needing a long, hot summer to fruit well. In a cool climate such as that of the UK, where it is not safe to set out such tender plants until early summer, it needs to be sown under glass and to be potted on regularly so that it does not receive any check to its growth. It should then be planted in a really hot position, preferably at the foot of a south wall. When it is happy it makes a sprawly, large-leaved plant, bearing its pale grains in quite small panicles.

Zea

There are just a handful of really large annual grasses suitable for use as specimens or in large, sub-tropical bedding schemes, or indeed just for use to ameliorate the rigidity of the plants in perennial borders. The best-known of these is *Zea mays* (Indian corn) which in its largest varieties, when well grown, can reach as much as 3.6m (12ft), though fortunately it is usually seen rather smaller, 2.4m (8ft) being the very most that can be expected in the UK. There are, or have been, a great many varieties, though many have been lost with the passing years. Basically they fall into two groups: those that are grown for their variegated or coloured leaves, and those grown for their cobs. Each needs slightly different treatment, but what both groups have in common is that they require an exceptionally long growing season, and therefore must be started under glass, the large seeds sown in individual pots as early as midwinter in the UK. They then need to be moved on frequently to larger pots so that there is no check to their growth.

Where they differ in their treatment is that whereas those varieties grown for their foliage can be planted out singly, dotted among other plants, those grown for their cobs need to be planted in blocks or groups to ensure pollination and the production of cobs. The reason for this is that, unlike most other grasses, they carry their male and female flowers on different parts of their anatomy, the male flowers (known as tassels) being carried at the tops of the culms, as with other grasses, while the female flowers (known as silks) are at the side of the main culm, about halfway up. The staminate tassels are many-fingered plumes, while the silks appear as a mass of long, silky threads protruding from the leafy sheath enclosing the pistillate flowers which later turn into the cobs.

The plain, green-leaved plant is suitable for use in sub-tropical bedding schemes, for the leaves can be as much as 90cm (3ft) long and 11cm (4½in) wide, though

variegated forms are generally preferred. *Z. m.* 'Variegata' ('Albovariegata') has leaves longitudinally striped white, as does *Z. m.* var. *japonica*, which however is a dwarfish variety, growing to only 1.2m (4ft): *Z. m.* 'Quadricolor' has leaves striped green, white, yellow and pink, while *Z. m.* 'Harlequin' has leaves striped red and green, and red cobs. Of the varieties grown of their cobs, which are a feature of harvest and Thanksgiving festivals and of dried winter decorations, the cultivar called *Z. m.* 'Indian Corn' has multicoloured grains, while *Z. m.* 'Strawberry Corn' has small, burgundy grains in yellow husks and *Z. m.* 'Fiesta' has long grains coloured white, yellow, red, blue and purple in patches.

Sorghum

Sorghum bicolor (true or great millet) is sometimes grown in sub-tropical bedding schemes. It is a huge plant, growing in the tropics to 6m (20ft), but still imposing at the 2.4m (8ft) that can be attained in Britain. It produces an abundance of lush, rich green foliage, each leaf up to 90cm (3ft) and 10cm (4in) wide. From among these leaves the panicles appear, rather in the manner of the silks of Indian corn, often white, pink or purple, followed by orange seeds. It is a native of tropical savannahs and needs to be sown under glass in order to give it a long growing season.

Panicum

Panicum miliaceum 'Violaceum' (purple hog millet) has about the most eye-catching panicles of any annual grass, green when they come into flower in midsummer but gradually becoming rich, deep violet-purple. The panicle is much-branched, but the branches tend to run nearly parallel so that it looks more like the head of a miscanthus than of a panicum, drooping attractively under its own weight. It grows to about 90cm (3ft) and is most effective grown in groups. It makes an interesting neighbour for *Sorghum nigrum*, which grows to much the same height and has dense panicles of large, black seeds. They both look well grown in groups among large, dusky-flowered autumn plants such as *Eupatorium purpureum* (Joe Pye weed), preferably in one of its smaller forms, or among the fading heads of hortensia hydrangeas, the combination sharpened by the addition of several spikes of *Aconitum carmichaelii* in one of its darker forms.

Deschampsia caespitosa 'Goldgehänge' blends easily with other plants in sun or shade.

Part Four Orchestrating the Grasses

11 | The Modern Grassery

Because their beauty lies more in their structure than in their colouring, it is perfectly possible to make an entirely satisfying garden picture using only grasses. In the making of such gardens there are three guiding principles. The first is the creation of dynamic groups – that is, groups in which the shape of each element complements the shapes of the others, for example by placing a vertical against a horizontal and linking the two together with a rounded shape. In classic landscaping terms such dynamic groups may be created using perhaps *Populus nigra* var. *italica* (Lombardy poplar) for the vertical, *Cornus controversa* for the horizontal and *Salix babylonica* (weeping willow) for the rounded shape: on a smaller scale the horizontal could be a recumbent rock, the vertical a small bamboo and the unifying rounded shape a tufted grass. In general the shape of a grass is that which it assumes when its flowers are at their fullest development, though sometimes it is just the shape of the leaf mound that is important, as with the cushion shape of the small fescues.

The second principle concerns voids and solids. In general landscaping terms voids are such open spaces as lawns while solids are such objects as trees or buildings. The most pleasing gardens are those in which voids and solids alternate in such a way as to create a rhythm through the garden. The concept of voids and solids is not absolute: there can be greater and lesser solids and, in a sense, greater and lesser voids. In plantings of grasses these should flow from one into the other, rather than being distinct as in formal landscaping.

The third principle is specific to the planting of grasses and concerns opacity. The panicles of grasses vary more than the flowerheads of other plants in the extent to which you can, or cannot, see through them. On a mature clump of *Calamagrostis* × *acutiflora* 'Stricta' the culms and panicles are so close together that you really do not see through them, while those of *Molinia caerulea* ssp.

arundinacea 'Transparent' are so diffuse that they scarcely obstruct one's view of whatever lies beyond. It is because of the contrast in opacity that these two look so singularly good when planted together. The same principle should be applied wherever one grass is used with another.

THE GARDEN AT APPLE COURT

In our own garden we have made a planting of grasses in a raised, rectangular brick bed at the centre of the daylily garden, which is itself a rectangle enclosed by 90cm (3ft) high copper beech hedges, crossed by mown grass paths which run around the grasses bed. The daylilies (*Hemerocallis*) are grown in beds edged with box (*Buxus sempervirens* 'Suffruticosa') which gives the area a rather formal look, but the ebullience of the daylilies and grasses is made all the more ravishing because of the contrast.

From a design point of view the grasses bed was divided into three parts of which the end two were squares and the middle one rather less than a square. The intention was to fill the two squares with largish grasses creating solids, and to use the gap between them as a void, visually carrying the path across the bed, but in different grasses. The starting point for the planting of the squares was the need to create a vertical emphasis to counterbalance the horizontal lines of the brick sides of the bed. *Calamagrostis* × *acutiflora* 'Stricta', which grows to about 1.2m (4ft), was chosen for one square, with *Miscanthus sinensis* 'Malepartus', which grows to about 1.8m (6ft), providing the equivalent vertical in the other. These were placed diagonally opposite each other in their squares, so that when seen along the long axis they would close the sight line. To block any remaining gap between these two, and to give more height, *Miscanthus floridulus*, which grows to about 2.4m (8ft), was added.

The three grasses that best associate with *Calamagrostis* × *acutiflora* 'Stricta' are *Panicum virgatum*, whose panicles are so diffuse as to be almost transparent, *Pennisetum alopecuroides*, with panicles like soft brown bottle-brushes, and *Molinia caerulea* ssp. *arundinacea* 'Karl Foerster', all of which make a dynamic contrast with the narrow vertical panicles of the *Calamagrostis*. These grasses were all planted in interlocking square or rectangular blocks. Further rounded shapes, to link the verticals and the

The raised bed at Apple Court. In the top picture the planting has been designed to block the view across the bed, while in the bottom one the objective is to see straight across it. Note how strongly the *Pennisetum villosum* at front right and the *Miscanthus sinensis* 'Malepartus' draw the eye in the top picture

horizontals, were added: *Stipa calamagrostis* and the low-growing *Miscanthus yakushimensis*; *Eragrostis curvula* and *E. chloromelas*; *Helictotrichon sempervirens* for its rigid blue leaves; *Stipa tenuissima* for its softness; *Pennisetum villosum* for its irresistible white panicles; and a few annuals, including *Briza media* 'Limouzi' (quaking grass), *Lagurus ovatus* (hare's tail grass) and its dwarf form *L. a.* 'Nanus', *Agrostis nebulosa*, *Lamarckia aurea* and *Catapodium rigidum*, both to create interest early in the year and to underplant the taller elements.

The narrow centre section, the void through which the path appeared to continue, was planted with a pattern of interlocking rectangles of little blue fescues, *Festuca glauca* 'Harz' and *F. g.* 'Aprilguen' with *F. g.* 'Elijah Blue' as the dominant element, making a carpet of varying blues no more than 23cm (9in) high so that one could see straight across the daylily garden and grasses bed unimpeded.

The new grassery

This grasses bed was for some years the culmination of the gardening year, following on from the daylilies by which it was surrounded and being in its own right rich and varied. However, it was always too small, and so a decision was taken to create a new grassery in an open area in front of the house, recombining many of the same grasses. At the same time it became apparent that one could use the blue grasses in the raised bed to create as it were a sense of hollowness at the centre of the daylily garden, akin to the sense of distance one would create were one to use blue trees and shrubs at the far end of one's garden. By happy chance several new American grasses with blue foliage were just then becoming available. Without them, and in particular without the new, larger-growing selections of *Panicum virgatum*, the scheme would not have been possible.

The basic layout of the bed has been retained – that is, the two square solids at each end and the less-than-square section in the middle being a void. The void has remained unchanged and still contains an interlocking pattern of blue squares each made up of a different form of the little blue fescues. Height is provided by the rounded shapes of *Panicum virgatum* 'Blue Tower' and *P. v.* 'Cloud Nine', both of which are intensely blue, and by *Miscanthus sinensis* 'Giganteus', whose foliage is grey-green. Other blues are provided by *Panicum virgatum* 'Heavy Metal', *P. v.* 'Pathfinder', *P. v.* 'North Wind', *Helictotrichon sempervirens*, *Sorghastrum nutans* 'Sioux Blue', whose foliage is

silvery blue, *S. n.* 'Indian Steel' (greyish-blue), *Elymus hispidus*, *E. magellanicus* and the much larger, non-invasive *E. canadensis glaucifolius*. Underplanting these are the top-shaped *Poa labillardieri*, *Schizachyrium scoparium*, *Koeleria glauca*, *Alopecurus alpinus* and the prostrate *Muhlenbergia japonica*, with *Poa colensoi* used to bring blue to areas shaded by taller growing grasses.

The new grassery is set out like the spokes of a wheel, except that the spokes are strongly curved and there are two separate hubs. The aim was first to produce wave after wave of grasses in flower, each a little taller than the one before, with lower, mainly earlier-flowering grasses in between each wave, and secondly to create the illusion as one walked past them on a curving path that they were revolving.

This basic layout itself creates an alternating pattern of voids and solids with the tallest grasses nearest the centre. The sequence from left to right, smallest to largest, is *Miscanthus sinensis* 'Little Kitten', which will grow to about 30cm (12in) in flower; *Pennisetum alopecuroides* 'Woodside', 60–75cm (2–2½ft); *Miscanthus oligostachyus* 'Purpurascens', 70–90cm (2½–3ft); and *Calamagrostis × acutiflora* 'Karl Foerster', 1.5m (5ft). Beyond these is *Miscanthus sinensis* 'Malepartus' at 1.5m (5ft). When seen from the other end the sequence of grasses is *Stipa calamagrostis*, which grows to about 45–60cm (1½–2ft) *Stipa (Calamagrostis) brachytricha* at about 90cm (3ft) and the 'Malepartus'.

The voids between these have been planted with mainly lower-growing, green-leaved grasses: *Melica ciliata*, *Deschampsia wibelliana*, *Nassella trichotoma* and *Molinia caerulea* ssp. *caerulea* 'Moorhexe'. Among these have been planted some taller blue grasses, *Festuca dalmatica*, *Schizachyrium scoparium*, *Andropogon gerardii* and *Sorghastrum nutans* 'Sioux Blue', to create a pattern of alternating green and blue. However, at one end the blues are replaced by coppers, partly because this seems a natural progression, but more immediately because the planting marries up, across a wide strip of grass, with brick-edged borders whose planting is in salmon and peach tones. Here *Chionochloa rubra* is grown with *Carex secta* var. *tenuiculmis*, both being far subtler in colour than the more commonly grown New Zealand sedges, and with the bright red *Carex uncifolia*.

These brown grasses blend well with small, brown daylilies – the dark mahogany *Hemerocallis* 'Brunette', the much lighter *H.* 'Jenny Wren', *H.* 'Frank Gladney', *H.* 'Cajun Lady' (a subtle salmon-bronze), and *H.* 'Silkwood' (bronze-brown), and the slender, autumn-flowering

A modern grassery is built up of contrasting forms rather than contrasting colours, the visual interest being afforded by the juxtaposition of different shapes.

Kniphofia triangularis 'Nelsonii'. A single plant of *Ilex crenata* 'Hetzii' is being clipped into a smooth cone whose shape will afford a ravishing contrast to the elegant informality of the grasses.

Spring planting

Though still in its early years, the whole scheme is starting to cohere, with wave on wave of foliage and flower developing as the year advances. It has to be said, however, that there is one brief season when this grassery, like others, looks less than ravishing, and that is in the six weeks or so that elapses between the late winter when the grasses are cut down and mid-spring, when they have made sufficient new growth to have regained their good looks – a small price to pay for 10½ months of foliage and flower. This space of time is best filled with bulbs. At Apple Court the sequence starts with snowdrops followed by scillas and then by daffodils, so arranged that they blend from white at one end of the grassery through creams and pale yellows to strong yellows and then to the amber of *Narcissus* 'Ambergate' to marry in with the borders of peach, salmon and apricot flowers across the grass walk from the grassery. These are followed by tulips – many of which, if planted with 20cm (8in) of earth over their noses, will prove perennial in many gardens – which flow in a sequence from pale yellow to the peachy

The Campbell-Sharp grassery. The areas to be planted were treated with weedkiller, the outline having first been marked out with canes. Ideally, weedkilling should be done nine months before planting.

The grasses set out in their pots groups prior to planting. On this intractable, flint-infested ground the grasses were planted in individual holes, but generally it is best to dig over the whole area.

colours of tulip 'Artist' nearest the peach, salmon and apricot borders, and finally by camassias, which move from the pale creamy white of *C. leitchlinii* 'Alba' through pale blues through deeper blues to *C. scilloides*, the darkest of all. By the time these are in flower the grasses are growing with sufficient vigour to assert their own presence once more.

A GRASSERY IN WILTSHIRE

The Campbell-Sharps' grassery is by comparison with Apple Court a free-hand fantasy. It was created on a hilly promontory in the garden, which lies on a west-facing slope of the Marlborough Downs in Wiltshire, England. From the house one goes down some steps and across a herb garden to reach a kidney-shaped pond crossed by a small bridge. This lies at the top of the knoll and is the focal point of the garden when seen from the house. Beyond the pond are a large *Juniperus sabina* 'Tamariscifolia', a *Photinia davidiana* and a 3.6m (12ft) *Taxus baccata* (English yew) through which climbs a vigorous *Clematis tangutica*. Beyond this the ground falls away and then levels off into lawn. The ground consists of a thin layer of turf and very little soil over a mixture of chalk and flint.

The grassery has been planted on the falling ground and was devised as a string of interlocking island beds with a mown path running through them. The steepness of the slope was deliberately exaggerated by planting the smallest grasses at the bottom and the tallest at the top: *Miscanthus tinctorius* 'Nanus Variegatus', which grows only 30cm (12in) high, was placed at the lowest point of the grassery, with *M. s.* 'Malepartus', which grows, to some 1.8m (6ft), at the highest point. The effect of this

planting is that the slope appears to increase in steepness with the passage of the year until by early autumn the apparent slope is far steeper than the true slope, which is revealed again in late winter when the grasses are cut down.

The grassery started from a simple desire to have a sunny hillside filled with *Stipa gigantea*, much as it grows in the wild, but this needed to be separated from the herb garden and so a low hedge of *Stipa calamagrostis* was planted. To these were added *Panicum virgatum* 'Rehbraun', *Pennisetum alopecuroides* and *Stipa tenuissima*. These three grasses, together with the *Stipa gigantea*, come into bloom in a sequence that starts in late spring and ends in early autumn, but will remain attractive until midwinter.

The next island bed called for taller grasses so that some at least could be seen above and beyond the first island bed. The lowest was *Deschampsia caespitosa* 'Goldtau', used both because it is evergreen and because it flowers earlier than the others, in late spring and early summer, and then, in ascending order of height, *Miscanthus yakushimensis*, *Calamagrostis × acutiflora* 'Stricta' and *Molinia caerulea* ssp. *arundinacea* 'Karl Foerster'. In this grouping *Stipa gigantea* will be the first to flower, to be joined about a month later, in early summer, by the *Deschampsia* with both the *Calamagrostis* and the *Molinia* coming into flower by early to midsummer. The last element to flower is *Miscanthus yakushimensis*, which does not flower until late summer, by which time the *Molinia* and *Calamagrostis* will already be taking on their first tints of autumn.

Both of these beds are positioned so that when seen from the house they have the sun beyond them for much of the day and for most of the year. This exploits to the

Once planted the beds were mulched with pea-grit. In other gardens forest bark might have been more suitable. Spacing is such that the grasses will grow together into a weedless carpet.

Midsummer following autumn planting and the grasses are starting to look well established. By the following summer they should all be flowering freely.

maximum the way in which the panicles of grasses can capture and hold the light and even draws the greatest possible benefit from the feeble light of the low winter sun, bringing to the tan and biscuit winter colours of the leaves an added warmth of hue which would not be seen were the light to be falling on them rather than through them.

The third bed is somewhat shaded by the promontory itself and the grasses used in it are more shade-tolerant: *Deschampsia caespitosa* 'Bronzeschleier', *D. c.* 'Goldtau' and *Miscanthus oligostachyus* 'Purpurascens', which abuts a pre-existing group of tall shrubs. The *Deschampsia* and *Miscanthus* both grow to much the same height and so have been studded with specimen grasses much as conifers were once used as specimens among heathers. One single *Miscanthus sinensis* 'Malepartus' and three *M. s.* 'Flamingo', each spaced about 1.8m (6ft) apart, punctuate this planting and wave their pale curling plumes above the whiter plumes of the *M. oligostachyus*.

The seat, which gives a commanding view of the grassery to each side, is itself flanked on the one side by a specimen *Miscanthus floridulus* and on the other by a clump of striped eulalia, *M. sinensis* 'Variegatus', underplanted with drifts of dark-leaved *Deschampsia caespitosa* which extend to the prostrate *Juniperus sabina* 'Tamariscifolia' on the one side and the *Taxus baccata* on the other. And since the soft, flowing qualities of grasses are always enhanced by contrast with strong, clean lines, the latter has been topiarized into a slender, interrupted cone. In winter, when the background trees have lost their leaves, the sere forms of the grassery blend to perfection with the Marlborough Downs beyond.

In this chapter we have looked at how grasses may be used when viewed purely from a structuralist point of view. In the following chapters we shall look at other ways of using them, in increasingly naturalistic combinations and by mixing them with other plants.

Eighteen months after planting the grassery is in full flower. Foreground: *Stipa tenuissima*; Middle: *Stipa gigantea*; Middle left: the purple haze of *Panicum virgatum* 'Warrior'.

12 The New Classicism and the Hummelo Effect

The current popularity of grasses has done little to resolve the old debate between formalism and naturalism in gardens, though it has added new challenges and a new dynamism to both approaches. Until recently the very idea of using ornamental grasses in a formal garden would have been perceived as an attempt to marry incongruous elements. Yet the contemporary Belgian designer Jacques Wirtz has done just this, and with great success, in the garden of La Petite Garenne at Schoten, east of Antwerp in Belgium.

At La Petite Garenne near Schoten in Belgium the formality is softened by parterres of ornamental grasses.

This garden was laid out in 1989, in what had formerly been the grounds of a great 18th-century estate, though no trace remained of any garden except for mature woods in the distance. To the west of the house, on level ground, Jacques Wirtz laid out a garden which in many ways resembles one of the great 17th-century gardens such as Vaux or Versailles, though trees, grass, gravel and water, the classic elements of Renaissance gardens, have been employed in entirely new ways. The garden is composed of triangular beds that fan out to form a semi-circle, with the house at its base and a formal circular pond inside a circle of yew at the very centre of the composition. Beyond this are four beds

of low beech hedges clipped into freestyle versions of 17th-century *parterres de broderie*, each bed being slightly different and yet all of them conforming to an essential unity.

From the plan, without a key to the planting, one would imagine entirely formal plantings, yet the experience of moving through the gardens at ground level is in fact quite different. The triangular beds are treated as informal parterres filled with ornamental grasses and, as these are separated from each other by broad paths of mown grass, the effect is very much that of close-trimmed lawn and rough grass, only more emphatically so. The particular grasses used are *Pennisetum alopecuroides*, which is the outer element, with *Molinia caerulea* ssp. *arundinacea* used inside it in order to give height. These grasses enclose drifts of grey willows (*Salix*) at the centre of the beds. The contrast between the formality of the concept and the ebullient informality of the actual planting creates dynamic tensions which are quite ravishing to the eye.

THE HUMMELO EFFECT

Piet Oudolf is as much Holland's leading contemporary garden designer as Jacques Wirtz is Belgium's and yet, though they both take an essentially structuralist approach, the gardens they create could scarcely be more different. Wirtz's gardens, for all their modernity, are still essentially Cartesian and even in his wildest gardens the unifying rhythm of the underlying formality comes through. In Oudolf's gardens the underlying principles of organization are less apparent, so that it seems almost as though his plantings have been imported from some Utopian wilderness.

Oudolf has summed up his planting philosophy by saying that structure is more important than flower, and that colour should be used to produce mood – and, somewhat gnomically, that plants have a mathematical and hierarchical relationship which has to be understood to achieve harmony. The gardens he creates are neither neat nor fashionably colour themed: indeed they seem rather larger than life. He seeks to evoke echoes of wild landscapes with an abundance of flowering and other plants, relying on the shape and form of the plants for his effects, and on making groups of what he calls 'good neighbours', that is, plants that not only look well together but grow happily with each other. His approach to form is very similar to the structuralist view in the planting of grasses, that is that the flowerheads achieve

a new dynamic once the petals fall away, and that the seedheads can contribute as much to the planting as the flowers.

The palette he uses to achieve these effects is highly personal and owes nothing to Jekyllian concepts; the keynote is exuberance, rather than control. Typically he creates bold groups composed of giant angelicas, fennels, large, late-flowering eupatoriums, filipendulas and tall thalictrums, with lesser perennials such as polygonums and persicarias at their feet. Grasses, typically *Molinia caerulea* ssp. *arundinacea* or *Miscanthus*, hover on the edges of these groups, or in the linking passages between them, catching in their flowers the light from the sky and bringing it down into the borders, just as water does. Interestingly, he seldom uses grasses with coloured or variegated leaves.

He sees a particular affinity between the grasses and certain other groups of plants noted for their architecture rather than their colour: umbellifers, for example, with their rounded or flattened heads, including the tall *Angelica gigas* with its dark, purplish-red heads, the more refined pale pink *Pimpinella major* 'Rosea', the black-leaved, pale-flowered *Anthriscus sylvestris* 'Ravenswing', the sharp, greenish-yellow of *Angelica archangelica*, the mauvey-pink of *Chaerophyllum hirsutum* 'Roseum', and the dark-leaved, pink-flowered *Angelica sylvestris* 'Purpurea'.

Another group Oudolf uses frequently which associate particularly well with the grasses are plants which bear their usually small flowers in thin spikes: mauve *Agastache foeniculum*, of which there is also a good white form, *A. f.* 'Liquorice White', *Persicaria amplexicaulis* in dark crimson, pink and white, *Lythrum salicaria* whose flowers come in every shade of pink as well as dark purple and bright red, *Verbena hastata* and *Veronicastrum virginicum* as well as various *Digitalis*, *Asphodelus*, *Salvia* and *Epilobium*. He also uses ball-like flowerheads, for example *Echinops*, and loosely paniculate, such as *Phlox*, contrasting all these four key flowerhead shapes with grasses, the latter making up about 20 per cent of the plants in a border.

Planting combinations

In his own book, *Prachtig Gras*, Oudolf lists the plants that he likes to use in combination with particular grasses as follows:

Calamagrostis × acutiflora with *Echinacea*, *Eupatorium*, *Phlox*, *Rudbeckia* and *Veronicastrum*;

Stipa (*Calamagrostis*) *brachytricha* with *Echinacea, Kalimeris, Monarda, Rudbeckia* and *Verbascum*;

Carex species with *Asphodeline, Campanula, Geranium, Rodgersia* and *Salvia*;

Chasmanthium with *Anemone, Lobelia, Scutellaria* and *Tricyrtis*;

Deschampsia with *Astrantia, Hosta, Lobelia, Luzula* and *Persicaria*;

Festuca with *Achillea, Geranium, Dictamnus, Lavandula* and *Origanum*;

Hakonechloa with *Aster, Ceratostigma, Epilobium, Scutellaria* and *Tricyrtis*;

Luzula with *Euphorbia, Geranium, Hemerocallis, Persicaria* and *Pulmonaria*;

Miscanthus with *Anemone, Aster, Eupatorium, Helenium* and *Vernonia*;

Molinia with *Echinacea, Eupatorium, Lobelia, Monarda* and *Salvia*;

Panicum with *Achillea, Helenium, Lavatera, Monarda, Sedum,* × *Solidaster* and *Verbena*;

Sesleria with *Achillea, Amsonia, Astrantia, Geranium* and *Polemonium*;

Spodiopogon with *Aconitum, Aster, Echinacea, Persicaria, Rhazya* and *Sanguisorba*;

Stipa with *Artemisia, Eryngium, Origanum, Papaver* and *Salvia*.

The Hummelo beds

In a planting in the stock beds of his nursery at Hummelo near Arnhem which is typical of his style and palette, Oudolf has the heavy mauve of *Eupatorium maculatum* 'Atropurpureum' and the purple of *Vernonia crinita*, 1.8–2.4m (6–8ft) tall, as the centrepoint of a group which then descends through the pale pink but dark-eyed *Phlox paniculata* 'Lichtspel' to the dark-coned pink daisies of *Echinacea purpurea* 'Magnus' and pale pink *Anemone hybrida*, with pinky-mauve *Saponaria* × *lempergii* 'Max Frei' at its feet. Next to them, the vinous reds and pinks that flush the flowers of a 1.2m (4ft) *Miscanthus* pick up the pinks and darker tones of the border.

Piet Oudolf's garden at Hummelo in Holland. About 20 per cent of the planting consists of ornamental grasses, the grasses becoming the dominant visual element in the late summer and autumn. Here *Stipa (Calamagrostis) brachytricha*, which has been in flower since early summer, is joined by *Miscanthus sinensis* 'Kleine Silberspinne' (centre) and *M. s.* 'Silbersturm' (top right).

13 The New Wave Gardens

Wolfgang Oehme and James van Sweden aim, like Piet Oudolf, to bring echoes of wild landscapes into their gardens, but the particular wild landscapes they seek to bring in are rather different – those of the now rapidly disappearing American prairie. In so doing they are creating gardens in a uniquely American idiom and on a truly American scale, with vast sweeping horizontals of yellow prairie daisies and monotypic stands of largely native grasses that connect with the vaster landscapes beyond, either in reality or through the mind's eye.

The resulting gardens are, to English eyes, singularly un-English, and this is very much to the point, for while the Oehme, van Sweden partnership is reaching forward to the American dream of the limitless prairie it is consciously rejecting the European, and particularly the English, concept of a garden, which traditionally revolves around perfect lawns, neat edges and herbaceous borders and entails endless mowing, tying in, cutting down, dividing and replanting. By contrast Oehme, van Sweden gardens need little more than to be cut to the ground once a year, and even that can be done without bending one's back, with a strimmer. A few plants, such as some of the clumping grasses, may need dividing once in a while.

In European gardens colours and incidents are held firmly in place by a rigid framework of hedges and static evergreen shrubs. By contrast Oehme, van Sweden gardens flow across their defined spaces with drifts of fine-foliaged grasses and largely native perennials waxing and waning with the seasons, moving and rustling with the wind. Through these flowing masses there are taller plants, usually miscanthus or bamboos, but occasionally fine-leaved trees, which create rhythm, pattern and dynamic visual tensions. Usually about 80 per cent of the planting is perennials and a considerable proportion of that percentage is grasses, which are important because they contribute so much to the gardens over such a long period.

In order to create the high-interest low-maintenance gardens for which the partnership is now famous, great care is taken with the selection of the plants. Every grass, perennial, tree or shrub in an Oehme, van Sweden garden is chosen because it is aesthetically remarkable not just in one way but in several, by virtue of its foliage, colour, form, texture or flower, and because it is by nature well-suited to both site and climate, self-sufficient, reliable, drought-tolerant and heat-resistant, and even deer-proof if need be. While colour is not particularly important, it should be capable of flowering for at least six to eight weeks and contributing to the pleasure of the garden either with its seedheads or its texture throughout most of the year, winter included. Such demanding criteria inevitably restrict the palette.

PLANTING COMBINATIONS

Though the New Wave gardens are famed for their miscanthus, molinias, pennisetums and calamagrostis in combination with *Eupatorium purpureum*, *Sedum* 'Herbstfreude' ('Autumn Joy'), *Rudbeckia fulgida* 'Goldsturm', *Lythrum salicaria*, *Liatris spicata* and *Liriope* species, Oehme and van Sweden employ a much wider palette, the following being the grasses they use most and the plants with which they combine them:

Calamagrostis × *acutiflora* 'Stricta' with *Aster, Pennisetum, Rudbeckia* and *Sedum*;
Carex morrowii 'Variegata' with *Bergenia, Epimedium* and *Rodgersia pinnata*;
Carex pendula with *Astilbe, Bergenia, Epimedium, Hosta, Ligularia* and *Rodgersia pinnata*;
Cortaderia selloana 'Pumila' with *Eupatorium* and *Lythrum*;
Deschampsia caespitosa with *Bergenia, Epimedium, Hosta* and *Ligularia*;
Helictotrichon sempervirens with *Artemisia, Nepeta* and *Stachys*;
Imperata cylindrica 'Rubra' with *Bergenia* and *Stachys*;
Miscanthus floridulus with *Hibiscus* and *Rudbeckia*;
Miscanthus sinensis 'Gracillimus' with *Aster, Pennisetum, Rudbeckia* and *Sedum*;
Miscanthus sinensis **'Purpurascens'** with *Rudbeckia, Sedum* and *Yucca*;
Molinia caerulea ssp. *arundinacea* 'Transparent' with *Coreopsis* and *Sedum*;
Panicum virgatum **'Hänse Herms'** with *Aster, Boltonia,*

The New Wave gardens seek to bring a real sense of the American prairies into town gardens. Front right is *Calamagrostis* × *acutiflora* 'Stricta'

Sedum and *Yucca*;

Pennisetum alopecuroides with *Aster*, *Eupatorium*, *Rudbeckia*, *Sedum* and *Yucca*;

Sesleria autumnalis with *Ceratostigma*, *Chrysanthemum pacificum* and *Sedum*;

Spodiopogon sibiricus with *Aster*, *Rudbeckia*, *Sedum* and *Stachys*;

Stipa (Calamagrostis) brachytricha with *Liriope*, *Rudbeckia* and *Sedum*.

SPRING BULBS

Most of their gardens are dependent on spring bulbs, particularly tulips, to bridge the gap between the time that the grasses and other perennials are cut down and when they have made sufficient growth to become interesting again. The tulips are usually the red, orange and yellow 'Emperor' varieties, followed by the lily-flowered 'Red Shine', 'Jacqueline' and 'West Point', which are not only later but longer in flower. These are followed by *Allium giganteum*, *A. aflatunense*, *Camassia cusickii* and *Fritillaria persica*. Care is taken not to plant the tulips with sedums or with calamagrostis, both of which start into growth early enough to hide the tulips with their foliage. They are best planted among pennisetums, rudbeckias, asters, *Miscanthus oligostachyus* 'Purpurascens' and anemones. Oehme and van Sweden particularly like combining bright tulips with the blue flowers of brunneras, and daffodils with hostas and ligularias.

THE MARTIN BUILDING GARDENS

The gardens for which James van Sweden and Wolfgang Oehme are most famous are those surrounding the Federal Reserve's 1970s Martin Building in Washington DC. In the year in which they became partners a unique opportunity came their way. An exceptionally severe winter had killed some 90 per cent of the municipal evergreens with which the Federal Reserve's gardens had until then been planted, and a decision was taken to improve the gardens. Oehme and van Sweden were invited to submit designs and the garden that resulted has changed the face of Washington.

Oehme and van Sweden created a broad central lawn looking across towards the Martin Building from Pennsylvania Avenue, with a single rectangular bed right in front of the building. In that bed they designed a scheme in which *Miscanthus sinensis* 'Gracillimus' is used to anchor the planting, much as other designers might have used shrubs. One whole corner, underplanting three of the six *Miscanthus*, is filled with *Pennisetum alopecuroides*. Next to this, running diagonally from the approximate centre to another corner, is a broad rectangle of *Calamagrostis* × *acutiflora* 'Stricta', with the corner diagonally opposite filled with *Liriope muscari* 'Big Blue'. The remaining space is filled with *Bergenia cordifolia*. At each

In this New Wave garden rounded tufts of *Miscanthus sinensis* 'Gracillimus' stabilize naturalistic drifts of *Hemerocallis*.

side of this bold central vista, behind massive plantings of *Rudbeckia fulgida* 'Goldsturm' and beneath glades of fine-foliage trees such as *Zelkova serrata, Sophora japonica, Quercus rubra* and *Q. phellos*, they have created shaded sitting areas that are screened from busy streets by earth berms and dense plantings, bringing human scale and comfort to a city that is monumentally institutional in its architecture.

In spring, beneath the white blossoms of *Pyrus calleryana* 'Bradford' and the yellow of *Hamamelis*, drifts of single red, orange and yellow tulips blend with drifts of white or yellow daffodils. Later, grasses and yellow-rayed daisies take over. By autumn, beneath the colouring leaves of native oaks, the flat red heads of *Sedum* 'Herbstfreude' ('Autumn Joy') provide an eye-catching display between the spiky leaves of drifts of *Yucca filamentosa* and the hairy spikes of *Pennisetum alopecuroides*, with the wheat-like colours of *Calamagrostis* × *acutiflora* 'Stricta' in the background.

A GARDEN IN GEORGETOWN

The philosophy of bringing the prairie into the city does not depend on scale; rather it depends on the plants used, and on the dominance of grasses in the planting scheme. James van Sweden's own small garden in Georgetown shows what can be achieved. Measuring 5.2 × 16.8m (17 × 55ft), it is enclosed by wooden fencing and dominated by a large *Ailanthus altissima*, probably planted more than a century ago when the house was built and now draped with *Hedera helix* (English ivy). The garden is entered from the house through French windows which lead on to a narrow terrace, beyond which a retaining

wall 60cm (2ft) high holds back the garden and raises the planting almost to eye level when seen from the house. Steps go from the terrace to a small landing, from which a diagonal line of stepping leads through the planting. The soil in the garden is raked like a stage, higher at the far end, lower nearer to the house, enabling the eye to see further into the garden than it would were the soil level.

From the house, the eye is led through the slender grey limbs of a multi-stemmed *Magnolia virginiana* to a sculpture of four balls created by Grace Knowlton. Each ball is of a different size and their positions in the garden are changed from time to time, though they also have a life of their own, tending to move gradually down the sloping garden towards the house. In winter other shrubs add to the structure of the scene, a *Hamamelis mollis* at the far end of the garden, and an evergreen *Mahonia bealei*.

The season starts when the grasses are cut down. Attention is drawn from their brown stubble by drifts of white tulips and of parrot tulips in reds and yellows. As the year progresses other plants grow up, changing the dynamics of this small space, so that by midsummer it is filled with the fragrance of the *Magnolia virginiana* and the varied textures of restful greenery: ferns such as *Adiantum pedatum, Osmunda regalis* and *Polystichum acrostichoides*; grasses including *Carex morrowii* 'Variegata', *Miscanthus floridulus, M. sinensis* 'Gracillimus', *Pennisetum viridescens, P. alopecuroides* and *Calamagrostis* × *acutiflora* 'Stricta'; and *Epimedium* × *versicolor* 'Sulphureum', *Acanthus hungaricus, Liriope muscari, Rodgersia pinnata, Hosta plantaginea, H. sieboldiana, Brunnera macrophylla* and *Hibiscus moscheutos,* punctuated by the mauve globes of *Allium giganteum*. Bright colours are kept to the foreground and planted in pots.

In autumn and winter, periods which together embrace nearly half the year, the whole scene, stripped down to its essential structure, becomes not so much a symphony but rather a sonata in the key of beige in which the grasses are the collective soloists. For it is the strong verticals of the grasses that lead the eye through the garden, creating tall masses above the void left by the other plants, now broken by frosts or flattened by snows.

If such a garden, lacking the strongly structured framework of yews and beech hedges, looked to English eyes like a wilderness, no doubt Wolfgang Oehme and James van Sweden would feel they had succeeded in bringing nature into the city – yet their gardens are far more structured than those of the new naturalism.

14 The New Naturalism

Gardening, like sex and food, lies somewhere between art and nature, being wholly neither yet partly both. At different times, in different cultures, one or other has predominated in gardens. Historically, especially in England, especially in the 20th century, it has been art. However, the balance may now be shifting towards greater naturalism, for man is increasingly seen as the destroyer of nature, and gardens increasingly as a means of redemption.

The basic tenet of the new naturalism is that gardens have habitats akin to wild habitats and that only those plants should be grown in a garden that are found in that habitat in the wild. Thus chalk gardeners should grow only chalk lovers, and those on acid soils only calcifuge subjects, and so on. The seminal book on the subject is *Perennials and their Garden Habitats* by Richard Hansen and Friedrich Sachs, who identify seven types of garden habitat and the plants that grow naturally in each. All categories are further defined by other factors such as climate, light availability, soil moisture content, availability of nutrients and humus type. One might have, for example, dry woodland or damp woodland, and either might be rich or poor in nutrients, on acid or alkaline soil and so on. Since grasses are found in almost every type of wild habitat, they have a key role to play in these ecological gardens.

Gardens created along these lines look very different from conventional gardens, presenting a wilder aspect and resembling, as indeed they are supposed to, natural associations of plants. Lacking the formal framework of lawns and hedges that characterize traditional gardens, the plants drift across the internal space of a garden, relying on the repetition of rhythms and patterns to give a sense of cohesion. These rhythms and patterns are created by theme or key plants, which are typically plants of striking habit, exceptional flower colour or extraordinary freedom of flower. Grasses, especially tall grasses such as *Miscanthus* or *Stipa calamagrostis*, are ideal as theme plants, and it is always the theme plants that are positioned first

Westpark in Munich is the seminal garden for those interested in ecologically correct gardens.

in the planning or planting of a garden. Lesser themes can then be designed to wander in and out through these, making sub-themes and counter-melodies.

The classic example of the new naturalism is a scheme designed by Rosemarie Weisse and planted at Westpark in Munich in 1983. Here the planting drifts as if of its own volition through lawns towards the edge of woodlands, while paths meander between the plants. The plants are not graded as in conventional borders with the tallest at the back, but set out in seemingly natural groups, each based on a theme plant which is then associated with the plants that would naturally grow with it. Such plantings, however, are not static. In time perennials, including grasses, wander, and this is allowed to happen. They may also seed themselves where they were not originally placed, and this may be acceptable. And if by chance flowers from elsewhere seed themselves into the scheme, they too may be allowed to remain, for they have plainly found their ecological niche. Weeds, as Emerson pointed out, are a problem of perception. They are, after all, just wild flowers, at home among other wild flowers but out of context in highly organized plantings.

DRY HABITATS

The Westpark garden, being on poor, dry, gravelly soil, is deemed to have a habitat similar to that of the steppes. Typical theme plants for steppe habitats include hardy *Yucca*, *Verbascum*, *Eremurus* and *Allium* and a large number of grasses including *Elymus arenarius* and *E. canadensis*, as well as the dramatic early summer-flowering *Stipa gigantea* and the later-flowering *S. calamagrostis*. The steppes themselves are one of the great centres of diversity for grasses, and abound with ornamental species. The choice is wide, ranging from the small but early-flowering *Sesleria rigida*, *S. caerulea* and *S. albicans* to the early summer-flowering *Helictotrichon sempervirens*, *Melica ciliata*, *M. transsilvanica*, *Festuca mairei*, *Poa glauca*, *Sesleria heufleriana* and *S. nitida* to the later summer-flowering *Stipa calamagrostis*, *S. tenuissima*, the coarser *S. tenacissima*, the prickly *Festuca punctoria*, *Koeleria glauca*, *Chrysopogon gryllus*, *Bouteloua gracilis*, *Stipa extremiorientalis* and *Eragrostis curvula*. Still later are *Pennisetum alopecuroides*, *P. a.* 'Hameln' and *P. orientale* and, last of all, *Sesleria autumnalis*.

To this already extensive palette can be added several showy grasses more often associated with border perennials, including *Miscanthus sinensis* in all its varieties, *Panicum virgatum*, again in variety, *Calamagrostis × acutiflora* 'Karl Foerster', *Hystrix patula*, *Panicum bulbosum* and

Sorghastrum nutans. The main difference between the use of these grasses in dry habitat plantings and in more conventional plantings is that in the former they tend to be used as single clumps, rather than in bold drifts, though the single clumps are arranged rhythmically in threes or fives, but with space between them where other plants may be grown.

The long-awned feather grasses, such as *Stipa barbata*, *S. joaniis*, *S. pennata* and the earlier flowering *S. ucranica*, as well as the amazing *S. tirsa* with its extraordinarily long, feathery awns and the rarer *S. papposa* and *S. pulcherrima*, need to be grown on their own partly because they are not well able to withstand competition but also because in isolation the beauty of their long awns trailing in the wind can better be appreciated. They tend to be short-lived perennials and so need renewing from time to time, which most of the other grasses do not. They also tend to fall apart from the centre of the clump after flowering and benefit from being cut down at that time.

The perennials that are associated with these grasses in steppe plantings tend to be wild species or simple selections from them, rather than the more usual border perennials which are often the product of hybridization and which on the whole demand richer soils. In steppe habitats the planting should be quite sparse: there are insufficient nutrients in the soil to sustain dense plantings. The perennials that are typically used with the grasses in these plantings include a number of spiky plants such as *Carlina acanthifolia*, *Eryngium alpinum*, *E. amethystinum*, *E. bourgatii* and *E. × zabelii*; and several bulbous subjects including *Allium sphaerocephalum*, *Gladiolus communis*, *Tulipa sylvestris*, *Lilium croceum* and *Paradisea liliastrum* as well as several rhizomatous irises such as *I. pallida*, *I. p. dalmatica* and *I. germanica*. More conventional perennials include *Paeonia tenuifolia*, *Asphodeline lutea*, *Aster laevis*, *A. mongolicus*, *Phlox arendsii*, *Solidago* ssp, *Limonium latifolium* and *Veronica incana*, *Centranthus ruber*, *Gypsophila paniculata*, *Crambe cordifolia*, *Nepeta faassenii*, *Oenothera missouriensis*, *Phlomis samia* and several sedums for autumn display.

An early summer vignette might show cream or yellow hybrids of *Iris germanica* close to the pinky-purplish spheres of *Allium sphaerocephalum* with the white trumpets of *Paradisea liliastrum*, while in the autumn the mauve daisy flowers of *Aster mongolicus* might be found next to the flat pink or mauvish heads of sedums with a backdrop of *Pennisetum*, *Stipa* (*Calamagrostis*) *brachytricha* and tall miscanthus. If we compare this with an ecologically correct planting for a wet habitat, it at once becomes

At Westpark naturalistic plantings drift through the landscape of trees and grass. *Stipa calamagrostis* is in the foreground

apparent, because the wet habitat flora is more familiar, just how reliant on frequent watering most gardens are.

WET HABITATS

The spring-flowering perennials for wet habitats include many plants widely grown in gardens where habitat has never even been considered, as for example *Cardamine pratensis, Filipendula ulmaria, Geranium pratense, G. psilostemon, Geum rivale, Polemonium caeruleum, Trollius europaeus* and *T. chinensis*. Familiar early summer-flowering species include *Althaea officinalis, Boltonia asteroides, Camassia cusickii, C. quamash, Hemerocallis, Iris ensata, I. pseudacorus, Lythrum virgatum* and *Veratrum album*. These can be planted quite densely to give a luxuriant look, and indeed perennials need to be planted more closely on moist soils if they are to join up into a weed-suppressing community.

The range of grasses suited to moist habitats is limited compared with those suitable for dry habitats, though this is somewhat offset by the potential for growing some variegated grasses, which on the whole would not do well in dry soils fully exposed to sun and weather. Of the tall theme grasses the full range of miscanthus can still be grown, including *Miscanthus floridulus*, which is intolerant of summer dryness, and the various striped

miscanthus. In addition *Cortaderia* species, which again dislike summer dryness, come into their own, and *Arundo donax* is completely at home in moist soil. Other tall potential theme grasses include *Molinia caerulea* ssp. *arundinacea* 'Transparent', 'Zuneigung' and others, *Spodiopogon sibiricus, Spartina pectinata*, usually grown in its variegated form, *Panicum clandestinum* and *Pennisetum alopecuroides*. Most of these are familiar garden grasses, as are the variegated grasses best suited to moist garden habitats, *Glyceria maxima* var. *variegata* and *Phalaris arundinacea*.

MAINTENANCE

It is claimed for such ecologically correct schemes that the amount of maintenance needed is less than in conventional gardens, the theory being that the perennials, completely at home in their habitat, not only knit together leaving no spaces for weeds to invade but maintain themselves in balance with each other and so do not need dividing and replanting every two or three years. The Munich planting, however, depends for much of its success on the poorness of its soil, this having been deliberately impoverished by the lavish admixture of large quantities of grit and gravel. Since the plantings are not watered in summer, the theory being, after all, that if the plants are right for their habitat they will survive, weed seeds cannot germinate since the perennials have already exhausted the available moisture.

PLATE VII
Bamboo leaves (yellow)

× *Hibanobambusa tranquillans*
'Shiroshima'

Pleioblastus chino
'Murakamianus'

Pleioblastus akebono

Pleioblastus shibuyanus 'Tsuboi'

Pleioblastus auricomus

All plants shown approximately ½ size

15 Flowering Lawns

Flowering lawns are neither so neat as mown lawns nor so rough as meadows, but because of their relative tidiness are suitable for highly visible areas. Lawns, by definition, are mown, but the frequency of mowing can be varied. The prime purpose of mowing is to prevent coarser grasses, perennials and shrubs from establishing themselves in the grass, as they would were it never cut.

The cycle of mowing that best fits in with flowering lawns is to make the first mow in midsummer and then to keep mowing until early autumn when autumn flowers such as crocuses begin to appear, starting the cycle all over again. The mower blades should be set no lower than about 10cm (4in), thereby creating a rougher texture than that of closely mown grass. Such treatment will give the majority of the grasses that are commonly found in lawns time enough to flower before being cut.

LAWN GRASSES

The prime requirements of lawn grasses are that they should be able to withstand trampling and mowing, and give a seamless greensward all year round. Since the number of grasses that can do this is rather small, most English lawns contain much the same grasses, whether grown from seed or turf or simply produced by mowing rough grass. However, since flowering lawns are not mown nor trampled on as much as normal lawns, a few less tolerant grasses can be admitted.

The three grasses most frequently found in lawns are *Agrostis tenuis* (brown top), *Festuca rubra* var. *commutata* (Chewings fescue) and *F. r.* ssp. *rubra* (red fescue). Of these *Agrostis tenuis*, which flowers from early until late summer, has small, almost pyramidal panicles of small brown spikelets creating *en masse* a light, airy haze of brown; *A. canina* (velvet bent grass) is very similar. *Festuca rubra* var. *commutata* flowers profusely in early summer, with rather stouter spikelets which *en masse* create a highly decorative carpet of a pale pink or purplish tinge, while *F. r.* ssp. *rubra*, which flowers from late spring until midsummer, has more substantial panicles over a longer period, again pink or purplish. *Cynosurus cristatus* (crested dog's tail grass), which is often added to lawns to make them

harder wearing, has quite different panicles, these being upright and spike-like, green with a brown tinge, produced from early until late summer. The panicles of *Phleum bertolonii* (smaller cat's tail grass) are similar in form, and are again produced from early until late summer. *Lolium perenne* (perennial rye grass) is sometimes found in lawns, though it is really more of a meadow grass. Flowering from late spring until midsummer, it produces narrow spike-like panicles that are flattened, with the spikelets to left and right.

To these can be added, to further enrich the flowering texture of the lawn, *Festuca ovina*, which flowers from late spring until early summer and has much smaller, more refined panicles than *F. rubra*, *Holcus mollis*, whose dense, pyramidal panicles are flushed purple when in flower from early to late summer, or the very similar *H. lanata*, *Poa trivialis* and *Deschampsia flexuosa*. The latter two plants both have broadly pyramidal panicles that are very open in structure, creating a most airy effect when massed in the garden. Finally, *Anthoxanthum odoratum*, which is one of the earliest lawn grasses to flower, from mid-spring until midsummer, has dense green ovoid panicles, and the whole plant smells of coumarin (new-mown hay) when crushed underfoot.

WILD FLOWERS

Most lawns, even if mown, will contain a mixture of wild flowers, as long as weedkillers are not used. The commonest are *Bellis perennis* (daisies), *Ranunculus acris* (buttercups), *Prunella vulgaris* (self-heal), *Leontodon hispidus* (hawkbit), *Primula vulgaris* (primrose) and *P. veris* (cowslip) either in their native pale yellow or other colours. These can be supplemented with *Lotus corniculatus*, with its red-stained yellow pea flowers, *Thymus serpyllum* (common thyme), and camomile, both for their fragrance, *Leucanthemum vulgare* and clouds of *Anthriscus sylvestris* (Queen Anne's lace or cow parsley). If these are supplemented with spring and early summer bulbs such as snowdrops, snowflakes, daffodils and narcissi, with perhaps some species tulips, bluebells in blue, white or pink and tall blue camassias, as well as *Cyclamen repandum*, with its long-eared flowers in spring, a very long season of interest can be created.

Flowering lawns can be as colourful as meadows until the time comes when they are mown.

On damper soils, where *Holcus mollis* is likely to be one of the dominant grasses, celandines may easily establish themselves, along with *Fritillaria meleagris* (snake's head fritillaries). Under trees, *Anemone blanda* and *A. nemerosa* (wood anemones), in pink, white or blue, may seed themselves around, to be followed by pale mauve *Cardamine pratensis* (lady's smock). On acid soils, where *Festuca tenuis* and *Deschampsia flexuosa* (wavy hair grass) are likely to be dominant and the growth of the grass is less dense than it tends to be on damp, alkaline soils, species

daffodils may seed around, particularly the lovely pale citron form of *Narcissus bulbocodium*, while on damper acid soils *N. cyclamineus*, with its reflexed petals and rich yellow flowers, will do better.

In any patch of grass that is mown as recommended above, the number of wild flowers will gradually increase, both in quantity and diversity, over the years, even if no deliberate attempt is made to introduce them. But to be effective a flowering lawn needs to contain an abundance of flowers, since it is the massed effect that matters, not the individual flowers. Different species will tend to congregate in different areas, depending on small differences in soil moisture levels or acidity.

16 Meadows

Meadows differ from lawns first by the greater height of their grasses and flowers and secondly by their being mown only once or at most twice in a season. What both lawns and meadows have in common is that the massed effect is more important than the individual flower, and that overall the plants in a meadow are all approximately the same height, though the particular height changes as the plants grow up through the season. The greater height gives scope for greater diversity of grasses and flowers than can be used in lawns.

Prairies and meadows are sometimes confused with each other, but although they may look similar they are in fact quite different. Meadows are by definition mown (from the Old English word *mawan*); once the mowing stops other plants such as brambles, elders and blackthorn invade and the character changes until ultimately the area becomes woodland. Prairies by contrast are climatic climax vegetation and have maintained their equilibrium for centuries without human intervention. More importantly, from a gardener's point of view, prairie perennials such as rudbeckia and echinacea can coexist with native grasses because those grasses need high temperatures before they get going, giving the perennials a chance to be well into growth before them. If one were to try to grow these perennials on equal terms with the grasses in a British meadow they might well fail because in British meadows the grasses start into growth while temperatures are still low, and indeed grow in the winter, which they do not in the prairies. Moreover, they would be exposed to pests unknown in the prairies; it has been estimated that meadows contain the same weight of slugs and snails as vegetation.

THE MAKING OF A MEADOW

It is important to be clear what kind of meadow one is aiming for, since there are meadows and meadows. Natural meadows are highly complex communities not only of visible grasses and herbs but also of unseen mycorrhiza and micro-organisms and have taken hundreds of years to evolve. They contain, moreover, the optimum vegetation that that piece of land will support under a regimen of regular mowing, and as such are highly

stable. Meadows made now, no matter how much they may seek to look the same as natural meadows, cannot but be highly stylized, lacking as they do the rich variety of mycorrhizal and micro-organismic associations. As such they are unstable and subject to change both in the short and in the long term. For example, in new-made meadows some annuals such as *Papaver rhoeas* (red poppies) and a few short-lived perennials such as *Leucanthemum vulgare* (ox-eye daisies) will dominate for the first few years, turning the meadow first red then white but virtually dying out in the succeeding years. Moreover, as the equilibrium of natural meadows is lacking, weeds (especially woody ones such as hawthorn, blackthorn and ash) can invade and even desired plants get out of hand. The idea that naturalistic modes of gardening save a lot of work may be somewhat fallacious.

Nor does everyone have the same expectation of what a meadow should look like. To some a meadow is a parcel of ground that is sown with a mixture of annual grasses and flowers, resown every year; to others it is specifically a perennial grass matrix spangled with wild flowers, while others will admit bulbs to their meadows to extend the season of interest. Most people think of the grass matrix as being green, but it is possible to make a meadow of predominantly blue grasses, and of flowers in the blue or mauve spectrum, creating an illusion of distance. And some perceive a meadow as containing much the same grasses and flowers as a border, but differently arranged, though this is really a wild garden.

DISTRIBUTION OF SPECIES

When one first glances at a meadow it tends to look as though the grasses and flowers are spread evenly across the whole area, but on closer examination it becomes apparent that within the general evenness of distribution there are greater concentrations of some species in some places, usually because the ground itself is not entirely even, containing small areas that are damper or drier than the rest, in which species favouring those conditions tend to congregate. It takes hundreds of years for species to migrate to these most favoured places, but the general illusion that this has happened can be created by having greater concentrations of one grass or one wild flower in a particular area. The distribution of the grasses and flowers can also be arranged so that species that flower together occur in separate parts of the meadow.

Meadows can be made by adding bulbs and flowering plants – annuals and biennials as well as perennials – to the existing rough grass of an orchard or field, or even an uncut lawn, since meadow gardening is essentially a matter of growing flowers in a matrix of grasses. In general, meadows are most easily established on poor soils, since on richer soils vigorous grasses and weeds such as thistles, nettles and even brambles tend to get the upper hand. For this reason it is not wise to make a meadow on an abandoned lawn which has been heavily fed, nor in a vegetable garden, where again the soil will be too rich. Bulbs can easily be planted in rough grass, and flowering plants can be grown in plugs and added as and where desired. However, if you want to have control over which grasses are grown it is necessary to clear the ground and to start the whole meadow from seed, though it can be nudged towards maturity by adding bulbs and plants from plugs. Seed merchants have grass and wildflower seed mixtures suitable for most kinds of soils. Once planted, meadows need constant reappraisal, for some species will tend to become dominant and will need controlling while others will tend to die out and need replacing.

The overall effect of a natural meadow is that all the plants in it are approximately the same height. In fact there are usually subtle variations, grasses on damper ground growing taller than those on drier ground. It is difficult to achieve this in a new meadow, but if there is an obvious centre to the meadow the taller grasses and flowers should be placed towards it, and taller plants towards the back. In wild meadows occasional tall plants do crop up, drawing the eye as specimens do in beds and borders. Similar effects can be achieved in new meadows, but care needs to be taken as to which species are used. *Arundo donax* would be quite out of keeping, as would *Miscanthus floridulus* or *M. sacchariflorus*, but grasses whose leaf mound conforms to the general height of the meadow, but whose flowering culms are much taller, as for example *Molinia caerulea* ssp. *arundinacea* or *Erianthus ravennae*, would be ideal. Which raises the fundamental question as to whether meadows should be composed wholly of native species, or whether aliens can be admitted. In the narrow ecological view meadows by definition can only be composed of natives, but a greater range of both visual and seasonal interest can be obtained

if a greater or lesser number of aliens, both grasses and flowers, are included. Since contemporary meadows made specifically for their ornamental value cannot be, in the short term, anything other than stylized, it would seem worthwhile to admit aliens as long as the overall effect of the massed grasses and flowers is greater than their individual importance.

ANNUALLY RESEEDED MEADOWS

The most colourful of all meadows are those that are annually reseeded. This may sound very unnatural, but there are a number of wild habitats in which virtually the only vegetation is annuals. It is possible to obtain seed mixes for annual meadows which contain only broad-leaved annuals such as *Agrostemma githago* (mauve corn-cockle), *Papaver rhoeas* (red field poppies), *Nigella damascena* (blue or white love-in-the-mist), *Chrysanthemum segetum* (yellow, daisy-like corn marigolds), and *Limnanthes douglasii* (poached egg plant) – all plants that made the corn-fields colourful until modern seed-cleaning techniques and selective herbicides came along. To these might be added the clear blue of *Borago officinalis*, the soft pink of *Clarkia amoena*, the red-eyed yellow of *Coreopsis tinctoria*, the orange poppies of *Escholschzia californica*, the pinks, whites, reds and purples of *Papaver somniferum* (opium poppy) and the dark red of *Scabiosa atropurpurea*.

Such plantings, though colourful, hardly constitute a meadow which, by definition, is essentially grassland, and in fact the planting will be far more effective over a longer season if the annuals listed above are sown in a matrix of annual grasses such as *Agrostis nebulosa* (cloud bent grass), *Aira elegantissima*, *Apera spica-venti* (loose silky bent) and *Panicum capillare*, all of which have diffuse, cloud-like panicles of tiny spikelets; *Lolium temulentum*, *Phalaris canariensis* and *P. minor*, which have spike-like panicles; *Cynosurus echinatus*, *Echinochloa crus-galli*, *Lagurus ovatus*, *Lamarckia aurea*, *Polypogon monspeliensis* (annual beard grass) and *Setaria glauca*, all of which have feathery or bristly panicles; and some with more distinctly individual panicles such as the digitate *Eleusine indica*, the oat-like *Avena sterilis*, the greater and the lesser quaking grasses, *Briza maxima* and *B. minor*, and the various annual brome grasses such as *Bromus madritensis*, *B. arvensis* and *B. macrostachys*.

The plants suitable for annually reseeded meadows are mostly natives of disturbed ground, and as such they need annually tilled bare soil in which to grow. Left to seed themselves year after year, some annuals would flourish

while others would fade away and ultimately all would succumb to competition from tougher perennials. The technique is therefore to clear the ground in the autumn once flowering is over, to use a herbicide to clear the ground of any remaining weeds, and then to reseed. Over the years a proportion of self-sown seeds will germinate, gradually changing the proportions of the species, but this is only a problem if one or two species become dominant at the expense of the others. Just occasionally, perhaps at intervals of 20 years or so, it may be necessary to leave the ground fallow, using a herbicide to clear the ground of all the plants that germinate.

THE BRITISH MEADOW

In the UK, native meadows are composed of about two-thirds grasses and one-third wild flowers. The seed mixes from which new meadows are made usually contain the same ratio of grasses to wild flowers, but some of the grasses, and indeed some of the wild flowers, may be aggressive species that soon dominate. Generally meadows are made of much the same grasses as lawns: *Agrostis tenuis* (browntop), *A. canina* (velvet bent grass), *Anthoxanthum odoratum* (sweet vernal grass), *Cynosurus cristatus* (crested dog's tail grass), *Festuca ovina* (sheep's fescue), *F. rubra* (red fescue), *F. pratensis* (meadow fescue), *Holcus mollis* (soft velvet grass) and *Alopecurus pratensis* (foxtail grass). There are usually also a few that are more vigorous, or taller, such as *Festuca arundinacea* (tall fescue), with its tall arching stems dangling at their tips large, long-awned spikelets; *Hordeum secalinum* (meadow barley), with angled heads and symmetrically spaced long awns; *Trisetum flavescens* (yellow oat grass),with open heads of golden spikelets; *Koeleria macrantha* (crested hair grass), which is quite different, with upright spikes; *Deschampsia caespitosa* (tufted hair grass); *Phleum pratense* (Timothy grass), a plant with 90cm (3ft) slender wands bearing slim green cylinders of spikelets at the tips, named for Timothy Hanson, who introduced it to America in the 1720s; and *Briza media* (perennial quaking grass).

The British native wild flowers that would naturally occur in meadows include *Trifolium pratense* var. *serotinum* and *T. hybridum* (red and white clover); *Salvia pratensis* (meadow clary), which has spikes of purple, or sometimes pink or even white, flowers over a long season; *Sanguisorba pratensis* (salad burnet), with pinnate leaves

About two-thirds of the plants in a native British meadow are grasses, the rest being wild flowers.

and round heads of white flowers; *Pimpinella saxifrage* (burnet saxifrage), with pale pink or more usually white flowers like those of cow parsley; *Hieracium aurantiacum* (orange hawkweed), with orange dandelion flowers; *Achillea millefolium* (yarrow), with flat heads of usually white flowers; *Campanula glomerata* (clustered bellflower); *Chrysanthemum leucanthemum* (white ox-eye daisies); and the blue *Geranium pratense*, the pink *G. sanguineum* and *G. versicolor*, with thin, pencilled lines on its pale pink petals. However, as compared with native American or European flora, the British flora is a lame affair, and meadows relying for their effects wholly on the British flora will seem poor things by comparison. On balance, a mixture of native and exotic plants will be both visually and texturally more interesting.

Introducing non-natives

Once one admits some aliens to a meadow – a possibility that may be abhorrent to the ecologically pure but is generally acceptable to gardeners – it is possible greatly to extend the season of interest and the visual impact of a meadow. The season could, for example, start in late winter with the golden saucers of winter aconites and bulbs such as *Chionodoxa luculiae* or *Crocus tomasinianus*, both of which form small bulbs that can be planted relatively shallowly, and which naturally spread quite quickly. The crocus, once established, will vary in colour as it spreads across a meadow, darker in colour in some parts, paler in others, a tendency one could encourage by planting deeper named forms in some areas and paler or white forms in others. These could be followed by the chequered flowers of the native *Fritillaria meleagris* (snake's head fritillaries) in pale or deep maroon or white.

These in turn could be succeeded by daffodils and early-flowering tulips, species rather than hybrids being appropriate to a meadow setting, and then early summer-flowering perennials such as *Leucanthemum × superbum* and its varieties (Shasta daisies) and *Papaver orientalis* (oriental poppies) which disappear after flowering at the same time as the first of the grasses, *Melica ciliata*, *M. transsilvanica*, *Helictotrichon sempervirens* and the lowly festucas. By midsummer these grasses are joined by seslerias and *Calamagrostis × acutiflora*, while *Panicum virgatum*

is already coming up towards flowering. These can be interplanted with tall alliums, *Lilium martagon* (turk's cap lilies), *Achillea millefolium* (yarrow), and even, if one does not mind leaning towards the prairie, *Rudbeckia fulgida* 'Goldsturm' and thread-leaf tickseeds.

By late summer and into autumn the warm-season grasses should be dominant – *Panicum* (switch grasses), *Pennisetum* (fountain grasses) and *Miscanthus* - with purple asters and pink sedums, while *Rudbeckia* (cone flowers) and *Coryopsis* (tickseeds) will have lost their petal colour and turned to sere browns and beiges. These will last well into winter, mostly turning to browns and beiges, though the foliage of the tickseeds turns grey and the sedums tend to turn copper-coloured. Then in late winter the meadow needs to be cut down so that the cycle can start again.

FAR MEADOWS

The overall effect of most meadows is green, and such meadows are sometimes known as near meadows to distinguish them from far meadows, in which the grasses are predominantly blue- or grey-leaved, and the flowers are predominantly on the mauve, blue or purple wavelength, giving the viewer the impression of being further away than near meadows. The main grasses used in such meadows are *Koeleria glauca*, *K. vallesiana*, *Sesleria caerulea*, *S. nitida*, *Helictotrichon pratense*, *H. sempervirens*, *Eragrostis chloromelas* and *Elymus arenarius* with a small admixture of blue- or grey-leaved switch grasses such as *Panicum virgatum* 'Heavy Metal', *P. v.* ' Pathfinder' or *P. v.* 'North Wind' and the grey-blue Indian grass *Sorghastrum nutans* 'Indian Steel' or the blue *S. n.* 'Sioux Blue'.

The effect can be enhanced if among these grey-leaved grasses blue-flowered plants are grown, starting in spring with *Chionodoxa luculiae*, *Scilla sibirica* and *Crocus tomasinianus*, followed by such perennials as mauve *Cardamine pratense*, sky-blue *Linum anglicum*, *Geranium sylvaticum*, *Anchusa sempervirens*, *Galega orientalis*, *Allium giganteum*, *Nepeta*, *Perovskia*, *Campanula lactiflora* and *C. glomerata*, not forgetting the misty blues of the camassias and the distant mauves of scabious. Subtler, and more difficult to achieve is a drift from the greens of near meadows to the blues of far meadows.

17 Wild Gardens

The term wild garden is an oxymoron, for a garden is by definition cultivated. Yet the term has persisted across the centuries, meaning different things at different times. Western gardens have evolved to assert man's dominance over nature and this has been expressed through geometry in terms of order and symmetry, the Cartesian garden itself representing an ordered society. But times are changing, and as modern life moves further from any form of existence that could be considered natural, and as the sprawl of cities and motorways destroys the habitats of wild plants, the strictures of modern living stimulate a compensating desire for wilder gardens which themselves will provide a safe haven for threatened native species.

In wild gardens the individual grasses and flowers assume a greater importance than they do in meadows, where it is the overall effect that matters most. Grasses more than other plants have overtones of wildness and so must be the dominant plants in any form of wild garden; the use of them in quantity will in itself induce a sense of wildness. But there are wild gardens that are wild as opposed to well-manicured, and there are wild gardens that are filled with wild rather than exotic plants. The differences are substantial. In the first type of wild garden, grasses from different parts of the world may rub along promiscuously together, so long as an untamed effect is achieved; *Cortaderia* from the Argentine or New Zealand may rub shoulders with *Pennisetum* (fountain grasses) from Australia and Ethiopia, *Eragrostis* (hair grasses) from Europe and America, *Stipa* from Camschatka, and tall *Miscanthus* from China. However, to achieve a garden that is wild as opposed to exotic takes a little learning.

NATIVE PLANTING

The essential source books for such gardens are native or regional floras, and books dealing specifically with the particular grasses or sedges of particular countries or regions: notably C. E. Hubbard's fascinating *Grasses* and A. C. Jermy and T. G. Tutin's *British Sedges* for the UK, A. S. Hitchcock's monumental *Manual of Grasses of the United States* for the USA and Nancy Burbidge's *Australian Grasses* for Australia which, though it is not encyclopaedic,

contains most of the grasses that Australians are likely to be able to use.

Even a quick look at a local flora or one of these more specialized books will reveal just how many of the grasses we grow in our gardens are natives – such is the range and variety that it is possible to make a visually stimulating garden using only these plants. British native grasses include such highly decorative species as *Deschampsia flexuosa* (wavy hair grass), *D. caespitosa* (tufted hair grass), *Molinia caerulea* ssp. *caerulea* (purple moor grass), *Briza media* (common quaking grass), *Glyceria maxima* (sweet reed grass), *Festuca arundinacea* (tall fescue), *Bromus* species, *Koeleria cristata* (crested hair grass), *Elymus arenarius* (blue lyme grass) and many others. There are also several sedges such as *Carex pendula* (pendulous or great weeping sedge), *C. flacca* and *C. panicea* (carnation grasses), lovers of wet ground such as *C. riparia* (greater pond sedge), and *Cyperus longus* (galingale), a whole range of *Luzula* species (woodrushes), *Schoenoplectus* (clubrushes), *Juncus* (reeds) and *Eriophorum* (cottongrasses).

From such a wealth of material it is possible to make a wild garden full of interest, bearing in mind that the difference between a garden and a wilderness is that gardens are organized according to rhythms and patterns that are instantly perceptible to the mind at levels just below the conscious, while wildernesses follow natural laws. In order to create a garden that will look authentically wild, one must lay aside all preconceptions of aesthetics and instead set out to imitate natural, native plant associations. The best wild gardens are those that seek to copy a single ecological entity, with all the native plants that occur together naturally being grown together.

PLANT DISTRIBUTION

One of the most significant distinctions between grasses in gardens and grasses in the wild is the way they are distributed. In gardens they are grouped to please our own eyes, while in the wild they are loosely distributed through all parts of the environment but are particularly prominent in clearings among shrubs or among taller perennials. The reason for this is that the grasses as a family are generally sun-lovers, and relatively few have evolved to grow in shade.

The tiny spikelets and open panicles of *Panicum virgatum* 'Rubrum' give an almost transparent effect.

Even in quite a small space, it is possible to make a wild garden running from woodland and woodland species, represented by the shade of a hedge or a few small trees, through a stretch of seemingly open meadowland to a wetland habitat at the edge of a small pond. Such a garden would contain a considerable diversity of grasses, not only those from woodland, meadow and waterside, but also many transitional species. The woodland might contain, for example, *Milium effusum*, drifts of the tall rangy *Festuca arundinacea* as well as *F. heterophylla* and *F. tenuifolia*, *Bromus ramosus*, *Brachypodium sylvaticum*, the broad-leaved *Poa chaixii* and *P. nemoralis* as well as *Hordelymus europaeus* and the slowly running *Melica uniflora* mixed with wild native daffodils and pink, white and blue *Anemone blanda*. These might be followed by drifts of *Hyacinthoides non-scripta* (bluebells) and the spears of *Digitalis purpurea* (foxgloves), *Iris foetidissima*, *Convallaria majalis*, the various native *Polygonatum* (Solomon's seals), *Ruscus* (butcher's broom) and sinister *Arum maculatum* (lords and ladies) with their lurid spathes and spadices and poisonous red berries.

In the meadow area, which is open to the sun for most of the day, many of the same grasses as are found in lawns will do best – *Agrostis tenuis*, *A. canina*, *Cynosurus cristatus*, *Anthoxanthum odoratum*, *Festuca rubra*, *F. ovina*, *F. pratensis*, *Holcus mollis* and *Alopecurus pratensis*, the latter two liking damper ground. Then there are the taller, showier grasses, *Hordeum secalinum*, *Trisetum flavescens*, *Koeleria macrantha*, *Briza media* and *Phleum pratense*. Among these there might be *Chrysanthemum leucanthemum* (ox-eyed daisies), *Campanula glomerata* (clustered bellflower), blue and pink *Geranium* (cranesbill), the deep blue spikes of *Salvia pratensis* (meadow clary), *Sanguisorba pratensis* (salad burnet), *Pimpinella saxifrage* (pink cow parsley), *Hieracium aurantiacum* (orange hawkweed), *Gladiolus illyricus*, *Leucojum aestivum* (summer snowflake) and *Knautia arvensis* (field scabious).

At the pond's edge one might grow *Glyceria maxima*, *Zizania aquatica* (Indian rice), *Phalaris arundinacea* (ribbon grass), *Molinia caerulea* ssp. *caerulea* (purple moor grass), drifts of the reeds *Scirpus* and *Schoenoplectus*, *Juncus effusus* (soft rush), and galingale, as well as *Carex elata* and the blue-leaved, invasive *C. riparia*, interspersed with stands of *Lythrum salicaria*, *Osmunda regalis* (royal fern), *Dactylorhiza fuchsii* (marsh orchid), *Orchis mascula* (purple orchid), *Anacamptis pyramidalis*, *Iris pseudacorus*, *Angelica archangelica*, *Alisma plantago-aquatica* and flowering rush. *Typha* and *Phragmites* might look quite in keeping but would soon take over the pond to the exclusion of all else.

THE ROBINSONIAN GARDEN

If, however, you wish to make a wild garden as advocated by William Robinson in *The Wild Garden*, first published in 1870, then you are looking at something entirely different. Robinson's idea of a wild garden was of one that was not cultivated and in which plants were established and then left to fend for themselves against the native vegetation. In such a garden *Cortaderia* species would be quite in keeping, as would *Miscanthus*, *Stipa gigantea* and *S. calamagrostis*, *Panicum* (switch grasses) and *Pennisetum* (fountain grasses), *Spodiopogon sibiricus* and some of the coarser grasses such as *Stipa tenacissima*. Charming effects can be created by combining these with *Papaver orientale* (oriental poppies), daylilies such as the fragrant yellow *Hemerocallis lilioasphodelus* or the larger fulvous daylily *H. fulva*, *Paeonia* species and large umbellifers such as *Angelica gigas* or *A. archangelica* with *Geranium pratense* or *G. psilostemon*.

18 Wetland and Waterside

Water, and the wet ground beside it, provide an opportunity to grow to their full glory a number of grasses that never attain such luxuriance in ordinary earth. Quite the most magnificent of these is *Arundo donax* (Provençal reed) which can be grown either as a marginal or with its feet in water and which, once established, can reach some 4.6m (15ft). The variety *A. d.* 'Macrophylla' has larger, bluer leaves, while *A. d.* 'Variegata' (var. *versicolor*) is richly variegated creamy-white, but is rarely hardy out of doors in the UK. The typical species is probably best grown in isolation as a specimen or, if a sheet of water is large enough, repeated at intervals round the margins. Few other grasses are bold enough to match it, and if it is to have companions they

need to be giants in other genera: *Lysichiton*, *Gunnera*, *Osmunda regalis* or huge hostas, the chartreuse *Hosta* 'Sum and Substance', the silvery-blue *H.* 'Jade Cascade', or the rugose *H.* 'Blue Mammoth'. The other option is to grow it with tiny-leaved grasses or little bamboos such as *Pleioblastus humilis* var. *pumilus* or *P. pygmaeus*.

The other species of *Arundo* provide charm rather than drama, the most striking being *A. pliniana*, whose leaves are only 10cm (4in) long but sharp enough at the tip to pierce the skin. It forms a fascinating grey-blue tracery of upright and arching culms beset with small

Carex elata 'Sue Ward' is a singularly bright solid gold seedling from the green-edged *C. e.* 'Aurea' (centre).

stiff leaves. It travels at the root rather more than *A. donax*, and is perhaps not so hardy.

Phragmites australis (common reed) is an aggressive colonizer and quite unsuitable for all but the very largest parks and gardens. It is quite variable, though few forms have been brought into gardens. It can grow up to 3.6m (12ft) tall but is usually about 2.4m (8ft), and typically has tapering grey-green leaves and large plumes which in the wild may be as much as 45cm (18in) long, in green, white, purple or almost black. *P. a.* 'Pseudodonax' is a form with extra-thick culms and oversized leaves resembling the Provençal reed, *Arundo donax*. There are several variegated forms which interestingly grow happily in ordinary earth and do not run excessively. *P. a.* 'Variegatus' has dark green leaves with a rich, golden-yellow variegation; *P. a.* 'Striatopictus' has cream-striped leaves and is more vigorous. *P. a.* 'Candy Stripe' has pale, minty green leaves and culms that are brightly striped white and pink. *P. karka* 'Variegatus' is similar. These variegated forms seldom grow to more than 1.8m (6ft).

CAT-TAILS

The cat-tails or reed maces (*Typha*) are essential plants but can become excessively invasive. *T. latifolia* can grow 2.4–3m (8–10ft) tall, and is best in 15–30cm (6–12in) of water. It is an architecturally superb plant, its culms rising out of the water stiff and straight with to each side of them the flat, blue-green leaves arching upwards and outwards. The dark brown, cigar-shaped flowers, which can be 30cm (12in) long and 5cm (2in) thick, are produced at the tops of the culms from the midsummer onwards into autumn, and last well into winter. The leaves assume yellow and brown tints in autumn, and decay in the winter. *T. l.* 'Variegata' is far less vigorous, reaching only 1.2m (4ft), but still needs confinement in a container. It is a most attractive form, its leaves longitudinally striped white.

There are several smaller species that are eminently suitable for smaller ponds and gardens. The smallest of these is *T. minima*, which grows only some 60cm (2ft) tall. It blooms early in the year, the small, ball-like inflorescences emerging green then turning light brown, and looking their best in early and midsummer. *T. shuttleworthii* differs markedly in having very narrow, almost rolled leaves. It grows to about 90cm (3ft) tall.

The dwarf cat-tail *Typha minima* is ideal for smaller gardens and flowers earlier than most other types.

T. angustifolia grows to 1.5m (5ft) at most, and flowers in mid and late summer.

The cat-tails, large or small, make attractive companions for water lilies, creating strong vertical accents against the flat pads of the lilies. The decorative qualities of the small cat-tails is such that they are sometimes grown on terraces or in conservatories in large pots which in turn are stood in saucers of water to ensure that they never dry out.

RUSHES

Quite different in character are *Schoenoplectus* and *Scirpus* (club rushes), which have osier-like clumps of upright stems. These stems, which are often mistakenly referred to as leaves, are cylindrical and hollow. The true leaves are usually reduced to scarcely noticeable sheaths, and the flowers are produced at the tips of the stems but appear to be borne at the side, about three-quarters of the way up. This is because two bracts extend upwards past the flower and appear to be a continuation of the stem. The true clubrush or bulrush, *Schoenoplectus lacustris*, which grows to about 1.5m (5ft), has grey-green stems which are scarcely ornamental enough to admit to a small garden. However, the two variegated forms of the subspecies *tabernaemontani*, *S. l.* ssp. *t.* 'Albescens' and *S. l.* ssp. *t.* 'Zebrinus', are by contrast in the first rank of ornamental water plants. 'Albescens' has stems longitudinally striped bright white, or occasionally entirely white, while the stems of 'Zebrinus' are transversely banded white. Both will grow to 1.8-2.4m (6- 8ft) tall and reach some 1.2m (4ft) across the base. There is a third plant which, though usually listed as a scirpus, almost certainly belongs here. This is *Scirpus* 'Golden Spear', which differs from 'Albescens' only in that the variegation is bright yellow early in the season, fading to green. All are clump-forming, and look best grown in submerged tubs or barrels. They should have no more than 7.5cm (3in) of water over their roots. Because of their extraordinarily vertical emphasis these rushes afford a useful contrast to the flatness of lily pads, and are good for visually breaking up the harsh margins of ponds.

The true rushes are not in the main sufficiently ornamental to grow in gardens, though *Juncus* 'Carmen's Gray', which grows to some 60cm (2ft), is remarkable both for the blueness of its foliage and the copious profusion of its flowering, while *J. pallidus* is notable for its arching pale green stems. It reaches about 1m (3¼ft) high. Both grow taller in wet ground. *J. effusus* 'Gold Strike' is an

Arundo donax 'Variegata' (striped Provençal reed) is a moisture-loving grass but only suitable for the mildest areas.

eyecatching American selection whose leaves are striped gold and green. Unlike the old *J. e.* 'Vittatus', it is stable. It grows to about 75cm (2½ft), taller in damp ground.

There has been a passing craze for rushes whose stems instead of being straight are curled. Of these, *J. e.* 'Spiralis' is known as the corkscrew rush and is supposed to look like a bundle of overgrown green corkscrews sticking out of the ground. Its stems are a deep, shining green. *J. balticus* 'Spiralis' is similar but runs at the root, forming drifts or patches rather than clumps. In the USA this plant has been widely sold as *J. effusus* 'Spiralis' for some years. *J. inflexus* is the hard or inflexible rush, and its curly form is known as 'Afro'. It is quite distinct in that its stems are grey, not green, and in that it will grow well in ordinary earth. *J. glomeratus* 'Spiralis' is quite different again, being of diminutive stature, growing no more than 15cm (6in) and looking more like a ball of rusting wire wool than a clutch of corkscrews. The problem with these curly rushes is that in time the clumps come to contain more dead leaves than green ones.

SEDGES

There are some bright sedges that will grow with their feet in water, though they are more usually grown as marginals. The first is *Carex elata* 'Aurea' (Bowles' golden sedge), which forms dense tussocks of long, arching leaves which are rich yellow thinly edged with green: *C. e.* 'Knightshayes Form' is brighter, lacking the green margins. *C. e.* 'Sue Ward' is even brighter. Both grow to 75cm (2½ft) tall and 90cm (3ft) or more across and are striking

in early summer. When in sun the foliage assumes an almost brassy brightness, but is a lime-yellow in shade.

Another is the striped riparian sedge, *Carex riparia* 'Variegata'. In spring the new leaves, which build up into a round mound of arching foliage some 60cm (2ft) tall, emerge whiter than white, gradually acquiring thin green margins which deepen in colour as the season wears on, while the pristine whiteness of the central variegation gradually fades to light green. The foliage is deciduous. The flowers are very showy and are produced in the spring, just after the leaves, the terminal male tassel being foxy reddish-brown while the female spikes are shining jet black. It looks best in a container; when allowed its freedom it runs and becomes too diffuse to be effective. The danger is not merely that it will run, but that it might revert to the non-variegated form, which is an aggressive colonizer. It will grow with about 5cm (2in) of water over its roots. *C. r.* 'Aurea' is a newer selection with yellow-flushed leaves.

I have seen *Carex elata* 'Aurea' and *C. riparia* 'Variegata' used to great effect at the side of formal, brick-edged tank in company with shaggy, maroon-leaved *Rheum palmatum* 'Atrosanguineum' and the digitate, coppery leaves of *Rodgersia podophylla*. Shrubby, white-variegated *Cornus alba* 'Elegantissima' echoed the white of the *Carex riparia* 'Variegata' and the yellow leaves of *Sambucus racemosus* 'Plumosa Aurea' echoed those of *Carex elata* 'Aurea'. To this one might add the sumptuous blue leaves of a large hosta of *H. sieboldiana* derivation such as *H.* 'Mira' or *H.* 'Big Daddy' and the vertical accent of the leaves of Siberian irises (*Iris sibirica*), their flowers perhaps picking up echoes of other plants nearby. Several carices such the clumping *Carex morrowii* 'Variegata' or *C. m.* 'Fisher's Form', or the slowly running *C.* 'Silver Sceptre', *C.* 'Ice Dance' or the blue *C. flacca* might be used an an underplanting.

Quite different from any of the above is *C. secta*, which is usually found in the wild with its feet in water, though it has no absolute need for saturated soil. It is a tussock-forming sedge which will gradually form a trunk, ultimately some 90cm (3ft) tall, composed of dead roots and leaf-bases. It is grown for this curious habit, neither the leaves nor flowers being notably beautiful.

CYPERUS

The *Cyperus* genus (umbrella plants) are as indispensable as the carices and introduce a different note, for at the tops of their upright stems they carry wheel-like whorls of leaves which support often diffusely ball-like heads composed of slender stalks tipped with brown spikelets. Three species are generally hardy in the average climate of the UK, and at least two are natives. The larger and showier of these is *C. longus* (galingale, or sweet galingale), which grows to about 90cm (3ft) and is probably the hardiest of the genus. It produces its flat umbels of brown flowers at the top of the stem surrounded by several extraordinarily long green bracts of unequal length. It is soundly perennial, and clump-forming. The other British native, *C. fuscus* (brown cyperus), is by contrast an annual, and a diminutive plant at that, growing to no more than 15cm (6in) tall and producing at the tops of its slender stems reddish-brown flowers on short stalks, beneath which are two green bracts, one of which is usually quite long. More showy is American galingale, *C. eragrostis* (*C. vegetus*), which forms a loosely tufted perennial growing to about 90cm (3ft) and from midsummer until autumn produces ball-shaped heads of pale brown flowers beneath which is a collar of slender, pointed green bracts.

C. ustulatus is by comparison a somewhat coarse plant, but useful because of its size, growing to 1.8m (6ft) tall, and for its broad, striking leaves, which are of parchment-like texture and an unusual lime-green stained pale café-au-lait with a conspicuous reddish-brown midrib. The flowerheads resemble those of *C. eragrostis*, but are presented in larger, showier clusters. It will grow with water over its roots but is surprisingly happy in ordinary earth.

In addition to the grasses mentioned above, most forms of *Miscanthus sinensis* will flourish in moist ground, as will the very tall *M. sacchariflorus* and the various forms of *Cortaderia selloana*, as well as both *C. richardii* and *C. fulvida* and many bamboos.

DESIGNING FOR SHAPE

Most of these waterside grasses are strongly upright in their emphasis, but many also have leaves that create counterbalancing horizontals against the verticals of their stems. The subtle differences between these varying verticals and horizontals can be pointed up by the careful positioning of the plants. *Arundo donax*, though it grows tall, has a strongly horizontal effect because of the way its leaves are held, making it a perfect backdrop to stately clumps of *Schoenoplectus lacustris* ssp. *tabernaemontani* 'Albescens', whose seemingly leafless stems seem all the more erect against the leafiness of the *Arundo*. A slightly different emphasis can be achieved if *S. l.* ssp. *t.* 'Zebrinus'

is used instead of 'Albescens', the alternating white and green of the transverse banding picking up the alternating pattern of the leaves and the spaces between them on the *Arundo*. If in front of this is grown one of the *Cyperus* genus, *C. eragrostis*, for example, whose stems arise straight and leafless from the water but are topped by a horizontal whorl of bracts, this not only echoes the flatness of the water but also marries the visual emphases of the other two plants, picking up the vertical of the *Schoenoplectus* and the horizontal leafiness of the *Arundo*. The use of arching leaves, such as those of *Spartina pectinata*, also helps to marry verticals and horizontals.

Such compositions can be enriched if broad-leaved plants are used to accentuate the linearity of the grasses. Suitable waterside plants include *Gunnera manicata*, the less massive *Lysichiton* (false skunk cabbage), the tall-stalked *Darmera peltiphyllum* and *D. p.* 'Nana', the ubiquitous *Ligularia dentata* 'Desdemona' with its dark leaves and gaudy orange flowers or the less familiar *L. d.* 'Othello' with flowers of a clearer yellow and *L. przewalksii* with shaggy palmate leaves and flowers produced on tall, swaying wands. *Cardiocrinum giganteum* (giant lily), with its huge, highly polished, heart-shaped leaves, is particularly valued for the fragrance produced by its massive creamy-white trumpets, carried on stout 3m (10ft) stems.

As tall or taller, and suitable for making a late autumn picture with the plumes of *Miscanthus*, *Cortaderia*, *Panicum* and *Pennisetum*, are the swamp chrysanthemum, *Chrysanthemum serotinum* (*C. uliginosum*), with stems 1.8–2.4m (6–8ft) tall bearing clusters of white Shasta daisies which

Cyperus longus, a British native, is most at home growing beside water, as seen here.

PLATE VIII
Miscanthus

All plants shown approximately ½ size

Miscanthus sinensis 'Kaskade'

Miscanthus sinensis
'Sirene'

Miscanthus
oligostachyus
'Africa'

Miscanthus sinensis 'Spatgrun'

Miscanthus sinensis
'Yakushima Dwarf'

Miscanthus sinensis
'Flamingo'

Miscanthus transmorrisonensis

turn to follow the sun across the sky, the blue *Aconitum carmichaelii* 'Arendsii', and the giant maroon eupatoriums *Eupatorium purpureum*, *E. p.* ssp. *maculatum* 'Atropurpureum', *E. p.* 'Chocolate' and *E. p.* 'Purple Bush'.

Lesser companions that will grow with their feet in water include *Zantedeschia aethiopica* 'Crowborough' (arum lily), *Calla palustris* (bog arum), which has broad glossy leaves and stumpy white arum flowers, *Sagittaria sagittifolia* (common arrowhead), with arrow-shaped leaves and white flowers, *Menyanthes trifoliata* (bog bean), which produces fringed, pinky-white flowers over spreading leaves, and *Caltha palustris* (common marsh marigold), which bears its golden, cup-shaped flowers in spring.

Floating water plants contribute strongly structural shapes on the surface of the water to counterbalance the sheer linearity of the grasses. Take, for example, the perennial *Stratiotes aloides* (water soldier) with floating rosettes resembling pineapple tops and *Hydrocharis morsus-ranae* (frog-bit), which resembles a miniature white-flowered water lily, and tender plants such as *Eichhornia crassipes* (water hyacinth), which floats on inflated green bladders, or *E. trapa* (water chestnut) which produces, above rather holly-like green and bronze leaves, small white flowers followed by large black spiny seeds resembling large horse chestnut seed-cases.

There are smaller grasses and smaller companions to grow with them beside the water, among the best of which are the moor grasses, including the lovely cream-striped *Molinia caerulea* ssp. *caerulea* 'Variegata' as well as the short *M. c.* ssp. *c* 'Moorhexe' and *M. c.* ssp. *c* 'Moorflamme', *Deschampsia caespitosa* (hair grass) in its many forms, *Luzula nivea* (snowy woodrush), its leaves edged with white hairs, cloud-like drifts of *Panicum*, the white-striped *Dactylis glomerata* 'Variegata' and the yellow-striped *Alopecurus pratensis* 'Aureomarginata'.

PLANT ASSOCIATIONS

Many hostas grow well in wet situations, particularly some of the new fragrant American sun-loving varieties derived from *H. plantaginea*, such as *H.* 'Guacamole', *H.* 'Sweetie', *H.* 'Summer Fragrance' and *H.* 'Summer Bouquet', while many of the older varieties, usually considered shade-lovers, will in fact grow well in sunny positions if they have sufficient moisture at their roots to sustain them, though varieties with white variegation should be avoided. Some moisture-loving ferns will flourish in sun if their roots are in saturated soil, *Onoclea sensibilis*

(sensitive fern), for example, as well as *Osmunda regalis* (royal fern) and *Thelypteris palustris*.

Such combinations rely primarily on the architecture of the plants. If variations on themes of colour are added, the picture becomes much richer. A starting point might be to plant a tall, white-variegated pampas grass, such as *Cortaderia selloana* 'Silver Beacon', and carry on the white theme with other white-striped grasses, including *Phalaris arundinacea* 'Feesey', *Miscanthus sinensis* 'Morning Light' or *M. s.* 'Cosmopolitan'. Next add white-variegated plants from other genera such as *Hemerocallis fulva* 'Kwanzo Variegata', which has longitudinally white-striped leaves, or pick up the whiteness in the flowers of *Senecio smithii* or *Aruncus dioicus*. If a framework of key plants is established in this way a great variety of other plants can be used without losing the sense of harmony.

In a smaller space, one could play variations on a yellow theme, for example, using *Glyceria maxima* var. *variegata*, *Milium effusum* 'Aureum', *Spartina pectinata* 'Aureomarginata' and *Carex elata* 'Aurea'. Plant them with *Iris pseudacorus* 'Variegata', *Sisyrinchium striatum* 'Aunt May', tall spuria irises, *Alchemilla mollis*, and *Primula florindae*. All this could be underpinned with a counterpoint of blue-grey shades, for example the blue *Hosta* 'Halcyon', *H.* 'Buckshaw Blue', *Carex glauca* or the taller *C. flaccosperma* and the greys of the small willows *Salix helvetica* or *S. lanata* as well as the grey leaves and tall stems of the moisture-loving *Eryngium yuccifolium*. Mix in a minor theme of white provided by some *Holcus mollis* 'Albovariegata' at ground level and some *Cornus alba* 'Elegantissima' in the background.

All of this planting presupposes banks that are saturated where they meet the water, but ponds are often constructed of concrete or with impermeable liners which keep the ground at their edge as dry as dust, and this can present problems because the expectation is that the vegetation around a pond will be lush with vigour. Since the plants of dry soils never appear to have rude vigour the answer seems to be to sink large buckets in the ground, with about 15cm (6in) of soil above the rim, to provide an unseen reservoir. Just a few buckets strategically placed are all that is needed, since a mere handful of waterside plants will lend the illusion of wet-ground lushness continuing beyond the pond. The key plants to grow in the concealed buckets would be *Zantedeschia aethiopica* 'Crowborough', *Lysichiton*, *Ligularia* and *Astilbe* species and *Osmunda regalis* or a clump of the shuttlecock fern.

19 Woodland and Shade

The true grasses are essentially plants of open, sunny places and relatively few flourish in woodland, though the few that do are sylvan delights. Far better adapted to woodland are the carices and woodrushes which may be relied upon to thrive, contributing both flowers and foliage.

Quite the most visually arresting of the flowering grasses for woodland and shade are *Deschampsia caespitosa* and its varieties (tufted hair grasses), with their diffuse heads of tiny, shimmering spikelets. They are natives of wet woodlands, poorly drained meadows and damp moorland and as such are more plants of woodland margins than of dense shade deep within a woodland. Perhaps more beautiful but slightly less dramatic is *Deschampsia flexuosa* (wavy hair grass), which bears similarly diffuse panicles of tiny spikelets at the tops of slender beige stems but differs in its much lower mounds of dark green foliage and in its tendency to spread, in time making small drifts rather than the tight clumps of *D. caespitosa*. Flowering as these grasses do through the early and middle weeks of the summer, they follow on from the hectic display of the rhododendrons and azaleas, bringing a quieter mood to woodland and glade, bridging the gap until the hydrangeas begin their display. Their tiny spikelets afford a complete contrast to the large leaves of so many rhododendrons and bring relief from the funereal gloom which descends on woodland gardens heavily dependent on ericaceous plants.

D. flexuosa is notably a plant of acid soils and is sometimes used as a lawn grass on soils too acid to grow a more conventional turf. Indeed, it can be used in open acid woodland where a wild (that is, uncultivated) look is desired as a matrix in which to grow spring and summer bulbs, including lilies, many of which grow in the wild with their feet cooled by native grasses. *D. caespitosa* is not so fussy and is easily grown in most soils.

Almost as beautiful are the quaking grasses (*Briza*) which flower in the first half of the year, their dry heads continuing to contribute beauty to the garden until late summer. They are characterized by their dangling, locket-shaped spikelets composed of overlapping scales borne at the tips of slender branchlets drooping from arching culms. They are at first a mysterious pale green, as though

Hystrix patula (bottlebrush grass) is one of the few true grasses that will flourish in woodland or on woodland margins.

carved with infinite patience from tiny pieces of jade, but gradually turn to pale browns. *B. maxima* (larger quaking grass) is an annual and a native of dry, rocky places around the Mediterranean, in spite of which we have had it growing for many years in a damp border, shaded by *Phyllostachys dulcis* and a hedge of *Podocarpus salignus* where it not only flourishes but seems to last longer in flower and to scatter its seeds with greater freedom than in dry, sandy soil. *Briza maxima* 'Rhodes Form' is dwarfer, with larger spikelets. *B. media* (lesser quaking grass) is perennial and will also flourish at the edge of woodland, damp or dry. Both become dormant in the heat of summer and start into growth again in autumn, just as the colchicums come into flower.

Similar in the structure of its spikelets is *Chasmanthium latifolium* (northern sea oats), though it has little else in common, being a warm-season grower from the southeastern United States and Mexico, where it grows in moist, fertile woods. It differs from the quaking grasses in its much larger spikelets, which are flattened as though they have been ironed. They are olive green at first, becoming a well-tanned bronze for winter. It makes an excellent complement for *Hystrix patula* (bottle-brush grass), which flowers at much the same time and enjoys much the same conditions. Its 10cm (4in) upright heads are composed of widely spaced, horizontally held, double-awned spikelets which are jade green tinted pink at the base. It flowers through mid and late summer, shattering in early autumn. In shade or woodland both can be inter-planted with *Anemone blanda* (woodland anemones), com-ing up once those die down, and with the hardy begonia *Begonia grandis* ssp. *evansiana*, which scarcely comes out of the ground until early summer and whose pale pink flowers match exactly the pink of the *Hystrix*. They also associate particularly well with hardy ferns and, having rather weedy foliage themselves, benefit from having this deficiency somewhat hidden by lacy fern fronds.

EUROPEAN NATIVES

There are three grasses that are natives of Europe, includ-ing the UK, which grow naturally together in the wild and which associate well with each other in the garden. These are the tall, rangy *Festuca gigantea* (giant fescue), which produces 1.5m (5ft) stems topped with arching, one-sided panicles of dangling green spikelets, the shorter (90cm/3ft) *Brachypodium sylvaticum* which bears arching panicles of narrow, fine-awned spikelets above yellowish-green leaves and *Bromus ramosus* (wood brome), which again bears its spikelets from pendulous branch-lets in an arching panicle. It grows to about 1.2m (4ft). All three flower in mid and late summer. For the eco-logically correct it is perhaps enough to grow all three together in beech or oak woods, their tufts of leaves emerging from ground carpeted earlier in the year with bluebells. However, the sheer panache of their arching panicles may be shown to better advantage by associa-tion with plants of greater substance such as acanthus or hostas, planted in drifts with other shade- and moisture-lovers like *Ligularia* 'The Rocket', *Petasites paradoxus*, *Astilbe* and *Rodgersia* with a background of *Mahonia × media* 'Charity' or the more spreading *M. japonica*. All three grasses also mix well with *Digitalis* (foxgloves), their vigorously upright and arching stems contrasting with the stems of the foxgloves which are, by the time the grasses flower, heavy with seed and usually leaning in all directions.

AUTUMN COLOURS

Other grasses can contribute autumn foliage colours to the woodland scene. The best known of these is flame

grass, *Miscanthus oligostachyus* 'Purpurascens' (syn. *M. sinen-sis* 'Purpurascens'), which is in effect like a thin-leaved *Miscanthus sinensis*, the thinness of its leaves making them vulnerable to scorching in hot sun. Grown in shade or at the edge of woodland, where the light is good but little direct sun reaches it, it will start to take on its colour-ing by mid to late summer, the leaves becoming tipped with vinous purple, a colour which gradually suffuses the whole leaf so that by early autumn it is as red as a good claret held up to the light, its colouring made all the more intense by the singularly white plumes which are produced at the same time. To be seen at its best it should be side- or back-lit against a dark background, but even with the light falling on it it can be conspicu-ous because its colouring is a blue-red, as opposed to the predominant yellow-reds and scarlets of the season.

Spodiopogon sibiricus, especially in its 'West Hills' form, can be almost as showy in the autumn, and is, on the whole, a better garden plant at other seasons, carrying itself stiffly upright with the leaves held out horizontally, or slightly drooping below the horizontal. Indeed, in its

Hakonechloa macra 'Alboaurea' (golden Hakone grass) thrives in woodland but assumes subtler colouring than it displays when grown in a sunny position.

general carriage it looks rather like a small bamboo. It is a cool-season grower, in spite of producing its flowers in late summer and early autumn. These are ovoid panicles of green, grey and purple spikelets. In late summer the leaves become tipped with vinous purple which gradually seeps down the leaves, but by autumn they have also taken on brighter reds and yellows, though never quite so bright as the fiery maples. It grows most erect in cool climates, in the UK and in the more northerly states of the USA, tending to flop in the heat of North Carolina and thence southwards.

These two grasses gain by being placed where they form a visual entity with another grass or plant whose autumn colouring is a lucent yellow. Among grasses *Molinia caerulea* ssp. *caerulea* and its varieties (purple moor grasses) turn first butter yellow but then acquire a hint of amber in their colouring, while *Panicum virgatum* 'Strictum' stays a clear butter yellow for several weeks. Both the *Molinia* and the *Panicum* grow better in good light at the edge of woodland, rather than in deeper shade. Among woody plants *Cladrastis lutea* (yellow wood) has

leaves that turn clear yellow before falling, as do the leaves of the scandent or climbing *Celastrus orbiculatus* while at the same time, if the summers are hot enough, covering itself with scarlet- and gold-spangled fruits. When mature, and again if the summers are hot enough, yellow wood produces long, drooping, wisteria-like panicles of fragrant white flowers.

SEDGES FOR SHADE

Of the sedges only *Carex pendula* (pendulous sedge) can really be said to contribute much in the way of flower power to woodland or shade, its stems (which usually grow to about 90cm/3ft, but occasionally more) arching towards the tips and bearing pendulous, catkin-like spikes of flowers. In some gardens it may seed itself with a freedom that can be troublesome. Where this is the case *C. trifida* and *C. boottiana* can provide similar bulk and foliage, but are less decorative in flower, these occurring in a fist-like cluster that scarcely shows above the leaves. The various forms of *C. morrowii* such as *C.m.* 'Variegata' and *C.m.* 'Fisher's Form' contribute spikes of good dark flowers in spring and make excellent groundcovers among bamboos or shrubs, their leaves and flowers providing a textural contrast with the glossy, dark green leaves of camellias, the tracery of *Hamamelis* or the spiky, pinnate leaves of mahonias.

Almost as distinct in a totally different way and eminently suited to woodland and shade is *C. muskingumensis* (palm leaf sedge), which forms 60cm (2ft) high slowly spreading clumps with strongly three-sided stems and the leaves arranged in three ranks but mostly gathered at the top of the stems. The flowers are little brown pompoms of no great decorative value, but in the autumn the whole plant assumes smouldering tones of ochrous yellow. *C. m.* 'Oehme' is a selection with striking gold-edged leaves. *C. m.* 'Little Midge' is a dwarf about 23cm (9in) high, while *C. m.* 'Wachtposten' ('Watchtower') is notably taller but has sickly yellow leaves.

C. plantaginea and the green-leaved form of *C. siderosticha* both have broad pleated leaves and flower in early spring, just as their leaves are emerging, the dark flowers, beset with pale anthers, being produced with great freedom. Both prefer dampish ground and can look singularly effective used in drifts among small species

Narcissus such as *N. bulbocodium* and *N. cyclamineus*, among the unfurling leaves of hostas or contrasting with the apoplectic puce of emerging paeony leaves. However, quite the most unexpected of the sedges is *C. fraseri*, which comes from deep, rich, moist woodlands in the south-eastern United States. It has leaves that might be mistaken for those of a tulip, so broad are they, 2.5cm (1in) or more across and finely toothed. The flowers look like tiny white drumsticks. We grow it with *Athyrium filix-femina* 'Plumosum Druery', whose finely cut leaves are texturally so different, next to the gently white-variegated *Melica uniflora* 'Variegata' (wood melic) and the mottled, heart-shaped leaves of asarums such as *Asarum shuttleworthii*, *A. splendens* and *A. asaroides*.

WOODRUSHES

Luzula species (woodrushes) are not in the first rank of ornamental plants but have the great advantage that they will tolerate shade, even quite dense shade, and will grow either wet or dry, making them singularly useful where few other plants will grow. *L. sylvatica* (greater woodrush) and its forms grow happily in shade that is too deep for sedges. A number of green-leaved selections have been made over the years, of which the most distinct are 'Auslese', with broad but light green leaves which are distinctly twisted towards the tips, 'Tauernpass', which again has very broad leaves but of a rich, dark green, and 'Wäldler', which has bright green leaves and is reputed to be of hybrid origin. 'Hohe Tatra' is quite distinct from all other cultivars in its upright habit of growth, the leaves ascending somewhat in the manner of a *Billbergia* rather than flat as in other varieties. Sometimes a yellow-leaved variety, presumably *L. s.* 'Aurea', is sold under this name. Perhaps the most remarkable of the green-leaved varieties is a giant selection grown at Trompenberg, near Rotterdam in Holland, called 'Bromel'. The name is short for bromeliad, for the very long leaves are presented in an upright, cup-like arrangement, much in the manner of a *Billbergia* or *Aechmea*, and at 45cm (18in) are more than half as long again as the leaves of the typical species. The flowers are borne well above the leaves but the stem that supports the flowering umbel continues to lengthen after flowering, as with other varieties, and can be over 90cm (3ft) long by the time the seeds are ripe.

Of the varieties showing colour *Luzula sylvatica* 'Taggart's Cream' is the most fascinating. Its new leaves in spring emerge pure white, slowly turn cream, then assume thin green edges and then, by early summer,

become suffused with green and finally turn wholly green. It reaches 45cm (18in) high. We grow this in a far corner of our white garden, in deep shade, in the company of *Arum italicum* 'Pictum', *Sarcococca orientalis*, snowdrops and white *Helleborus orientalis*, all plants which are visible when at their showiest in winter but which will be hidden later by taller spring- and summer-flowering plants. *L. × borreri* 'Botany Bay' is similar to 'Taggart's Cream' but is very much smaller, growing to no more than 20cm (8in) at most in flower. It is good in dry shade. More subtle in its variegation is *L. sylvatica* 'Marginata', which has hairy, satiny, broad leaves edged with no more than the thinnest of white or creamy-white lines. In continental Europe a selection with creamy margins is grown under the name *L. s.* 'Gilt', but it may be the same.

There are several other woodrushes that flourish in woodland and shade, though they are less often seen. *L purpureosplendens* looks like an elegantly refined version of *L. sylvatica*, with svelte, narrow, dark green leaves covered with soft hairs. From mid-spring until early summer it produces an abundance of purplish flowers, while *L. nivea* makes dense tufts of leaves that are covered with showy white hairs and produces flattish heads of white flowers on tall narrow stems in late spring and early summer. *L. plumosa* and *L. alopecuroides* are both dwarfs, growing to 15cm (6in) in flower. All make useful ground cover in shade.

COLOURFUL FOLIAGE

What many grasses, in the looser sense, contribute to woodland is the colour of their foliage. Perhaps the brightest and best known of these are *Hakonechloa macra* 'Alboaurea' and *H. m.* 'Aureola' (golden Hakone grasses), which in the wild grow in woodsy soil in shade. The two differ in that while 'Aureola' is bright golden yellow thinly striped green, 'Alboaurea' has in addition flecks of white in the yellow. Both these and the green-leaved form make enchanting rounded mounds of arching leaves that turn vinous red in autumn then foxy brown for the winter. They can be used in woodland or shade at random, or in more considered blue and yellow schemes. For many years there was a planting of golden Hakone grass at the gardens of the Royal Horticultural Society at Wisley in which more or less square blocks of the Hakone grass alternated with similar blocks of the steely blue *Hosta* 'Halcyon'. I have also seen it used to great effect in a tiny blue and yellow front garden where a path lined with clipped balls of *Euonymus* 'Emerald 'n' Gold' grown as standards underplanted with blue violas and violets turns aside down old brick steps to plunge through a laburnum tunnel leaning against the house with the golden Hakone grass growing in its shade, backed in season by tall bearded irises in every colour from azure to indigo growing further from the house in sun. In a shadier situation one might use Siberian irises instead of the bearded irises.

Golden Hakone grass could just as well be used in a scheme of harmonizing yellows, mixed with hosta leaves striped, margined, centred or wholly yellow, with the softer yellow of *Milium effusum* 'Aureum', the viridescent *Carex pendula* 'Moonraker', *Haquetia epipactis* with its rich yellow buttons of flowers set in ruffled collars of greenery, the rich egg-yolk yellow of the annual *Smyrnium perfoliatum* and the more orangey-yellow flowers of *Adonis amurensis* or the later *A. vernalis*, their petals deeply burnished on the back. Alternatively, the Hakone grass could be grown at the foot of a shaded wall covered in yellow-variegated ivies and the gold-splashed × *Fatshedera lizei* 'Annemieke', with double primroses, pale yellow *Roscoea cautleyoides* or the darker *Cautleya spicata*, with maroon bracts around the flowers, beneath. It could also be centred around a golden holly such as the female *Ilex × altaclerensis* 'Golden King' or the slower-growing *I. × a.* 'Lawsoniana'. Earlier in the season, just as the Hakone grasses are emerging, the ground might be filled with *Uvularia sessilifolia*, whose primrose-yellow flowers dangle from arching stems, *Corydalis cheilanthifolia* bearing its small yellow tubular flowers above clumps of coppery, fern-like leaves, or *Erythronium* 'Pagoda', its rich yellow turk's cap flowers floating 30cm (12in) above the new leaves of the grass to be echoed later in the season by the speckled yellow turk's caps of *Lilium pyrenaicum*.

In such a scheme it is important to vary the yellows, lightening the effect by including drifts of *Molinia caerulea* ssp. *caerulea* 'Variegata' whose leaves are more cream than yellow, and to vary the shape, using perhaps the yellow-striped form of lily of the valley, *Convallaria majalis* 'Vic Pawlowski's Gold' to contribute upright, oval leaves or the huge heart-shaped leaves of the ivy *Hedera colchica* 'Sulphur Heart'.

On the whole such yellow schemes look all the yellower for containing some element of blue. Early in the spring an underplanting of blue crocuses and grape hyacinths may pass almost unremarked because the eye will be drawn to the more luminous yellows of the grasses, hostas and other foliage, but a little later in the season

the blues may compete better. One might emphasize the yellows of golden Hakone grass or of *Milium effuseum* 'Aureum' with the various blues of differing tones of *Corydalis flexuosa*, the dark-leaved *C. f.* 'Purple Leaf', the intense azure of *C. f.* 'Père David', the darker blue of *C. f.* CD&R 528, the capricious turquoise of *C. cashmeriana* or with *Meconopsis betonicifolia*.

Alternatively one might harmonize the blues, starting with the intense electric blue of *Carex glauca*, with its broad, pleated leaves. Next to this one might grow the taller, less intensely blue *C. flaccosperma*, which also has pleated leaves, or the narrow leaved *C. flacca* or *C. panicea*, both of which are called carnation grass from the fancied resemblance of their foliage to that of carnations. *Poa colensoi*, that New Zealand look-alike for the tufted blue fescues, will also grow well in woodland or shade, the fineness of its leaves setting it apart from the sedges. If these grasses are grown among blue-leaved hostas, or hostas with blue and white variegations, mixed with *Corydalis flexuosa*, blue primroses, single or double and grape hyacinths such as *Muscari azureum* or the powder-blue *M.* 'Baby's Breath', to be followed later by camassias in differing shade of blue, the effect can be quietly exciting. The linearity of grass and sedge leaves gains by juxtaposition with broader leaves, such as those of the Virginian cowslip, *Mertensia pulmonarioides* (syn. *M. virginica*), which produces in early summer, above oval grey-green leaves, cowslip flowers of the purest blue; or of *Pulmonaria* (lungworts), whose rough leaves are also oval and whose flowers range from deep blue to paler, watery shades often with a hint of mauve or violet. Among the bluest are *P. angustifolia* ssp. *azurea*, *P. a.* 'Munstead Blue' and *P. a.* 'Mawson's Blue'.

Whether one chooses to use one's coloured and variegated grasses in woodland in a yellow theme or a blue one, or mixed together, depends in part on whether one wants to shock the senses or soothe them, but also on whether one wants a particular group or part of the garden to advance or recede, the yellows advancing, the blues withdrawing into the distance.

WHITE PLANTS FOR SHADE

White plants will advance wherever you use them, and for this reason they are generally best used in the foreground, though they can be planted further away to draw the eye to a feature or a turning in the path. They are particularly useful in woodland and shade for the brightness they bring. The whitest of the grasses suitable

Luzula sylvatica 'Taggart's Cream' is a true woodlander. Its new leaves come through white and change through cream to green.

for such a position are *Arrhenatherum elatius bulbosum* 'Variegatum' (striped bulbous oat grass), and *Holcus mollis* 'Albovariegatus' (striped Yorkshire fog), both of which become dormant in the heat of summer, which may be just when you most need their presence. At Apple Court we grow these with drifts of *Lilium martagon* 'Album' and *L. regale* which grow and flower in time to draw the eye away from the decaying foliage; with *Begonia grandis* 'Alba' to bridge the midsummer period, with *Tricytis hirta* 'White Towers' (white toad lilies) and green-leaved *Saxifraga fortunei*, with its spidery, narrow-petalled white flowers to coincide with the emergence of the new growth in autumn; and with the rare and whiffy *Iris foetidissima* 'Fructoalba', whose dark green, sword-shaped leaves and ivory-white berries draw the eye in winter above a carpet of *Holcus mollis* 'Albovariegatus'.

We also grow in our white garden, shielded from direct sun by tall yew hedges and by the shade cast by the white-speckled *Catalpa duclouxii* 'Pulverulenta', *Aralia elata* 'Variegata', *Eucryphia lucida* 'Variegata' and green-leaved, white-flowered *Weinmannia trichosperma* among drifts of white foxgloves, *Campanula lactiflora* and that most finely cut of cow parsleys, *Selinum wallichianum*. They are accompanied by tall *Polygonatum* × *hybridum*, white trilliums and the lovely double white *Anemone sylvestris* 'Elisa Fellman', *Phalaris arundinacea* 'Feesey' and *Miscanthus sinensis* 'Morning Light'. Elsewhere, in the shade of *Sambucus nigra* 'Pulverulenta', we have the moist, acid-loving *Carex saxatilis* 'Ski Run', whose curly, white-striped leaves gradually form a carpet, and, shaded by a *Camellia japonica*, a drift of *Carex conica* 'Snowline', whose presence in winter is always welcome. At Kiftsgate Court in Gloucestershire this sedge, with clean, thin white lines along the edges of its leaves, is the only element in a planting of ferns that is not a fern, and the effect is highly pleasing.

20 Dry Gardens

Into this category fall gardens or parts of gardens that are situated in full sun, that are well-drained and that receive no watering beyond that needed to establish the plants. Such dry gardens may occur naturally on sandy or gravelly soils, or may be created by the laying of land-drains or French drains, or simply by the admixture of large quantities of grit to the soil, or by all three in varying degree. If drains are laid, then there must be some lower point into which they can drain, such as a ditch or soak-away. Drainage is crucial, because the kinds of plants that can withstand drought in summer cannot stand having their roots in wet soil in winter.

Dry gardens are typically surfaced with small stones, either pea-grit, which is round, or gravel, which has sharp edges. The effect is to suppress weeds and to retain deep moisture, though the use of these materials adds an aesthetic dimension. About a third of the surface pea-grit or gravel should be left showing once the planting has matured. Pea-grit or gravel may be used on its own, spread evenly over the surface of the garden as a mulch, with grasses and other plants dotted here and there, but on the whole the effect will be more interesting if there is some deliberate variation in the size of the pebbles or gravel used.

In order to survive in such adverse conditions a plant has to make certain economies, and to make growth at all it has to draw on its capital reserves. In hot, dry conditions these are hard to come by, so having invested in a leaf the plant does not want to lose its investment quickly: for this reason most plants of hot, dry regions are evergreen. But they can also insure their investment, and this they do by filling their leaves with aromatic oils, which may smell divine but often taste revolting. As a protection against desiccation many cover their leaves with fine hairs that trap a layer of cool air above the surface. It is these hairs that make so many of the plants of dry regions appear silver or grey.

BLUE GRASSES

Many of the grasses suitable for dry gardens have grey or blue leaves, a colouring they have developed as a defence against hot, strong sunlight. The one that seems best to typify aridity is *Festuca punctoria* (hedgehog fescue), a native of sunny, stony slopes in Greece. The blue leaves of this species are rigid and curved like upturned claws. Most of the blue cushion-shaped fescues and the similarly shaped koelerias will flourish in dry gardens, as will the larger helictotrichons, *Andropogon gerardii* and *Schizachyrium scoparium* (big and little bluestem), *Sorghastrum nutans* 'Sioux Blue' and the bluer selections of *Panicum virgatum*. All make good companions for such sun-lovers as *Thymus*, *Helianthemum*, *Oenothera missouriensis*, low-growing euphorbias and *Diascia*.

The cushion-shaped fescues retain their leaves through winter, though they do tend to lose their blueness. They also suffer the defect of spreading outwards from the centre over the years, turning in time into a ring of blueness with a dead centre. To avoid this they should be dug up and divided every three or four years. There are, however, two larger fescues which are worth considering for a dry garden and which are not so prone to dying out in the centre. These are *F. longifolia*, with needle-fine leaves that are blue with a whitish cast and which grows about 30cm (12in) tall, and *F. californica*, an American species with tight clumps of arching silvery-blue leaves about 60cm (2ft) tall.

Festuca punctoria is a native of hot, dry, stony hillsides in Greece and is ideal for sunny, dry gardens.

Of the other blue grasses suitable for dry gardens, *Helictotrichon sempervirens* (blue oat grass) is indispensable; a native of dry limestone rocks at the western end of the Mediterranean, it is a most architectural grass, with thin grey-blue leaves all seemingly radiating from a central point. *H. filifolius* has rather shorter leaves that are green on one side and silvery-blue on the other, attenuated into fine points which can pierce the skin. The large blue hair grasses, *Koeleria glauca* and the slightly larger *K. vallesiana*, are similar but smaller and could easily be mistaken for blue fescues.

Larger and decidedly less formal are the bluestems. *Schizachyrium scoparium* (little bluestem) produces upright clumps of slender blue stems with arching blue leaves, and *Andropogon gerardii* (big bluestem) makes strongly upright clumps of glaucous grey-blue leaves tipped with purple. *Leymus arenarius* (blue lyme grass) is even larger and is the most brilliantly blue of all grasses. It is eminently suited to dry garden habitats but runs in all directions at great speed and needs to be ruthlessly circumscribed. *Sorghastrum nutans* 'Sioux Blue' (blue Indian grass) is almost as blue but tightly clumping.

These blue grasses make excellent companions in the dry garden for grasses and sedges with bronze leaves such as *Uncinia rubra*, *Carex buchananii*, *C. comans* 'Bronze Form', *C. flagellifera*, *C. petriei* and *C. secta* var. *tenuiculmis* and those whose leaves turn purple late in the season such as *Panicum virgatum* 'Rubrum' and *P. v.* 'Rehbraun'. However, there is a problem: these grasses and sedges all prefer damper ground than the perfect drainage of the dry garden. The answer seems to be to make or retain pockets of ground that have been enriched with humus-forming materials such as garden compost, and then to plant the grass or sedge in the pocket and on the shaded side of a rock, which will cause moisture beneath it to condense out, making it available to the grass.

Blue grasses also go exceptionally well with pastel flowers, whose pale colours they seem to purify, and with plants with purple foliage or flowers such as *Salvia officinalis* 'Purpurea', the lovely *Geranium incanum* var. *multifidum* with its filigree silver foliage and opulent deep purple flowers, the shrubby *G. pulchrum*, the silver-carpeting *G. harveyi*, *Sedum* 'Bertram Anderson', the brown-leaved *S.* 'Arthur Branch', assorted sempervirens and the small, brown-leaved *Geranium sessiliflorum* ssp. *novae-zelandiae*. Vigorous grasses such as *Leymus arenarius* need to be matched in vigour by such flowering plants as *Geranium armenum*.

GREY GRASSES

There are several dry garden grasses which are grey, rather than blue. Among the best are *Sporobolus airoides* (alkali dropseed), which forms upright arching mounds of narrow grey leaves and *Eragrostis chloromelas* (Boer love grass) which forms low arching mounds. *E. curvula* (African love grass) is similar but with dark green leaves. *Muhlenbergia rigens* (deer grass) is also grey-leaved and produces erect whip-like panicles above dense 75cm (2½ft) clumps of leaves.

Grey-leaved grasses on the whole associate well with flowers of brighter colours than the pastels which are so good with the blues. They can take the scarlet and yellow of crocosmias or dahlias, or even of the later dendranthemums.

GREEN GRASSES

Of all the green-leaved grasses that will stand the rigours of the dry garden none, perhaps, is so spectacular as *Stipa gigantea* (Spanish oats), which comes from dry, sunny, rocky hillsides in Spain and produces huge heads of shimmering, coppery-gold spikelets in late spring. It is a plant of such architectural quality that it readily takes on the role of star in a dry garden, with lesser mortals at its feet.

Many good things, however, are to be found among these lesser mortals, including several stipas such as *Stipa tenuissima*, *S. calamagrostis*, *S. barbata*, *S. pennata*, *S. tirsa* and *S. capillata*. Other suitable green-leaved grasses include *Oryzopsis miliacea* (Indian rice grass), *Bouteloua gracilis* (blue gama or mosquito grass), *Melica altissima* (Siberian melic) and *Sesleria autumnalis* (autumn moor grass), which is the last of the truly drought-tolerant grasses to flower, being at its best in southern England through late summer and into mid-autumn. Because of its distinctly yellowish cast it goes well with blue grasses and with plants that have opalescent blue flowers such as *Penstemon* 'Sour Grapes'.

Both *Pennisetum* (fountain grasses) and *Panicum* (switch grasses) are excellent for dry gardens, the leaf colouring of the switch grasses in particular being far finer on dry soils than in ordinary garden earth, but *Miscanthus* prefer damper soils and are not so easily accommodated unless special provision is made for them.

DRY GARDEN STYLES

It is possible to make an entirely satisfying dry garden using combinations of grasses, gravel or pea-grit and

Carex flagellifera is one of several brown-leaved New Zealand sedges that will flourish in a well-drained, sunny position.

perhaps a few rocks by using the differing shapes of the various elements in counterpoint with each other – the craggy shapes of rocks, the reiterated roundness of pea-grit, the repeated verticals of the grasses. With some thought, effects can be build up using dynamic groups so that the eye explores the visual intricacies of first one group and then another, the light, airiness of the panicles of the grasses contrasting with the sheer weight of rocks.

Desert gardens

It is possible to create dry gardens that look positively desert-like, provided the drainage is perfect, by using sparse grasses in combination with real desert plants such as *Opuntia* species (prickly pears), a number of which have proved hardy both in London and in continental Europe over several decades, including *O. cantabrigiensis, O. compressa, O. englemanni, O. fragilis, O. humifusa, O. haematocarpa, O. linguiformis, O. phaeacantha, O. polyacantha* and *O. rhodantha*. Other amenable desert plants include hardy agaves such as *Agave gracile, A. parryi,* of which there are several subforms, *A. schottii, A. utahensis,* of which

again there are several subforms; the aloes *Aloe aristata*, *A. ciliaris* and *A. humilis*; the attenuated dasylirions of which *Dasylirion acrotrichum*, *D. longissimum* and *D. wheeleri* are all supposedly hardy; and some of the narrow-leaved yuccas such as *Yucca glauca* or the monocarpic *Y. whipplei*. Hardy *Nolina* species such as *N. erumpens*, *Chamaerops humilis* (European scrub palm), and some *Ephedra* (joint fir) species, which have no leaves but are made up instead of bundles of green stems with swollen joints, are other possibilities.

The best grasses for such schemes are those with a sparse appearance or with blue foliage, or both – the fescues for example, especially the prickly *F. punctoria*, *F. glauca* in its many forms, *F. cinerea* and the much larger, rather khaki-green *F. mairei*; the much taller *Andropogon gerardii*; both *Bouteloua curtipendula* and *B. gracilis*; the arching *Eragrostis curvula*, the steely grey-blue *Helictotrichon sempervirens*, the wispy *Schizachyrium scoparium* and the upright *Sorghastrum nutans*, especially the blue *S. n.* 'Sioux Blue' or the grey *S. n.* 'Indian Steel'. The occasional *Panicum virgatum* or *Miscanthus sinensis* could add to the scene but should be used sparingly: if too many are planted the appearance of prairie, rather than of a desert, is created. The appearance of a desert will be greatly enhanced if the ratio of bare ground, rock fragments or pebbles is not less than three to one.

Mediterranean gardens

A Mediterranean dry garden can be created by using more familiar flora, starting with *Lavandula* (lavender) and *Santolina* (cotton lavender), *Salvia officinalis* (sage) *Rosmarinus officinalis* (rosemary), *Thymus* (thyme) in several forms, *Cistus*, *Argyranthemum* (marguerites or Paris daisies), drifts of *Limonium* (sea lavender), *Convolvulus cneorum*, *C. sabatius* and *Centranthus ruber* (valerian). For variation in profile plant the taller *Asphodelus albus*, a groundcover of *Helianthemum* and *Ruta graveolens* (rue), and add real height with *Olea europaea* (olive), *Luma apiculata* (myrtle) and *Pittosporum tobira* with, if there is enough air movement, a gnarled *Cercis siliquastrum* (Judas tree) – unfortunately a plant always prone to coral spot fungus. The Mediterranean ambience could be further enhanced by adding in the background a fastigiate conifer, or even a group of them – not *Cupressus sempervirens* (pencil cedar), which is inclined to make a poor root system and

Carex petriei, C. buchananii, Stipa calamagrostis (right) and *Miscanthus oligostachyus* 'Purpurascens' (left) in a dry garden.

to blow over when planted away from the sun-drenched shores of the Mediterranean, but rather *Juniperus virginiana* in one of its fastigiate green forms or *Thuja occidentalis* 'Malonyana', which is well adapted to the British climate. As substitutes for citrus trees and clipped bays, those two most essential denizens of French gardens, there are two hardy citrus trees, *Citrus ichangensis*, a lemon which is reasonably hardy over much of the UK, and *Poncirus trifoliata*, which is even hardier (both can be clipped to shape), while *Quercus ilex* (holm oak) will do duty for the clipped bays.

In such a setting a wider range of grasses can be grown than in the desert garden, grasses which on the whole look more relaxed, including *Calamagrostis* × *acutiflora* 'Stricta' or *C.* × *a.* 'Karl Foerster', *Leymus arenarius* or *L. racemosus*, *Hordeum jubata* (squirrel tail grass) with its nodding iridescent pink barley heads, *Pennisetum*, especially *P. alopecuroides* and its cultivars, *P. macrourum* and pretty pink *P. orientale*, and the showy *Stipa gigantea*.

The English dry garden

It is also possible to make a dry garden in a much more English tradition using *Lavandula* species (lavenders), the woolly grey *Stachys lanata*, *Salvia officinalis* Purpurascens Group (purple-leaved sage) and spurges such as *Euphorbia characias* or *E. c.* ssp. *wulfenii* with a ground cover of helianthemums, interspersed with the native gladiolus *Gladiolus illyricus*, *Eryngium* × *zabelii* 'Jewel' and, perhaps, *Glaucium corniculatum* (horned poppy). Among these may be scattered clumps of the evergreen *Stipa gigantea*, *Hordeum jubatum* with its pink barley heads, *Calamagrostis* × *acutiflora* 'Karl Foerster', *Panicum virgatum*, possibly in one of its blue forms, *Helictotrichon sempervirens*, *Pennisetum alopecuroides*, *P. orientale* or *P. macrourum*, and some of the little blue fescues. Such a planting might look effective against the brickwork on the sunny side of a house, or set among rocks beyond a south-facing terrace. If sufficient space were left between the plants, autumn-flowering bulbs such as nerines and *Sternbergia lutea* might flourish.

PLANTING COMPANIONS

For those who prefer to combine their grasses with other plants the palette is still relatively limited, for dryness is very restrictive and the plants that evolve to survive it have little energy for flamboyance. Typically economic in their growth and flowers are the shrubs of dry regions: the grey, narrow-leaved *Lavandula* (lavender), fine-leaved *Rosmarinus* (rosemary), the shrubby *Salvia* species with their densely hairy leaves, the spindly, grey-leaved *Perovskia* and *Teucrium lucidrys*, again with grey leaves but a compact habit. All of these have flowers in shades of blues and mauves. Other choices are grey, woolly-leaved *Phlomis fruticosa* with its whorls of yellow flowers, *Ruta graveolens* with its rubbery blue leaves and the fragrant, white-flowered myrtles *Myrtus communis* or the shrubbier *M. c.* ssp. *tarentina*, which have two variegated forms, *M. c.* 'Variegata' and *M. c.* ssp. *t.* 'Microphylla Variegata'. All of these have leaves that are fragrant when crushed and often exude fragrant, volatile oils in hot, sunny weather.

Grey-leaved perennials abound in dry habitats and make excellent companions for the grasses: *Convolvulus cneorum* and *C. sabatius*, *Helleborus argutifolius*, *Romneya coulteri*, *Stachys byzantina* (always lovely with the mauve spherical heads of *Allium cristophii* rising from its midst on tall grey-green stems), tall *Cynara cardunculus* and *Onopordon acanthium*, cut-leaved *Achillea tomentosa* and daisy-flowered *Anthemis punctata* ssp. *cupaniana*, slender, feathery *Artemisia pontica*, trailing *Euphorbia myrsinites*, and sprawling, long-flowering *Nepeta* × *faassenii*.

There are also green-leaved perennials with which to create contrast: the giant, coarse, *Crambe cordifolia* producing huge panicles of tiny white flowers like an over-fed gypsophila on top of 1.8m (6ft) stems, *Acanthus spinosus* with its carefully sculptured leaves, coarsely hairy *Papaver orientale* (oriental poppy), lupin-leaved *Thermopsis villosa* with its spikes of yellow lupin flowers, the dazzlingly bright yellow *Oenothera missouriensis*, and the subdued, mauvey-blue *Limonium latifolium* (statice or sea lavender) with its broad, dark green leaves and airy umbels of tiny mauvey-blue flowers late in the year.

Bulbs and bulb-like plants are also plentiful in dry regions, and many are suitable to grow with grasses in dry gardens: *Allium cristophii*, *Alstroemeria ligtu* and other species, *Agapanthus* in variety, *Nerine bowdenii*, several species tulips including *Tulipa tarda* and *T. praestans*, *Asphodeline lutea* and *Eremurus stenophyllus*.

21 | Tussock Gardens

Tussock gardens evolved in New Zealand as a style of gardening particularly suited to the growing of native plants, and in particular the New Zealand tussock grasses, a term which embraces the New Zealand species of *Cortaderia* and *Chionochloa*, but which in a looser sense has also come to include those New Zealand sedges which are so distinct from the sedges of the northern hemisphere.

The earliest tussock gardens were designed around the concept of a dry river, the river bed itself being a winding path of small pebbles with planted areas to each side composed of somewhat larger pebbles and bounded on both sides by large rocks representing the river bank. The pebbles were sometimes graded from smallest closest to the central path to quite large near the rocks. In essence a tussock garden resembles a dry garden, except that there is no particular intention to create dryness. It is in the planting that it differs, New Zealand flora having an aspect all its own.

CORTADERIA

The showiest of the tussock grasses is *Cortaderia fulvida* (toe-toe, pronounced toy-toy), which is not at all a plant of dry habitats, growing more often than not at the edges of streams and lakes, frequently with its roots submerged, or in crevices in rocks seeping with water. In cultivation

Carex testacea shows its strongest colouring in a hot, dry position. In shade it tends to become a rather drab off-green.

it makes huge rounded mounds of broad, arching leaves and in early summer produces 2.4m (8ft) culms bearing huge, one-sided plumes of white or startling flamingo pink. In cultivation it needs abundant irrigation; if it gets at all dry bundles of leaves die off, making the leaf mound ugly. *C. richardii* is similar and hardy in all but the coldest parts of the UK, producing in early and midsummer tall arching culms bearing one-sided plumes that are cream at first becoming white. These plumes are rather svelte as compared with those of *C. fulvida*, which are decidedly shaggy.

CHIONOCHLOA

The snow grasses, *Chionochloa*, are one of the essential tussock genera, 22 of the 24 species being natives of New Zealand's alpine and sub-alpine tussock grasslands. Broadly speaking they resemble the pampas grasses, though they are on the whole smaller and more elegant. Sadly, few are wholly hardy in the UK. *C. conspicua*, known in New Zealand as Hunangamolio grass and elsewhere as plumed tussock grass, is the species most often encountered in the UK, forming tussocks of broad, light green leaves with an orange midrib about 1.2m (4ft) tall and producing green to cream one-sided panicles on arching, 1.8m (6ft) culms from mid-spring until the end of summer. The variety *cunninghamii* is indistinguishable in

Red New Zealand carices and New Zealand flax draw the eye in this small tussock garden.

the garden. The plumes of both are exceptionally good for drying.

Chionochloa rigida (snow tussock) grows to 90cm (3ft) and forms loose rather than compact tussocks, producing its flowering culms in mid and late summer. The plumes are a one-sided, much-branched panicle, the spikelets pale green, white or occasionally buff. Though attractive in flower it suffers the defect of hanging on to its old leaf sheaths, these making an untidy litter in the middle of the tussock unless raked out from time to time. *C. flavescens* (broad-leaved snow tussock) is reputed to be the hardiest of the species, making low tussocks of relatively wide leaves and producing its creamy or yellowish, one-sided panicles at the ends of outward-arching culms. *C. flavicans* is broadly similar in appearance but is slow-growing and requires a position in hot sun on a well-drained soil, preferably with shelter from winds.

Chionochloa rubra (red tussock grass) is distinct from the above species in forming clumps of upright-divergent leaves of a distinctly foxy red. The leaves are narrow and rolled, up to 75cm (2½ft) long, and the flowers, which are the same colour as the leaves, are borne in a loose panicle. In the UK it is too often seen as a rather dingy, greyish-red grass 30cm (12in) tall; the secret of producing good colour is to keep it plentifully irrigated, which also increases its stature. *Poa labillardieri* has a similar habit but is blue.

CAREX

The natural companions to these tussock grasses in New Zealand native plant gardens are the many and varied New Zealand sedges. The best-known of these are the bronze or brown sedges which even to the initiated can be hard to distinguish from each other, but there are also blond sedges such as *C. comans* and some useful green-leaved ones, including *C. forsteri* and *C. buchananii* 'Viridis'. These sedges can be grown with other New Zealand natives, many of which are hardy in at least the more southerly counties of England: *Phormium tenax* (New Zealand flax), *P. colensoi* (mountain flax), and their many colourful selections; *Cordyline australis* (cabbage palm), of which there are bronze-leaved and variegated selections;

A typical planting of tussock grasses and native plants in Maneurewa Botanic Gardens near Auckland, New Zealand. The tussock grasses are mixed with manukas and cabbage palms, as they would grow in the wild.

a multitude of *Hebe* species; *Pseudopanax ferox* and *P. crassifolius* (lancewoods) with their extraordinary long, narrow leaves; *Melicytus* species with their tiny, almost succulent leaves and white berries; *Notospartium carmichaeliae* with its leafless, flattened stems, weeping habit and pink and purple pea-flowers; *Sophora tetraptera* (kowhai), of which many different forms exist, some upright, some weeping, some with pale yellow flowers and some with a hint of orange; and the curious *Corokia* with its zig-zag stems and tiny leaves.

VARIATIONS IN HEIGHT

Less typically antipodean are *Leptospermum* species (manuka trees), which mostly make tiny-leaved bushes or small trees with exfoliating bark, covering themselves in flowers in mid or late summer. The hardiest are the silver-leaved, white-flowered *L. cunninghamii* and *L. lanigerum*, though some forms of *L. scoparium* which have pink or ruby flowers will endure out of doors for many winters, flowering profusely in summer. The Tasmanian *L. humifusum*, which has small green leaves and white flowers, is prostrate and forms mats or carpets, rooting as it goes, while *L. grandiflorum*, another Tasmanian with grey leaves and white flowers, makes a small tree and is hardier than is generally realized. In spite of their Tasmanian provenance these last two look at home in tussock gardens.

Other New Zealand plants which fit well in tussock gardens include *Olearia*, which has some enchanting grey-leaved forms and hybrids, and *Brachyglottis* (formerly *Senecio*), of which the silvery-leaved, yellow-flowered 'Sunshine' is widely grown. Several conifers are unique to New Zealand and may be used to give height: *Dacrydium cupressinum* (rimu) forms a small weeping tree cascading with pendulous, cord-like branches; the tall podocarps such as *Podocarpus totara*, of which there is a golden-leaved form, *P. t.* 'Aureus', and *P. hallii*; the lower growing *P. acutifolius*, which makes a curiously bronzed bush, brightest on poor soils, and the dwarf, ground-covering forms of *P. nivalis*, whose leaves may be green, blue or bronze.

In New Zealand these plants are sometimes combined in island beds in which manukas and cabbage palms are used to create a central spine surrounded by bold drifts of first one species tussock and then another, with *Cortaderia*, *Chionochloa* or *Carex trifida* var. *chathamica* as specimen plants in their midst. Such schemes can be highly ornamental and require little maintenance.

22 Subtropical Effects

The essence of subtropical gardening is to grow plants with luxuriant foliage reminiscent of the tropics in climates to which they are totally unsuited. In the Edwardian heyday of this fashion the plants used in the UK were mainly tender exotics grown under glass and bedded out or plunged in appropriate places outside during the hottest part of the year. The more modern concept seems to be to try to achieve similar effects with mainly hardy plants, chief among which are *Trachycarpus fortunei* (Chusan palm), *Musa basjoo* (Japanese banana), a selection of jungly bamboos and several tropical-looking grasses.

BAMBOOS

Since leaf size is important in this context, *Indocalamus hamadae* is a prime candidate for any subtropical garden, having the largest leaves of any bamboo that is hardy in Britain. When the plant is well grown in damp shade they can be as much as 50cm (20in) long and 8cm (3¼in) across, and are a rich dark, matt green with a conspicuous yellow mid-rib. The culms (canes) grow to 90cm (3ft) or more in length, but seldom achieve more than half that height, being bowed down by the weight of the leaves. It spreads persistently but not uncontrollably, and is ideal at the foot of a shaded wall or for ground cover among taller subjects, including other bamboos, palms and bananas. The sheer size of its leaves can be emphasized by planting a bamboo with tiny leaves nearby, placing it so that the shadows of the little leaves fall on the surface of the huge leaves of *Indocalamus hamadae*. *Thamnocalamus crassinodus* 'Kew Beauty' is probably the finest bamboo with which to do this, being in its own right a bamboo of the first order, having thick culms which are at first conspicuously whitened with a mealy powder and which gradually ripen through rich green to dusky red, against which are set a diffuse tracery of tiny leaves, almost ridiculously small for the size of the plant, which can grow up to 4m (13ft).

Both of these bamboos look excellent with *Farfugium japonicum* 'Aureomaculatum', not only because they both enjoy the same cultural conditions but also because the yellow spotting on the huge, round, glossy green leaves of the farfugium echo the yellow mid-ribs and deep green leaves of the bamboo of *Indocalamus hamadae*. *Farfugium japonicum* 'Crispatum', with its outlandishly crisped leaf edges, is an alternative for those who think *F. j.* 'Aureomaculatum' looks as if it has been sprayed with weed-killer.

Far more exotic is *Phyllostachys dulcis*, which has the thickest canes of any bamboo hardy in Britain and looks as though it hails straight from the torrid zones. The culms, which are rich, shining, dark green, can grow as thick as a man's forearm and as much as 9m (30ft) tall, and carry a dense canopy of dark green leaves, glaucous beneath. To look its best it needs shelter from strong winds, as indeed do most bamboos, and rich, moist soil. *P. vivax* is broadly similar, but shorter at 3.6m (12ft), more upright and tolerant of drier, sunnier conditions. Another very leafy bamboo is *Semiarundinaria fastuosa*, a notably straight-caned species 6m (20ft) tall, ideal for use as a screen. Equally leafy, but less tall and with more slender canes, is *Phyllostachys nigra*, whose canes ripen to jet black. Though this bamboo is often grown in shade, the canes turn black more quickly in sun, and on drier soil.

A more appropriate bamboo in smaller gardens is × *Hibanobambusa tranquillans*, a putative hybrid between a *Phyllostachys* and a *Sasa*, with large leaves that remain in remarkably good condition throughout the winter. It grows to about 1.8m (6ft) high, and is effective without being at all overpowering. Equally suitable is *Phyllostachys aurea* (golden bamboo), a densely leafy bamboo growing to about 4m (13ft) in the UK with yellowish-green culms and unusual congested basal nodes and internodes.

SUGAR CANE

Saccharum officinarum (sugar cane) not only looks tropical but is tropical, and as such is appropriate to a subtropical garden. The typical form makes upright arching clumps 3–3.6m (10–12ft) tall in a season, with rich green arching leaves that can reach as much as 1.5m (5ft) long and 7.5cm (3in) wide. Late in the season the lower leaves die off, revealing the reds, greens, mauves and violets that colour the culms.

In recent years several forms of sugar cane have been selected for their red- or yellow-striped leaves or canes, but one is outstanding. This is *Saccharum officinarum* 'Pele's Smoke', whose leaves and culms are a rich, reddish, horticultural purple. It makes a most pleasing picture when grown together with *Melianthus major* (honey plant), whose large, pinnate leaves are a luminous, glaucous grey-green, and with *Phormium tenax* (New Zealand flax), whose sword-like leaves are upright or upright-divergent in shades of grey, green or purple, variegated with cream, red or pink, and grow as much as 2.4m (8ft) tall. Other good companions are *Beschorneria yuccoides*, a giant Mexican plant related to the yucca with clumps of huge, wide, grey sword-like leaves, lurid pink 3m (10ft) flower stems and bracts and little dangling flowers, *Dasylirion acrotrichum*, which makes rosettes of tooth-edged leaves, and *Acanthus mollis* 'Hollard's Gold'. Normally treated as an annual or overwintered under glass to plunge or bed out in the summer, sugar cane is killed to the ground at 0°C (32°F), though some forms are hardier and can survive down to -12°C (10°F). All forms need rich soil and shelter from wind.

HARDY GRASSES

Of the really hardy grasses that can contribute to a subtropical garden the tall miscanthus *Miscanthus floridulus* and *M. sacchariflorus* are unbeatable. The former grows to about 2.4m (8ft), the latter to some 3m (10ft). Both are strongly upright and bear big green leaves, but there the resemblance ends, for *M. floridulus* is clump-forming and likes moist ground, while *M. sacchariflorus* is a runner. Neither of these grasses flowers regularly in the UK; of the miscanthus that do, the largest are *M.* 'Giganteus', which is thought by some to be a hybrid between *M. floridulus* and *M. sacchariflorus*, and *M. sinensis* 'Emerald Giant', which is a green reversion from *M. s.* 'Cosmopolitan'. Both have exceptionally large, showy plumes.

These vigorous hardy grasses look particularly tropical when grown in company with plants of a softer aspect, such as *Ischyrolepis subverticillata* (*Restio subverticillatus*) (rope grass), which can reach 1.8-2.4m (6-8ft), or the much dwarfer and hardier *Restio tetraphyllus*, which scarcely reaches 90cm (3ft). Both have green stems around which, at regular intervals, are produced whorls of green thread-like leaves or branches, slowly building into substantial clumps. *Ischyrolepis subverticillata* is hardy in sheltered gardens in the south-west of

Ireland, and in sheltered gardens in the south and west of the UK, but it is not hardy in the average British climate. *Restio tetraphyllus* does appear to be a little hardier but is so little known that it has scarcely as yet been tested.

TENDER GRASSES

Of the true grasses the variegated Provençal reed, *Arundo donax* 'Variegata', is without doubt the most tropical in appearance, growing 3.6–4.5m (12–15ft) in a season, with leaves 60cm (2ft) long and 6cm (2½in) wide, its leaves broadly margined and striped creamy white, as are its tall culms, the leaves shimmering with every breeze and rustling as the culms sway past each other. It is not hardy in the average climate of the UK, though it is worth bedding out in the summer, and bringing into the shelter of a greenhouse or conservatory for the winter. The typical form, with its blue-green leaves and culms, is just as exotic in its own way, but in a quieter key.

Two other grasses that contribute to the subtropical look are *Setaria palmifolia* and *Muhlenbergia dumosa* (bamboo muhly), neither of which is fully hardy in the south of England, though both have endured a few winters out of doors in our garden. The setaria makes dense, slowly spreading clumps about 90cm (3ft) high of upright divergent pleated mid-green leaves. The flowers are the same green as the leaves, which they scarcely overtop. Bamboo muhly produces slender, arching bamboo-like culms which branch to produce small, narrow, arching leaves, the whole plant looking like a miniature grove of weeping bamboo that sways with every sigh of a summer's day.

No sub-tropical garden would be complete without papyrus, either the true papyrus of the Egyptians, *Cyperus papyrus*, or the showier, more modern selection *C. p.* 'Mexico'. At the tops of seemingly bare, three-angled stems, papyrus carries almost spherical mop-heads composed of a hundred or more thread-like bracts: in the cultivar 'Mexico' these are twice-divided, making denser heads. In subtropical gardens in cold climates papyrus can only be stood out in summer, having been overwintered under glass, but few other plants can bring such an authentic air of the tropics. Ideally papyrus should be stood in a pool – where it makes a complete contrast with the round leaves of water lilies and the froth of the finely divided leaves of *Myriophyllum spicatum* (milfoil) – but failing that it can be stood in a deep saucer of water. It must never be allowed to become dry.

23 Bamboos

Bamboos are true grasses, though they differ from other grass genera in their woody culms, their branching habit and their often tree-like stature. Yet many myths and misunderstandings have grown up around them which make many gardeners reluctant to embark upon planting them.

The first myth is that bamboos run in all directions. In fact there are good and bad bamboos: the good ones stay where they are planted, and the bad ones run. Whether a bamboo is clumping or running depends entirely on its root system, and the roots of bamboos are classed as sympodial or monopodial. Sympodial bamboos form clumps: if you plant a young sympodial bamboo in your youth it is unlikely to be more than 1.8m (6ft) across when you celebrate your centenary. Sadly, most sympodial bamboos are tropical, and will take very little frost. The bad news is that most frost-tolerant bamboos have a monopodial root system, which means that they run, but the good news is that not all will take over half the garden every decade. *Shibataea kumasasa* runs so slowly, even in warm climates, that most people think it is a clumper. As a last resort any weedkiller that will kill grass will kill bamboo, so mistakes are not irreversible.

The second myth is that all bamboos of the same species flower at the same time all over the world, often after an interval of many decades or even a century or more, and then die. There are really two myths here: the first being that all bamboos of the same species flower at the same time, the second being that they die after flowering. The cycles of flowering in bamboos are not well recorded, and what triggers flowering is little understood. It is known that some species, *Chimonobambusa marmorea*, for example, are almost always in flower insomuch as that a search through an established clump will reveal an occasional flowering culm, while other species which have been known to science for many decades without flowering at all suddenly erupt into bloom, every twig on every branch of every culm breaking into flower and producing only a handful of leaves. Flowering is followed by seed production, and many bamboos produce an abundance of seed. After such a performance it is only natural to expect the bamboo to die of exhaustion. Yet the recorded evidence is that, while bamboos may look dead or at least very sickly for several years, most will eventually recover.

However, most of the documentation of bamboo performance comes from Europe and this distorts the picture, for bamboos are essentially plants of the tropics, needing long, hot summers for the full development and proper ripening of their culms. In Europe, and the UK in particular, such conditions do not exist and bamboos growing there are mostly at the limit of their tolerance of cold and moisture: the extra effort involved in flowering and the production of seed is a stress too many, and sufficient to kill them. In the warmer climates of the USA or Australia, the same bamboos often survive flowering and live to look lovely again.

A single plant of *Phyllostachys nigra* (black bamboo) was brought from Japan to England in 1827 by Freeman-Mitford, later Lord Redesdale, and in due course young plants were sent to the USA, New Zealand, Australia and other countries, so that all the plants of black bamboo around the world except in its native habitat were, for a long time, pieces of the same plant. It is consequently not surprising if they all flowered at the same time. If all the black bamboos had died after flowering there would now be no black bamboos, for black canes are the rarest of all cane variations. Luckily most plants recovered. A few set seed as well, and the black bamboo was saved until next time.

The exceptions to the rule that bamboos recover from flowering are those that are newly or relatively newly planted, and variegated bamboos, as variegated plants are generally of a weaker constitution than their green-leaved counterparts. Flowering cannot be averted: cutting off flowering culms will not prevent a bamboo that has started flowering from producing further flowering culms, or dying in the attempt. However, when one plants a bamboo the expectation is that it will flourish for many years.

ORIENTAL STYLE

In the West bamboos are used much like other ornamental plants, but in the East they have more particular roles assigned to them. The Japanese, who are masters of the art of small spaces, never try to fill small courtyards or gardens with riotous assemblies of flowers of different colours but rather seek to mirror the changing seasons by growing, against a background of bamboo and carefully placed rocks, only a single plant to represent each season – a cherry for spring, a paeony for summer, a chrysanthemum for autumn and a bamboo for winter. But the placing of the bamboos is crucial. The basic picture is composed of a tall bamboo juxtaposed with a small bamboo in a deliberately asymmetrical fashion in imitation of nature.

The Chinese are similarly masters of the art of small town or courtyard gardens which they never attempt to cram with flowers. Instead they manipulate the space. Typically they will plant a single, tall bamboo, this becoming the dominant element in the courtyard, the rest of the courtyard being paved. The great advantages of bamboos in such a situation is that they mature quickly, they are generally upright, taking up little space at ground level, and their foliage is often light and airy. A tree, by contrast, would present problems with its overhanging branches and its possibly dense leafiness.

Often the single bamboo is sufficient, but if there is space for other, smaller plants, they are usually grown in pots, and the pots are confined to particular parts of the courtyard rather than being scattered about. Very often the smaller plants will also be bamboos. Chinese courtyards are seldom completely enclosed, but usually have an opening such as a moongate, so positioned that passersby can see into the courtyard but not into the house.

The concept of borrowed views is also Japanese. The essence of this type of planting is to frame a piece of the landscape (or cityscape) so that it appears as part of your own garden, while at the same time concealing the proverbial glue factory. The view does not have to be of distant mountains or rolling hills: it may be something as close as a tree in the street outside. Bamboos are perhaps the best plants for framing a view, for their ultimate height is predictable, and they achieve it quickly: trees by contrast may take years to achieve their effective height. Bamboos are also predictable as to density, some being so densely leafy that they cannot be seen through while others have such light foliage that what lies beyond can be glimpsed through it, for it is often not necessary to hide unsightly objects in the landscape.

SPECIMEN PLANTING

Much of the beauty of a bamboo lies in its usually upright-arching culms, bare at the base but heavily leafy above.

Such a plant can best be displayed when it stands on its own. Sometimes the bamboo's form can be emphasized by placing beside it a large rock or stone water basin, or by surrounding it with gravel or sea-washed pebbles. Specimen bamboos are often seen at their best when planted by water, especially if their reflection can be seen in it. Other plants, especially other bamboos and large grasses or shrubs, should not be planted near enough to detract from the overall shape of the bamboo, though the taller the bamboo the nearer other plants can approach it.

The best bamboos for specimen positions are usually those with a fountain-shaped outline, such as *Phyllostachys decora*, and *P. nigra* (black bamboo), as well as some *Sinarundinaria* such as *S. nitida*, preferably in the clones 'Eisenach' or 'Nymphenburg' which have more pendulous tips to their culms than the species, or *S. murieliae*. *Pseudosasa japonica* has a stiffer habit of growth but is also suitable while *Chusquea culeou* (Chilean bamboo), with its stiffly upright habit and its new culms sheathed in what looks like white suede, is a good choice for a sheltered position in dampish soil. *Phyllostachys*, with their usually upright culms, are useful for giving height in narrow gardens and small spaces, while *Sinarundinaria* species, with their delicate patterns of growth, are light and airy enough for small gardens, as is the tall but tiny-leaved *Thamnocalamus crassinodus* 'Kew Beauty'.

BAMBOO HEDGES

Many of the same species can also be used to create hedges which require far less maintenance than conventional hedges and, being evergreen, are attractive throughout the year. The species most frequently used in the UK is *Pseudosasa japonica*, which makes a hedge some 3.6m (12ft) tall that in time becomes very dense. It makes a particularly good barrier against wind and noise, the relatively large surfaces of its leaves deflecting sound. *Sinarundinaria nitida* makes a more beautiful hedge, its slender culms bare for about half their height and so densely packed together you cannot see between them, while higher up the culms burst into cascading branches of fine, bright green leaves. It will grow about 4.5m (15ft) tall. In France *Semiarundinaria fastuosa* is often planted in towns along the front boundary of a property, between the street and the garden. It makes a rather taller hedge, to 7m (23ft) or more, but is not so dense, the dark-stained culms growing less closely together so that it is possible to see between them.

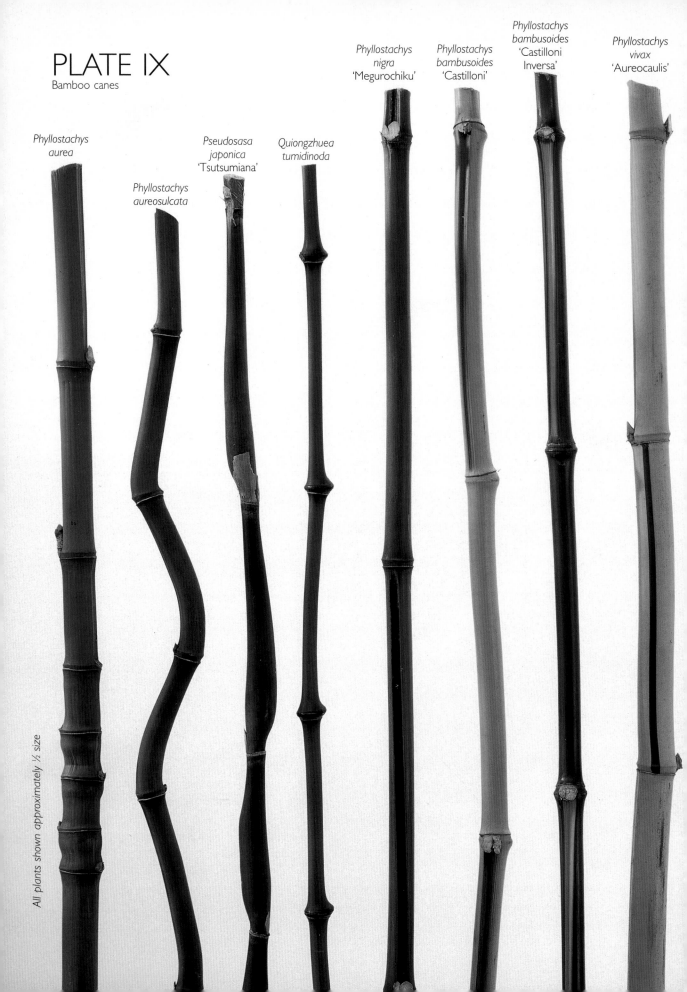

PLATE IX
Bamboo canes

Phyllostachys aurea

Phyllostachys aureosulcata

Pseudosasa japonica 'Tsutsumiana'

Quiongzhuea tumidinoda

Phyllostachys nigra 'Megurochiku'

Phyllostachys bambusoides 'Castilloni'

Phyllostachys bambusoides 'Castilloni Inversa'

Phyllostachys vivax 'Aureocaulis'

All plants shown approximately ½ size

*Phyllostachys
vivax*
'Aureocaulis'

*Phyllostachys
dulcis*

*Phyllostachys
bambusoides*
'Holochrysa'

*Chusquea
culeou*
'Breviglumis'

*Phyllostachys
violascens*

*Thamnocalamus
crassinodus*
'Kew Beauty'

Phyllostachys nigra

*Phyllostachys
nigra*
'Boryana'

In small gardens bamboo hedges will need to have their lateral spread limited, and this is easily done by annual cutting back of the rhizomes with a sharp spade: if the bamboos are allowed to spread the effort of cutting them back will be far greater. They may also need to be limited as to height. This cannot be done by the means with which conventional hedges are trimmed; the art is to thin every year, cutting out the older, less sightly culms at ground level.

BAMBOO SCREENS

Tall bamboos, such as *Phyllostachys* species, are generally too tall and not sufficiently dense to make good hedges, but they can make excellent screens, obscuring neighbours or unsightly objects without completely hiding them. I have seen *P. bambusoides* planted as a screen just outside the windows of a drawing room so that the occupants of the room could look through the bamboo into the garden, while those in the street could not look back into the drawing because of the changes in light levels, it being easier to see from darkness into light than from light into darkness. The best species for such screens are *Semiarundinaria fastuosa*, *Phyllostachys aurea* and *P. vivax*.

BAMBOO GROVES

Bamboo groves have a quality that no other kind of planting can aspire to: the quiet strength of the bamboo culms, the reassuring rhythm of their repetition, the symmetry of their spacing and the susurration of the wind through their leaves. Such groves can be created not only in large gardens but also to great effect in small ones, especially those that are enclosed. The art of the bamboo grove lies in the spacing of the culms, since it is the culms, rather than the leaves, that are most visible. Almost any tall bamboo is suitable, but particularly good are *Phyllostachys sulphurea* var. *viridis*, *P. vivax*, *P. dulcis*, *P. viridiglaucescens*, *P. decora*, *P. rubromarginata* and *P. bambusoides*. The grove can be started by planting three well-spaced bamboos and allowing them to grow together. It will take them about 10 years to reach their full height, but with each passing year they grow more strongly, and the spacing between the culms increases. At the end of 10 years you will have a grove of tall, clean canes with a heavy canopy of foliage overhead. To achieve the desired spacing of the culms these should be thinned every year. A few new culms should be allowed to develop each year; surplus ones can be suppressed by simply kicking them over as they appear in the spring.

A grass path winds mysteriously through groves of tall bamboos at Drysdale Garden Exotics in Hampshire.

Green gardens are similar but differ in that whereas the floor of a bamboo grove is littered with fallen leaves, in green gardens it is covered with greenery such as *Hedera helix* (ivy), *Parthenocissus*, *Pachysandra terminalis* or a fern such as *Matteuccia struthiopteris*. This can create a charmingly soothing effect.

BAMBOOS IN CONTAINERS

Many bamboos are also excellent plants for growing in pots or large tubs, indoors or out. The most important single consideration is that the container should be large enough; if there is insufficient space for the roots the top growth will become stunted and unattractive. As a rule of thumb the smallest bamboos need 41cm (16in) pots, while the larger sorts should be grown in tubs of 90cm (3ft) or more. The next essential is to maintain the balance between the top growth and the size of the container, and this is achieved by the regular removal of canes. As a general rule one should remove about one-third of the canes every year, preferably in late spring or early summer after the first flush of new canes, taking out the oldest canes and any very weak new ones. Feed the bamboo with proprietary slow-release, temperature-controlled granules or pellets just as the new culms start to appear then again in early summer and early autumn. It is vital that bamboos never dry out in their containers: if possible they should be watered with rainwater, especially in hard-water areas, since hard water leaches the nutrients out of the soil and makes it less capable of holding moisture.

By and large the most pleasing bamboos to grow in pots are the dwarf pleioblastus, which make dense mounds of small green leaves. Of the three dwarf species, *Pleioblastus pygmaeus* (formerly *Arundinaria pygmaea*) (dwarf fernleaf bamboo) is the smallest and most distinct, growing to 80cm (32in) high, or occasionally 90cm (3ft), and having strongly distichous leaves. The other two, *P. humilis* and *P. h. pumilus* (formerly *Arundinaria humilis* and *A pumila*), differ only in that the leaves of the former are glabrous (smooth) while those of the latter are pubescent, or hairy. Both grow to about 1.2m (4ft) tall, with slender canes and leaves no more than 12.5cm (5in) long.

More interesting in their overall texture are *Shibataea kumasasa*, which is a dwarf bamboo growing only to some 90cm (3ft) in the UK but about twice that in the USA and forming dense clumps of foliage, the leaves being extraordinarily wide for their length, and the winter bamboo *Chimonobambusa marmorea*, which grows to about 1.8m (6ft) and produces lime green young shoots marbled brown and white and streaked with pink at the tips. It often produces its new shoots long after other bamboos, hence its name, and will not endure any dryness at the root. *Quiongzhuea tumidinoda* (Addington bamboo) is

At Apple Court huge pots of Pleioblastus variegatus punctuate the pillared hosta walk, drawing the eye towards the end.

unusual in having swollen nodes on relatively slender culms which are yellow or olive green. It grows to 1.2–1.5m (4–5ft) with an arching or almost weeping habit, and shows itself particularly well in a pot.

Schizostachyum funghomii (formerly *Arundinaria funghomii*) is also highly suitable for pots, having an abundance of light green leaves which are quite remarkably long in relation to their width, some 18cm (7in) long by a mere 2.5cm (1in) wide. It has canes that are shiny green with orange markings, and grows to about 1.8m (6ft). *Arundinaria gigantea* ssp. *tecta* grows to much the same height but has a stiffly erect habit and is much more leafy. It has yellowish-green canes.

PLANTING ASSOCIATIONS

Bamboos, especially tall ones, are highly evocative of jungles, and jungly effects can be created by growing bamboos in association with palms such as *Trachycarpus fortunei*, *Butia capitata* or *Jubaea chilensis*. Other suitable plants are *Fatsia japonica*, *Acanthus* species, large-leaved bergenias such as *Bergenia ciliata*, with leaves to more than 30cm (12in) across, and coppiced *Paulownia tomentosa*, whose leaves can reach nearly 90cm (3ft) across when kept to a single stem and heavily fed.

Bamboos are sometimes recommended for ground cover beneath taller plants but the species which are most suitable are the low-growing bamboos such as *Pleioblastus pygmaeus*, *P. humilis* and *P. h.* var. *pumilus*, all of which run at the root and very easily get out of control.

PLATE X
Bamboo leaves (white)

Pleioblastus chino
'Aureostriatus'

Pleioblastus chino
elegantissimus

Pleioblastus variegatus

All plants shown approximately ½ size

24 Grasses for Containers

The growing of plants in containers for ornament is now more popular than ever, amounting to a minor art form. Yet, while grasses are among the best plants for container culture, giving a longer season of interest than most, the most effective ways of using them have as yet been little explored.

The selection of the containers is as important as the choice of plants to grow in them. As a general principle the pots are there to show off the plants, not to compete with them, and from this it follows that the simpler the surface of the pot the better. However, grasses break some of the rules. With their simple architecture and their linear emphasis they marry well with pots with bold but simple surface decoration, such as strapping. Highly glazed and highly coloured pots are on the whole inappropriate, though single-coloured glazed pots are sometimes suitable, especially for the larger grasses.

Pots and tubs are often most tellingly used near the house or in the vicinity of a garden house or garden room, because they carry the scale of familiar indoor things out of doors. This sense of the unity of scale can often be enhanced if similar pots with similar plants are used both inside and outside the house, carrying the theme from inside out. If large numbers of pots are to be used the plants are shown off to best advantage if the pots all have some common theme, either of size, shape or colour, or are deliberately chosen as variations on a single theme. Odd assortments of pots, on the other hand, can be given unity by using the same plant in all of them, or different cultivars of the same species.

CONTAINER PLANTING AT APPLE COURT

There are differing opinions as to how grasses should best be used in pots. My own preference is to go for the simplicity of a single species in a single pot, contrasting with other potfuls of single grasses and with pots containing plants of other types, especially broad-leaved ones. Simplicity is the hallmark of elegance. The alternatives are to grow two or three different grasses in a single pot, or to mix grasses with broad-leaved plants in the same pot.

At Apple Court parts of the garden are wholly dependent on the effects created by grasses in pots. My favourite (and probably everyone else's) for container planting is

The steely blue leaves of *Festuca glauca* 'Elijah Blue' make an excellent complement to this glazed blue pot.

Hakonechloa macra 'Alboaurea' (golden Hakone grass), which slowly builds itself up into rounded mounds of golden leaves striped with green and flecked with white which droop slightly over the rims of the pots, making the perfect shape to complement a typical pot. One of the first things we did here was to fill two inverted terracotta celery forcing pots with this grass. The pots are still outside the door from which we go from the potting shed into the nursery, standing at the foot of a brick wall up which *Microsorum diversifolium* is slowly climbing, but they are now filled with *Hakonechloa macra* 'Mediovariegata', which is less bright but more vigorous.

Even more dependent on grasses grown in pots is our hosta walk, where hostas are grown beneath a brick-pillared pergola beside a grass path. The brick pillars alternate with large pots of grasses set in gravelled squares. In the pots at the northern end, where we grow gold-leaved and yellow-variegated hostas, the pots contain golden Hakone grass, but at the southern end, where there are

Stipa arundinacea shares a pot with *Geranium* 'Mavis Simpson', pelargoniums and felicias.

blue-leaved and white-variegated hostas, the pots are planted with *Pleioblastus variegatus*, which is vigorous and effective. In time this will be replaced with *Hakoncheloa macra* 'Albovariegata', which will marry together both ends of the hosta walk rather better. This plant has leaves that are quite white by midsummer, though rather creamy in spring.

The two ends of the hosta walk are separated by an old stone seat set on a terrace of herringbone bricks with a stone surround, backed by a wisteria-covered wall. Here we grow a number of grasses in pots, though which particular grasses and which pots change from time to time. At the time of writing the most dominant is a 60cm (2ft) green glazed pot filled with a single specimen of *Stipa arundinacea* which makes a marvellously rounded plume of foliage, springing up in the centre and weeping over the sides, moving and rustling in the wind, changing colour slowly through the season until in autumn, when it produces its pendulous panicles which are almost lost among the profusion of foliage, it takes on tawny tints

of amber, orange, yellow, red and brown. This stands next to a giant long tom in which we grow the fragrant, sun-loving *Hosta* 'Summer Fragrance', which has white-edged green leaves that mound up and tumble over the rim of the pot, contrasting with the sheer linearity of the *Stipa arundinacea*.

At their feet are other pots and half-pots in which we grow various combinations of grasses. In the most successful of these we have *Carex dolichostachya* 'Kaga-nishiki' with *Helictotrichon sempervirens* and *Carex* 'Small Red', while in another, kept in a shadier position, we grow *Stipa tenuissima* with *Holcus mollis* 'Albovariegatus' and *Milium effusum* 'Aureum' (Bowles' golden grass). On the other side of the stone seat we have a large pot containing *Miscanthus oligstachyus* (flame grass), *Stipa tenuissima* and *Pennisetum villosum*, a combination designed to set the white scuts of the pennisetum against the burning reds of the flame grass, with the buff heads of the stipa to provide a colour bridge between the two. It is a combination that would work rather better were the pennisetum, which is a sun-lover, to be grown in one pot and the flame grass, which is happier in some shade and in damper soil, in another, the two being moved into juxtaposition in the autumn just as the flame grass becomes effulgent. Close to this is a large terracotta pot filled with *Leymus arenarius* (blue lyme grass), whose colour is the perfect complement to terracotta.

In our summer house, which is essentially a temple to hostas, we have a large pot filled with the tender red-leaved *Pennisetum setaceum* 'Burgundy Blaze', a superlative subject for container planting. One year we grew it with a ring of *Festuca glauca* 'Elijah Blue' just inside the rim of the pot, to colourful effect. Next to this we grow *Cymbopogon citratus* (lemon grass), whose grey-green leaves emit a delightful fragrance of lemons if crushed in the hand.

Over the years we have tried various combinations of white grasses, the most successful of which combined *Phalaris arundinacea* 'Feesey' with *Pennisetum villosum* and *Carex oshimensis* 'Variegata', which is attractive for months on end. This led to a planting in which we combined *Carex oshimensis* 'Variegata' with *C.* 'Frosted Curls' and the bamboo *Pleioblastus variegatus*, which remains effective in the shelter of the summer house almost until the spring, when it needs to be tidied up and given fresh soil. It is possible to make a gold version of this planting, using *Pleioblastus auricomus*, *Carex* 'Evergold' and *Luzula sylvatica* 'Aurea', though this lacks the sharpness of the white scheme and needs one of the bronze New Zealand sedges or hook sedges such as *Carex buchananii*, *C. petriei* or *Uncinia rubra* to sharpen it and to ameliorate that rather bilious feeling that tends to come with all-yellow plantings.

CONTRASTING FORMS AND COLOURS

In making plantings of grasses in pots, tubs or other containers it often helps to think first in terms of contrasting forms and secondly in terms of contrasting colours, and then to try to combine the best of both worlds. One might for example choose to combine the straight needle-thin leaves of *Helictotrichon sempervirens* with the diffuse haze of the flowers of *Agrostis nebulosa*, while at the same time being aware that the blue of the helictotrichon is a good foil for the nebulous brownness of the agrostis. In the same principle the pendulous leaves of *Elymus magellanicus* will act as a foil to the broad blades and upright carriage of *Chasmanthium latifolium*, with the blue of the former subtly complementing the green of the latter.

Much the same principles apply to combinations of grasses with broad-leaved plants, but the inclusion of the latter on the whole shortens the period during which the planting will be interesting, as compared with plantings of pure grasses. One has thus to think specifically of seasonal combinations. Sky-blue *Myosotis* (forget-me-nots) work well with *Holcus mollis* 'Albovariegatus' (striped Yorkshire fog), always one of the first grasses into leaf, and *Galanthus* (snowdrops) look good poking up through low-growing *Carex berggrenii*, but such effects are short-lived, as are red and yellow tulips in combination with the early leaves of yellow grasses such as *Milium effusum* 'Aureum' or *Carex elata* 'Aurea'. Longer-lasting effects can be achieved by combining grasses with annuals. For example one might combine sprawling salmon-pink *Diascia* which flower for six months on end with the upright blue tufts of fescues, the taller *Elymus hispidus* with flat-headed verbenas in pink, purple or scarlet, or red and orange nasturtiums with the blue of *Leymus arenarius* and the bronze of *Uncinia rubra*.

Hakonechloa macra 'Alboaurea' (golden Hakone grass) is one of the best grasses for pots, either in sun or shade.

25 Troughs, Sinks and Alpine Gardens

Many grasses are too large or vigorous to be let loose in troughs or alpine beds, but those few that are small enough are little gems, well worth the trouble needed to grow them.

The most beautiful and certainly the most challenging to grow is *Alopecurus lanatus* (woolly fox-tail grass), a tiny, woolly-white bundle of leaves which comes from sun-baked screes in Spain. It makes neither a mound nor a tuft, nor indeed any other clearly defined plant shape, but rather sends up short culms that are relatively thick as compared with the leaves, which measure 5cm (2in) long and 5mm (¼in) wide and are held horizontally to either side. The whole plant is blue, densely covered in silky white hairs, and grows to no more than 10cm (4in) tall in flower, with the leaf mound scarcely half that height, the flowers being minute, silvery fox-tails at the tops of silvery culms. It needs perfect drainage, a layer of grit around its collar to prevent rotting and a position in sun for most of the day.

Quite the smallest of the true grasses I have grown is *Festuca glacialis*, which makes tiny, dense mounds of slightly curving, needle-like leaves that are an intense whitish-blue in summer (though green in winter) and above which are borne violet flower spikes in early summer. The whole plant grows no more than 7.5cm (3in) high, and has a tendency (in common with most of the cushion-forming fescues) to die out in the centre, a tendency which is exacerbated if the drainage is not perfect. It is a lovely plant for a trough, where it can be divided and replanted from time to time. It comes from the high Alps and the Pyrenees, and again needs perfect drainage in full sun.

The perfect companions for these miniature, sun-loving grasses are small bulbs such as the very dwarf narcissi and bulbous alpine irises such as *Iris reticulata* or *I. histrioides*, as well as some of the late spring or early summer *Fritillaria* species, all of which need a good baking in the summer. Other diminutive plants with which these grasses associate well include the smaller campanulas, such as the blue *Campanula zoysii* or the white *C. cochleariifolia* 'Alba', dianthus such as *Dianthus alpinus* or *D. neglectus*, *Erinacea pungens* (hedgehog broom), silver-leaved *Euryops acraeus*, *Lewisia* species and the smallest of the *Phlox* species. The straight lines at the edge of the trough can be softened by growing over them the dwarf form of *Dryas octopetala*, *D. o.* 'Minor', *Dacrydium laxifolium* (pygmy pine) or the coarser conifer *Microcachrys tetragona*.

There are two *Poa* species which are almost as small and which make interesting contrasts with the dominant cushion form of alpine plants. The first is *Poa alpina nodosa*, which forms grey-green tufts to about 10cm (4in) tall in flower, while the second, *P. badensis* 'Ingelkissen', forms tufts of tiny, stiff, round-tipped leaves above which are borne fat green pompom panicles in late spring and early summer. It grows to 15cm (6in) in flower. *P. imbecilla* is rather larger, reaching 18cm (7in) high and producing from early summer until the frosts cloud-like panicles of tiny, bright green flowers that turn dark brown. They are held above tufts of fine, shining green leaves. This grass will grow in sun or shade.

Compared with these, *Alopecurus alpinus* (alpine fox-tail grass), a native of Scotland and alpine Europe, is a coarse plant and easy to grow, requiring only sun and a well-drained soil. In such a position it will slowly spread into a loose mat of intensely silvery-blue leaves, often tinged with purple, especially when young. The leaf mound grows about 12.5cm (5in) tall and 30cm (12in), with the flowers, which are again silvery-blue, reaching some 30cm (12in) high. It is a lovely plant for an alpine garden, but its spread may need controlling in a trough. The form *A. a.* ssp. *glaucus* does not seem to differ from the typical plant.

PLANTS FOR LARGER AREAS

A perfect plant for an alpine bed is *Carex conica* 'Snowline', which grows into a dense, compact tuft about 15cm (6in) in height and width, composed of narrow, very dark green leaves edged with narrow but clean white margins. It is a superb sedge in its understated way, and goes particularly well with lacy ferns, especially the less vigorous forms of *Adiantum pedatum*.

I have seen *Bouteloua gracilis* (mosquito grass) used to great effect in a large rock garden, where it formed an almost lawn-like carpet at the bottom of a wide valley between big rocks. Indeed, it is sometimes used in lawns and ornamental meadows. Its companions in this mock alpine valley were dense, rounded bushes of grey-leaved dwarf *Salix* (willows), dwarf pines which were kept remarkably tight by the simple device of pinching out their candles early every summer, and carpets of blue autumn-flowering gentians.

In larger alpine gardens the whole range of dwarf fescues can be grown, but particularly suitable are *Festuca gautieri* 'Pic Carlit' and *F. eskia*, both of which have richly green leaves, those of the latter lasting remarkably well through the winter while those of the former turn yellow in autumn and remain so through winter. 'Pic Carlit' grows to about 10cm (4in), *F. eskia* to 15cm (6in).

Agrostis canina (brown bent), a common grass in lawns, occasionally produces sports with variegated leaves. *A. g.* 'Silver Needles' (striped brown bent) is one such. It forms a dense carpet of narrow, white-edged leaves and in early summer produces a small forest of bright, foxy-red panicles that completely hide the foliage. It grows to 10cm (4in) in leaf, 20cm (8in) in flower, the flowers being on the whole showier than the leaves. It forms clumps that are inclined to die out from the centre, a tendency which can be reduced but not eliminated by regularly clipping it over with shears. Sooner or later it will need replanting, and this is probably best done every other year. *Holcus mollis* 'Albovariegatus' (striped Yorkshire fog) is broadly similar both in appearance but has wider, showier leaves, though the flowers are less showy, being greenish-white. It prefers damper soil than *Agrostis*, and is better with a little shade. It is in just the right scale to grow the black-flowered *Fritillaria camschatcensis* up through it, the fritillaria being in flower just when the new foliage of the grass is at its brightest.

Two rather larger grasses are sometimes included in alpine gardens. One is *Melica ciliata*, which makes neat tufts 45cm (18in) in height and spread and produces in late spring or early summer cylindrical panicles of white or off-white spikelets. The other is *Festuca punctoria* (hedgehog fescue) which has stiff blue, upright-pointing curved leaves which taper to horny points quite capable of piercing the skin. It grows about 12.5cm (5in) tall, and spreads slowly if well suited into clumps about 30 cm (12in) across. It needs a very sunny position and sharply drained soil.

SEDGES AND RUSHES

Three diminutive carices are eminently suitable for sinks, given a semi-shaded position in a peaty soil. The largest of these is *Carex berggrenii*, which forms tight clumps 10–12.5cm (4–5in) tall of flat, curving leaves that are brown with a curious greyish caste, producing its bundles of brown flowers and seeds almost hidden among the foliage. Several forms exist, some greener, some greyer, and some with narrower leaves. *C. ulophylla*, like *C. berggrenii*, comes from the mountains of New Zealand and forms dense tufts of recurving leaves no more than 4cm (1½in) long that are densely covered in short white hairs, especially at the margins, creating the effect of marginal variegation. A large, mature plant is smaller than one's fist.

Luzula × *borreri* 'Botany Bay' is a curious woodrush, also a native of the mountains of New Zealand, which forms tight rosettes of short leaves and whose new leaves in the spring are bright white, rather in the manner of *L. sylvatica* 'Taggart's Cream', but in miniature. *Juncus concinnus* makes a good companion for these two, growing to 10cm (4in) tall and forming tufts of curious olive-green leaves often tinged with red among which appear pale, creamy little drumsticks of flowers in mid and late spring, borne on green- and red-banded stems. This and the above will grow well in a trough in which a peat-soil mix is used rather than a sharply drained one, in which peat blocks or sea-washed driftwood is used rather than rocks, and which is placed in shade and kept moist. There are a wealth of little alpines needing similar cultural conditions including *Saxifraga fortunei* 'Mt Naichi', *Acorus gramineus* 'Pusillus', *A. g.* 'Masamune', tiny hostas such as *H. venusta*, *H.* 'Shining Tot', *H.* 'Masquerade' and *H. gracillima*, *Celmisia* and *Cassiope* species, *Dicentra peregrina*, tiny *Calceoleria* species, alpine *Gentiana* and small *Primula* species.

Carex firma is the smallest sedge I have come across. It forms a dense, compact tuft, usually no more than 5cm (2in) tall (though very old specimens sometimes attain twice that size), with narrow, wedge-shaped leaves about 2.5cm (1in) long and only 3mm (⅛in) across, three-angled, straight and rigid, terminating in a sharp point. The flowers are chocolate brown, borne on a short stalk. *C. f.* 'Variegata' is even more desirable, the leaves being boldly variegated creamy-yellow. Both can be increased by careful division or by cuttings taken in spring and rooted in pure sand under glass.

There is of course no absolute limit to the size of grasses that can be grown in sinks and rock gardens, but those mentioned above are among the smallest and most suitable. In larger rock gardens the choice is far wider.

26 House, Greenhouse & Conservatory

There are a number of good grasses that cannot be grown successfully out of doors because of the inclemency of winter and that come into their own given the warmth of a house or the shelter of a greenhouse or conservatory, most needing little more than to be frost-free and in good light. By far the most impressive of these is *Arundo donax* 'Variegata' (var. *versicolor*) (striped Provençal reed) which can make a specimen 4.6m (15ft) high, the stems symmetrically set with two ranks of broad leaves evenly spaced on the culm, each leaf nearly 30cm (12in) long, broadly margined and striped cream, as is the culm. It is a lovely plant for a greenhouse or conservatory where, because of its height, it should be planted in a border and the culms tied in to the wall, for left to their own devices they will tend to lean out across the room.

Saccharum officinarum (sugar cane) runs the variegated Provençal reed a close second when it comes to sheer stature, often growing to as much as 3.6m (12ft) each season. The culms (canes) are 2.5–7.5cm (1–3in) in diameter, while the leaves can be 2.5–7.5cm (1–3in) wide and 0.4–1.5m (1½–5ft) in length. The leaves are normally greyish-green, but in recent years several clones have been selected for their ornamental value, one with red leaves and green culms, one with red leaves and red culms and a third with red and green variegated culms, while *S. s.* 'Pele's Smoke', which grows to no more than 1.8m (6ft), is wholly a deep, rich, horticultural purple. The latter is as yet the only one to be named. Sugar cane rarely flowers outside the tropics, but the panicles, were they to appear, would be rather similar to those of the *Cortaderia* (pampas grass). In conservatories sugar cane needs a rich, moisture-retentive soil, and a position in full sun.

A lovely companion for these huge grasses is the bamboo muhly, *Muhlenbergia dumosa*, which is to the grasses world what *Salix babylonica* is to the tree world, for it throws up vertical, cane-like stems which, once they reach their full height, suddenly burgeon with leafy branches, the sheer profusion of the tiny, narrow leaves causing them to weep in a most graceful manner. It makes a most

Stenotaphrum secundatum 'Variegatum' (striped St Augustine grass) in the tropical water-lily house at Kew Gardens, London.

elegant plant in a large tub, and when grown thus will weep over the sides of the tub and almost touch the ground.

Oplismenus africanus, which is popularly known as basket grass because it is often grown in baskets, used to be known as idiot grass, *O. imbecillicus*, from its way of looking not like a grass at all but like a small-leaved houseplant tradescantia. The similarity applies not only to the arrangement of the leaves on the stems but also to the stems themselves, which are procumbent, becoming erect at the tips and rooting at the nodes. The form usually grown is *O. a.* 'Variegatus', or 'Vittatus', in which the leaves are striped white and often tinted pink as well, thereby still further increasing the resemblance to tradescantia. This grass has traditionally been grown in hanging baskets, but it is also excellent for low edgings in a greenhouse or conservatory, or for growing along the edge of staging where its leaves and stems will make a curtain to hide what is beneath. A native of tropical forests, it needs bright but indirect light and a fertile, moisture-retentive soil, and should be given plenty of water when in active growth. It needs a minimum winter temperature of 15°C (60°F).

Stenotaphrum secundatum 'Variegatum' (striped St Augustine grass) has similar uses but is altogether more vigorous, making a fast-spreading ground cover in greenhouses and positively cascading when grown as a basket plant. The leaves are both longer and wider than those of oplismenus, and have rounded tips. It needs rich, retentive soil in sun.

Cymbopogon citratus (lemon grass) is a clumping perennial 60–90cm (2–3ft) high, forming an upright-divergent tuft of grey-green leaves which are strongly lemon-scented, the fragrance being emitted when the leaves are crushed or squeezed. The leaves may also be used as a flavouring in cooking. It makes an attractive plant grown in a terracotta pot in a conservatory or greenhouse, though it is usually too large for a windowsill. A native of savannahs and other dry, open places, it needs full sun and a moisture-retentive soil, should be watered freely while in growth but scarcely at all when dormant, and must be kept above 10°C (50°F) in winter. It can often be found in the vegetable sections of supermarkets, the

Oplismenus africanus 'Variegatus' (striped basket grass) is an ideal houseplant for a position where its stems can trail.

PAPYRUS

More exotic still is the true papyrus of Egypt, *Cyperus papyrus*, a robust, clumping perennial whose leafless stems rise straight from the rootstock and are topped by a spherical umbel of spoke-like rays. It is the ideal plant for creating a tropical atmosphere in a conservatory or greenhouse but is not always easy to accommodate for, although it will grow well enough for a while in a pot stood in a saucer of water, it really needs the sort of high atmospheric humidity that can only be obtained by standing it in or beside a pool. It needs a minimum winter temperature of 5°C (41°F).

C. involucratus is rather smaller and easier to accommodate, growing to some 75cm (2½ft). However it differs from the true papyrus in that it is the collar of floral bracts that subtend the rays that is conspicuous, rather than the rays themselves. The collar is composed of 12–28 bracts arranged like flattened spokes around the top of the stem: each is dark green and tapers to a point. From summer to autumn these are topped by 14–32 thread-like rays bearing spikelets of yellowish flowers which turn brown once they have shed their pollen. *C. involucratus* is usually grown in its white-striped form, 'Variegatus', which is attractive but not particularly stable.

Cyperus albostriatus differs from the other *Cyperus* plants mentioned here in that it has basal leaves, these being about the same length as the stems, some 60cm (2ft). The stems are topped by the usual arrangement of floral bracts, though in this species there are only 6–9 of them. Above them are borne the showy spikelets at the tips of the rays. All these *Cyperus* need good light and high humidity, and should be stood in water. They are easily propagated by seed or division, or by inverting the umbels in water and potting the plantlets on as soon as they are large enough to handle. Though occasionally grown as house plants they are really better in conservatories, the atmosphere in a house usually being too dry for them.

SEDGES

There are two sedges that do make ideal conservatory or windowsill subjects, and that could scarcely be more different from each other. The first is *Isolepis cernua* (*Scirpus cernuus*), a curious rush that is sometimes sold as a houseplant. It forms a dense tuft of bright green, arching thread-like stems and leaves 15cm (6in) tall, resembling nothing so much as a head of green hair overflowing the sides of the pot. It is best grown in an acid potting mix

culm bases having been cleaned and trimmed so that it rather resembles a clove of fennel.

Another exotic grass sometimes grown in conservatories for its foliage effect and very suitable for large pots is *Setaria palmifolia*, sometimes known as palm grass. It makes wide clumps, sometimes as much as 3m (10ft) tall though more usually in cultivation not much more than 1m (3¼ft), composed of broad, conspicuously pleated, dark green leaves. The panicles are not conspicuous. *S. megaphylla* is similar.

Carex phyllocephala 'Sparkler' grows best in the shelter of a house or conservatory.

and kept rather wet, and is not soundly perennial. The other, *Rhynchospora nervosa* (syn. *Dichromena nervosa*), resembles *Cyperus* in that the very small flowers are surrounded by a collar of 3–8 leafy bracts, each broadly triangular tapering to a fine point, made conspicuous by being brilliant white on the upper surface, becoming green towards the tip. The bracts may be as much as 23cm (9in) long and the whole plant can grow to as much as 1.5m (5ft), though it is usually seen very much smaller, at 45cm (18in) or less. It needs to be grown in an ericaceous potting mix, and grows largest when kept quite wet, though it does not require saturated soil. Rated as a zone 9 plant in the USA, it will tolerate a frost-free greenhouse in the UK.

Of the several variegated sedges that make good plants for the home or conservatory *Carex phyllocephala* 'Sparkler' produces by far the brightest effect and is in any case a most arresting plant, for instead of growing into a lowly mound like other sedges it masquerades as a *Cyperus*, with a whorl of short, tapering leaves at the tops of erect, strongly three-sided stems 30cm (12in) tall. The leaves are 23cm (9in) long and 1cm (½in) wide, with bold white margins and a few whitish pencil lines

in the centre. Both they and the bracts are dramatically variegated creamy white, often strongly pink-tinted, especially early in the year. At the top of the stem, in the centre of the leaf rosette, are the flowers which, from an aesthetic point of view, finish the leaf assemblage without adding anything to it. They are composed of several spikes of short, erect, green female spikes at the centre of which is an insignificant, brownish male spike. It is slow to increase and difficult to propagate so will always be hard to find. It is not quite frost hardy with me but is happy in frost-free conditions. It does best in shade.

Carex muskingumensis (palm-leaf sedge) is similar in that it produces narrow upright stems about 30cm (12in) tall with the leaves arranged in three distinct ranks and mostly gathered at the tops of the stems. In the variegated form, *C. m.* 'Oehme', the leaves have golden-yellow margins and, since these are most noticeable at close quarters, this is an ideal plant for growing indoors.

Several other variegated sedges make ideal plants for house or greenhouse, and indeed this is how they were grown before it was realized that most were hardy. The most popular is *C.* 'Evergold', which makes dense round tufts of glossy evergreen leaves which are rich creamy-yellow with dark green margins; *C. oshimensis* 'Variegata' is similar but slightly smaller and with a white central variegation; and *C. brunnea* 'Variegata' is broadly similar in appearance, though more cream-coloured.

BAMBOOS

Bamboos make exotic and decorative plants for the home or conservatory, provided their needs are understood. Being rainforest understorey plants, their first requirement is for high humidity, which is often difficult to achieve in the home, and for more light than is generally found indoors – even the brightest rooms in a house are usually too dark, though supplementary lighting, as used in shops and offices, can help. Conservatories and greenhouses, with their higher light availability and potential for humidity, are really more suitable than the home for bamboos. The final limitation is one of height, for many bamboos are very tall and look absurd cut down to size.

Many variegated bamboos will perform better under cover than they will exposed to wind and weather out of doors. Perhaps the most desirable of these is × *Hibanobambusa tranquillans* 'Shiroshima', whose relatively large leaves, 23cm (9in) long and up to 4cm (1½in) wide, are dramatically striped creamy white, and are often tinted pink when young. It grows to about 1.5m (5ft) in containers, and has the particular merit of looking good through the winter. Rather taller, but just as striking, is *Pseudosasa japonica* 'Akebonosuji', whose 30cm (12in) long leaves are broadly striped yellow or creamy yellow. It will grow to 2.4–3m (8–10ft), and is quite stiffly upright, carrying most of its foliage high up, revealing the canes.

Of a much brighter white, and growing to no more than 90cm (3ft), the culms becoming pendulous with the weight of the leaves, is *Pleioblastus shibuyanus* 'Tsuboi', whose relatively small, round-tipped leaves are strongly white-variegated. The ubiquitous *P. variegatus* is similarly but less strikingly white variegated but is rather stiffly upright in containers. It grows to 1.2m (4ft) and spreads steadily. Far more subtle in its variegation is *Sasa kurilensis* 'Shimofuri', whose large leaves look as though thin white pencil lines have been drawn on them. It grows to about 1.8m (6ft) and spreads quite rapidly at the root.

Quite the strangest of the bamboos which do well in conservatories is *Pleioblastus akebono*, which is useless in the garden, scorching in strong light. It has slender canes that grow to no more than 75cm (2½ft) and small leaves, about 5cm (2in) long, that start wholly white, then become greener towards the base, the old leaves being almost entirely green. In a conservatory, provided it is grown where no ray of sun ever reaches it, it will remain in pristine condition and be a considerable adornment. It forms loose clumps, but never has sufficient vigour to be considered a runner.

Bambusa glaucescens (oriental hedge or golden goddess bamboo) is a most decorative house or conservatory plant, seldom exceeding 90cm (3ft) in a container. It makes a dense, upright and slightly divergent clump of slender, sparsely branched canes carrying all the leaves bunched together towards the tips. *B. g.* 'Alphonse Karr' is a showy selection with green stripes and rather pale leaves. Equally suitable for indoor cultivation are those phyllostachys with colourful canes or sheaths, since these can be appreciated better at close quarters than in the garden. *Phyllostachys nigra* (black bamboo) with its shiny, jet black culms is ideal, as is one of its sister clones, *P. n.* 'Boryana', whose culms are conspicuously speckled with brown. Several forms of *P. bambusoides* have thick canes which in the form 'Holochrysa' (syn. 'Allgold') are bright golden yellow, in 'Castilloni' yellow striped with green and in 'Castilloni Inversa' green with deep yellow internodal grooves. These will all grow to 4.5m (15ft) in the UK. Smaller, at some 3.6m (12ft) in cultivation, is *P. aurea*, whose yellow canes have the lowest internodal sections compressed and thickened. Again there is a selection called 'Holochrysa' which has bright yellow canes.

The most unexpected cane colouring is however to be found on *Himalayacalamus hookerianus* (syn. *Drepanostachyum hookerianum*), whose culms, if enough sunshine falls directly on them, will become a rich, deep pink, often marked with thin stripes of pale yellow, white or green. It will grow to 2.4m (8ft) tall and has pale, yellowish-green leaves, some of which are large and some of which are small.

It is surprising that grasses and bamboos are not used more in homes and conservatories as they harmonize happily with those other easy-care houseplants of Victorian drawings rooms – parlour palms and aspidistras, ferns such *Woodwardia radicans* (giant chain fern), whose stately fronds can grow to as much as 2.4m (8ft) long, the tree ferns *Dicksonia antarctica*, the black-stemmed *D. fibrosa* or the blue *Cyathea dealbata* whose trunk and fronds seem to have been whitewashed, the leathery *Blechnum chilense* and *Polypodium aureum* (syn. *Phlebodium aureum*) with its large, erect blue fronds and foxy-red rabbit's foot rhizomes. Other choices are fragrant gardenias, showy bougainvilleas and bright pelargoniums and busy lizzies (*Impatiens*).

27 Grasses in the Winter Garden

etween the first light frosts that brown the last dendranthemums and the flowering of the first snowdrops, grasses hold centre stage. In harmony with the low winter light, their flowers long past, their seeds scattered, the empty husks deck out the skeletal panicles against the pale winter sun, rimed in frost or spangled with raindrops, while the sedges and rushes, if evergreen, contribute the colour or colours of their leaves.

The winter picture is made from a narrow band of colours – sand, fawn, taupe, beige and biscuit – at least as far as the true grasses are concerned. Palest of all is *Phalaris arundinacea* (ribbon grass), like well-scrubbed Portland stone, while richest of all are *Molinia* species (moor grasses), an amber gold that looks particularly well

Most ornamental grasses hold their own against the attrition of winter until well into the New Year, and then go out in a blaze of glory whitened with hoar frost or spangled with snowflakes.

with the light browns of *Panicum* species (switch grasses) or the taupe of *Pennisetum* (fountain grasses). *Stipa tenuissima* bleaches like tow and contrasts well with the tawny straw of *Stipa arundinacea*. The sedges and rushes contribute more real colour – deep greens, browns, yellows and blues.

PLANTING COMPANIONS

There are various ways of composing a winter picture. A prairie-like effect can be created by planting drifts of *Miscanthus* contrasting with *Panicum* and *Pennisetum*, with the spaces between the grasses filled with drifts of *Coreopsis verticillata* 'Moonbeam', whose dark thread-like stems are tipped with tiny black cones, *Rudbeckia fulgida* 'Goldsturm', which creates much the same effect but on a larger scale, and *Sedum* 'Herbstfreude' ('Autumn Joy'), which creates a contrast in form with flat heads of dark brown.

Panicum virgatum 'Warrior' weighed down with hoar frost on a late winter morning

In a more English idiom one can combine single plants or twos or threes of various grasses – *Miscanthus, Andropogon gerardii, Schizachyrium scoparium, Pennisetum* and *Phalaris arundinacea* – with red- and yellow-stemmed *Cornus* and the cool green-flowered stinking hellebore *Helleborus foetidus* or the sun-loving Corsican hellebore *H. argutifolius*. As a background, plant yellow or blue *Chamaecyparis, Viburnum × bodnantense, Prunus serrula* for its polished bark, and *Buxus sempervirens* (box) for its rich greenery.

A more intimate grouping would be to use just one true grass, *Andropogon gerardii* for example, underplanted with single specimens of the dark green, white-edged *Carex conica* 'Snowline' and yellow-edged *C. dolichostachya* 'Variegatus'. The yellow theme could be continued with *Luzula sylvatica* 'Aurea', whose colouring will become brighter as winter progresses. Combine these with such broad-leaved winter treasures as *Cyclamen coum, Helleborus niger*, red-fruited *Aucuba* and dark *Danaë racemosa*.

Any winter tableau of grasses will be most effective if they are planted with a dark background, perhaps of conifers or rhododendrons, winter-flowering *Viburnum tinus* or clipped hedges of *Taxus* (yew), *Buxus* (box) or *Fagus* (beech) and sited so that the light can fall on them from behind or from the side. The scheme will be greatly enriched if planted where the skeletons of the grasses can stretch their shadows like malachite across the jade of green lawn, and if evergreen grasses such as *Deschampsia caespitosa* and *Luzula sylvatica* and dark green sedges such as *Carex caryophyllea* 'The Beatles' or *C. texensis* are included. These could be supplemented with the grass-

like ophiopogons or liriopes, or the frosty blues of *C. glauca* or *C. flaccosperma* could be used to increase the seeming coldness of the scene. A further dimension can be added by including here and there among the grasses the skeletons of broad-leaved plants – the ubiquitous *Rudbeckia fulgida* or the green-flowered *R. occidentalis*, both of whose cones are dark as bitter chocolate, the tall *Eupatorium cannabinum* 'Gateway', the etiolated fennels, the short astilbes, whose plumes turn darkest brown in winter, angelicas and *Sedum telephium*.

DESIGNING FOR COLOUR AND SHAPE

A greater sense of warmth and depth can be given to the planting if the warmest colours, the purple moor grasses (*Molinia*), for example, or *Stipa arundinacea*, are planted nearest the house with the palest grasses, such as the *Phalaris arundinacea*, further away. Sometimes artefacts such as statues or well-rounded oil jars can be used to increase the apparent desolation of the grasses, but living materials can often provide a more interesting contrast; neatly clipped cones or pyramids of *Taxus* (yew) or *Buxus* (box) provide solidity and strong, sharp lines which make the fluffy bleached heads of the grasses and their bundled culms seem all the more ethereal. It is also worth including in the scheme one of those bergenias whose round leaves become in winter as purple as the cheeks of an apoplectic colonel, *Bergenia* 'Sunningdale', for example.

The best grasses for winter effect are, on the whole, those that also contribute most in summer: *Calamagrostis, Miscanthus, Panicum, Pennisetum* and the evergreen *Deschampsia*, their forms and colours complementing each other as they do in summer. Of the lesser grasses, *Stipa* (*Calamagrostis*) *brachytricha* (Korean feather reed grass) has foliage of a richer hue than any other grass in the garden in winter, especially when wet, though *Sorghastrum nutans* (Indian grass) and *Spodiopogon sibiricus* run it close. *Stipa tenuissima* and *S. calamagrostis* contribute the fineness of their leaves and their movement. *Spartina pectinata* 'Aureomarginata' (striped prairie cord grass) holds itself together longer than almost any other grass in winter, except perhaps for *Typha* species (cat-tails), which hold their brown pokers aloft on straight rigid stems high above the arching ribbons of biscuit leaves.

For those who find the natural colours of grasses in winter too tame, there is an alternative: in at least one American garden the dry grasses are sprayed in a whole rainbow range of colours using aerosol car paints.

SEDGES

Any of the sedges with coloured or variegated leaves might be used to advantage: the familiar *C.* 'Evergold'; *C. oshimensis* 'Variegata'; *C. morrowii* 'Variegata'; *C. m.* 'Fisher's Form'; the New Zealand carices *C. dipsacea*, which is olive flushed with dull yellows, *C. testacea*, which is similar but brighter, *C. kaloides*, *C. buchananii*, *C. petriei* and *C.* 'Small Red', which are all browns; and the darker *C. flagellifera*, *Uncinia rubra* and *Ophiopogon planiscapus* 'Nigrescens', all of which can be used to make sharp contrasts with the icy blues of the American sedges *C. glauca* and *C. flaccosperma* and the running European blue sedges *C. panicea* and *C. flacca*.

In our own garden we put *C. glauca*, the brightest of the blues, next to *Luzula sylvatica* 'Aurea' which, though merely green in summer, turns to solid, brightest yellow in winter, with the mahogany *Uncinia rubra* beyond that, the emerging flowers of the golden *Luzula* in the early spring almost matching the colour of the *Uncinia*. On the far side of the *Luzula* we used *Carex flaccosperma*, with *C. dolichostachya* 'Kaga-nishiki' beyond it. These are all planted in broad, curving bands and are blended back into a border of mainly summer interest by a single plant of *Miscanthus sinensis* 'Adagio', a fairly dwarf miscanthus with a profusion of neat flowers held well through the winter, underplanted with *Poa colensoi*, a blue New Zealand grass that mimics the little blue fescues but has the merit of holding its colouring through the winter and of not minding the shade.

The same sedges could be used in different combinations and arrangements, and the overall effect would be enhanced were dark greens to be included, either in the form of one of the fragrant, winter-flowering Christmas boxes, *Sarcococca confusa*, perhaps, or the lower, more spreading *S. c.* var. *humilis*, possibly in an island bed together with *Hamamellis mollis* in one of its forms. There are several sedges that would provide the dark green: *Carex caryophyllea* 'The Beatles' forms low tufts of dark green leaves while *C. texensis*, the Catlin sedge, has thread-thin dark green leaves that tend to sprawl on the ground, making a hummock no more than 10cm (4in) tall but 30cm (12in) across. In both the flowers are of no ornamental significance. The Catlin sedge is currently being tested in the USA as a lawn substitute.

BAMBOOS

The bamboos, being evergreen, also have a part to play, contributing an abundance of foliage, usually most

Bamboos with coloured canes such as *Phyllostachys vivax* 'Aureocaulis' contribute colour to the winter scene.

welcome at this time of year. Those with coloured leaves can be particularly useful, the loveliest of these being *Pleioblastus shibuyanus* 'Tsuboi', whose leaves are heavily variegated creamy-white, *P. variegatus*, *P. chino elegantissimus*, *Sasa kurilensis* 'Shimofuri' and *Pseudosasa japonica* 'Akebonosuji', all of whose leaves are striped white or cream. *Pleioblastus auricomus* is notable for its bright yellow leaves.

Other bamboos contribute just as much welcome colour with their canes: the legendary black bamboo, *Phyllostachys nigra*, the tall, sun-tolerant *Phyllostachys vivax* 'Aureocaulis' and *P. bambusoides* 'Holochrysa' (syn. 'Allgold'), both with canes of a rich golden yellow, *P. b.* 'Castilloni', which has golden canes with striking green internodal stripes, and *P. aureosulcata* 'Spectabilis', with similar canes. The latter is the best golden-stemmed bamboo for colder gardens.

THE END AND THE BEGINNING

If they are left to their own devices the gradual attrition of the winter slowly erodes the grasses, scattering their leaves and sheaths on the ground. In the end the increasing litter negates their diminishing beauty, and the time has come to cut the grasses down and rake up the litter. By then the snowdrops are already in flower and the grasses are ready to start the cycle of the seasons over again.

28 Some Grass-Like Plants

There are a number of plants that look like grasses and are often included among them, though they are not related. The common names of several make some reference to grass, lily turf, for example, mondo grass, blue-eyed grass, scouring rush and so on. Most of these are sufficiently grass-like to make good companions for the true grasses, sedges, rushes and cat-tails. Any plant with the specific epithet *graminea*, meaning grassy or *graminifolia*, meaning grass-leaved, will also bear a resemblance to a grass, and there are many such, but most are just ordinary broad-leaved plants that lack the grace and beauty of the true grasses.

LIRIOPE

Liriope muscari (lily turf) is a member of the lily family. It produces its leaves directly from the roots and carries them in two ranks, from the centre of which the flower spike appears. The flowers, though not showy like those of the true lilies, are composed of the same floral parts. Their great virtue is that they make dense tufts of ever-green leaves and produce in late summer and autumn spikes of extraordinarily long-lasting mauve, lilac or white flowers that closely resemble those of a muscari. They are tolerant of sun or shade and if planted reasonably close will form a weed-suppressing ground cover. There are several named forms: 'Royal Purple' is an exceptionally strong purple, while 'Superba' is exceptionally pale; 'Majestic' is supposed to be a deeper colour than ordinary forms while 'Big Blue' is supposed to be taller, though in reality they differ little from wild plants; and 'Monroe White' has good white flowers but needs more sun to produce them than the others. There are several variegated forms, few of which seem to be entirely happy in the average climate of the UK. 'John Burch' is the best of those I have grown, with good yellow striping down the leaves and deep purple flowers: 'Silvery Sunproof' scorches in both sun and frost.

L. spicata has narrower leaves and poorer flowers than *L. muscari* but has a running habit, making it an excellent ground cover. *L.* × 'New Wonder' is a hybrid between *L. muscari* and *L. spicata* which combines the best characters of both. *L. minor* is a smaller plant, growing to about 10cm (4in) with narrow dark green recurving leaves

and a running habit. It makes more of a turf than any of the other species or varieties, and is conspicuous in autumn when it produces its large turquoise berries.

OPHIOPOGON

Mondo grass is a name strictly applied only to *Ophiopogon intermedius*, which was at one time *Mondo intermedius*, but it is now generally applied to all ophiopogons. *O. intermedius* forms low tufts of arching, dark, narrow ever-green leaves and grows only to about 15cm (6in) tall, but spreads by stolons, slowly forming extensive patches. In mid to late summer it produces arching stems of downward-facing mauve flowers, followed by dark mauve or lilac berries. In climates too arid to grow grass it is sometimes used as a lawn as it will stand occasional mowing and a little light traffic. *O. japonicus* is similar but smaller, with narrower leaves: *O. wallichianus* is variable, but broadly similar to *O. intermedius*, while *O. bodinieri* is more vigorous. These are useful plants to grow with grasses because their darkness provides a foil for the middling greens of most grass genera, and a dramatic contrast with variegated grasses such as *Miscanthus sinensis* 'Variegatus'. They are especially useful as a ground cover under and around specimen grasses, providing a dark carpet from the midst of which the specimen arises. They are rather better in this role than the majority of grasses. There is a charming dwarf form of *Ophiopogon japonicus*, *O. j.* 'Compactus', which grows to 5cm (2in) tall. *O. j.* 'Tamaryu Number Two', *O. j.* 'Kigimafukiduma' and *O. j.* 'Kyoto' may be the same plant.

O. planiscapus has much wider leaves, often of a lighter green. It grows to about 15cm (6in) tall and is a useful ground cover, but not a showy plant. The typical form has mauve flowers, but there is form with white flowers, which is rather showier. However, it is black mondo, *O. p.* 'Nigrescens' (syns. 'Ebony Knight', 'Black Dragon') that is outstanding, for this has jet black leaves which shine as though polished when wet with rain. The flowers are mauve but the berries are black, and if sown will produce about one-third black seedlings, the rest being green. It is startling when grown with blue *Festuca*, *Hakonechloa macra* 'Alboaurea' (golden Hakone grass) or *Imperata cylindrica* 'Rubra' (Japanese blood grass) and

The grass-like *Ophiopogon planiscapus* 'Nigrescens' with golden, moss-like *Sagina subulata* 'Aurea'.

lovely with snowdrops or white crocuses growing up through it.

ACORUS

The genus *Acorus* is generally considered grass-like, though it is an aroid with most ungrasslike spathes and spadices and produces its narrow leaves in flattened fans, which true grasses never do. The archetypal acorus is the sweet flag, *A. calamus*, which is usually grown in its variegated form, 'Variegatus', in which half the leaf is green and half creamy-white tinged with pink. The leaves grow to about 45cm (18in) long. Both leaves and roots contain the essential oil calamus which gives them a sweet, liquorice smell and is used in perfumes, beers and gins. *A. gramineus*, so-called for its resemblance to grass, is a far smaller plant, its narrow dark green leaves growing no more than 15cm (6in) long and making a carpet of greenery about 10cm (4in) high. *A. g.* 'Variegatus' has

leaves striped white, while in *A. g.* 'Ogon' they are striped green and yellow. *A. g.* 'Pusillus' is a miniature with leaves less than 5cm (2in) long of which 'Masamune' is a selection with wholly gold leaves, about 10cm (4in) long.

SISYRINCHIUM, IRIS AND LIBERTIA

Sisyrinchiums and some small irises can look very like each other, and both are sometimes mistaken for grasses. *Iris graminea* is, as its name suggests, grassy, making low mounds of dark narrow shining green leaves about 15cm (6in) high and producing in early summer, almost hidden among the foliage, rich violet and yellow flowers that smell strongly of rotting fruit. *Sisyrinchium angustifolium* is known as blue-eyed grass, because its 15cm (6in) tufts of grassy leaves are dotted in early summer with starry blue flowers. Several libertias have similarly grassy leaves, the grassiest being *Libertia peregrinans*, known as golden reed, which forms small tussocks of flattened fans of reed-like leaves which turn a unique golden-orange in sun. It grows 15cm (6in) tall, and has small, white, iris-like flowers in the summer.

Part Five Plant Care

30 Caring for your Grasses

One of the great virtues of grasses is that they demand little more than ordinary soil, a place in the sun, and sufficient watering to get them established. The sedges prefer a damper soil than the true grasses, and will stand shade rather better, while the rushes and cat-tails can take a lot more moisture and will even be happy with their feet in water.

Nor does the preparation of the ground before planting present any problems. The ground should be thoroughly dug over and the sods broken down where an extensive planting of grasses and companion plants is to be made, and for specimen grasses such as *Cortaderia* or *Miscanthus*, a hole should be taken out a 90cm (3ft) across and 45cm (18in) deep, and the soil returned to the hole and made firm before planting. Ideally this preparatory work, which loosens the soil and allows freer movement of air and water and hence greater root penetration, should be done six months before planting to allow the ground to settle again.

FEEDING AND WATERING

As a rule of thumb grasses should be fed lightly or not at all; over-feeding makes them grow out of character and renders them prone to attack by pests and to problems with diseases. Most general-purpose fertilizers are suitable for light feeding, and it is usually most convenient to apply whatever you are using on the other plants in the garden, but at only a quarter of the rate. For the largest specimen grasses, *Miscanthus* and *Cortaderia*, some organic manure may be incorporated into the planting hole, and the same material used as a mulch in subsequent years.

While most grasses should be watered during their first year to help them establish, the majority should be well able to withstand drought thereafter. Drought is nonetheless a stress for most grasses, and they will generally look better if that stress can be avoided. Mulching is a method of moisture conservation to which grasses seem to respond particularly well. The best materials for mulching are organic substances such as processed bark, which is low in nutrient value, or fine gravel or pea-grit, which will gradually work their way into the soil, improving drainage and aeration.

The sedges and rushes, preferring damper ground, are rather heavier feeders. As with the true grasses, it is usually simplest to apply whatever fertilizer is being used in the rest of the garden, but this time at the same rate. They can also take heavier mulching than the grasses, and of more nutrient-rich materials such as garden compost. However, in times of drought most sedges, if well established, can be left to cope on their own. The leaves may wither and the sedges may look rather wretched, but once rain returns they will recover.

Bamboos are quite different in their needs from the generality of grasses, being gross feeders. At planting time the prepared hole should be lavishly enriched with organic manure, and after planting the bamboo should be heavily mulched with a doughnut-like ring of manure. It should subsequently be fed with a general fertilizer as used in the rest of the garden, applied at the same rate. A yearly mulch of manure will be beneficial, not only for its nutrient value but also because of the moisture it conserves – important for bamboos, which also need to be grown in positions sheltered from winds for reasons of moisture conservation.

CONTAINMENT AND GROOMING

Most grasses form clumps that increase in girth slowly but steadily so that in time they may become too large for their space. In this case all that can be done is to dig up the grass, break it down into smaller pieces with a spade and put one of these back. There are, however, a number of grasses that run at the root, and sadly people often avoid planting these grasses for fear that they will take over. All that is needed is to cut the roots back with a spade to the desired circumference, and then to fork out any runners outside that area. The rule is little and often; if this is done two or three times a year, the spread of the grasses can easily be controlled. It is when the grasses are left for a year or two that problems arise.

Not all bamboos run, but those that do, such as the popular *Pleioblastus* and *Phyllostachys*, can be contained within a physical underground barrier. The taller the bamboo the deeper the barrier should be – a minimum of 30cm (12in) for the smaller species and 75cm (2½ft) for the larger ones. The earth should be scraped away from the top of the barrier once a year, and any runners that are trying to escape over it should be cut back. However, the spread of large bamboos such as *Phyllostachys* in the open ground can be controlled surprisingly easily as long as the new shoots are dealt with during the growing season, which only lasts for a few weeks in spring and early summer. At this time the shoots are soft and easily cut off below ground with a sharp spade or freezer knife. Go all round each bamboo in the growing season to ensure that all the runners have been removed. Smaller bamboos such as *Pleioblastus* grow throughout the summer and are best contained.

The only regular attention needed by most grasses is an annual grooming, and this is best done at the end of winter. Deciduous grasses that have lost all the colour in their leaves should be cut down close to the ground, the smaller ones to within 1–2.5cm (1–2in), while larger grasses such as *Miscanthus* should be cut down to 12.5–15cm (5–6in). Evergreen grasses, those which retain colour in a high proportion of their leaves, should not be cut down but merely trimmed over lightly to remove the scorched tips of the leaves, while dead leaves and debris should be raked out with the fingers or with a small garden fork.

It is usually as well to tidy the ground around the grasses at the same time, and to apply any mulches or fertilizers. The grasses can then be left to ebb and flow through another season, with little further intervention. Indeed, in most gardens the biggest problem with ornamental grasses is that weed grasses may seed themselves into the crowns of desirable species. It is important to keep on top of this and not allow the weed species to become established.

PROPAGATION

The propagation of grasses (including sedges and rushes) is on the whole simple and straightforward. All species and their botanical varieties, including the annuals, can be raised from seed, and contrary to the general rule, variegated grasses will produce about 20 per cent variegated seedlings. Most seed needs some pregermination treatment, but all that grass seed requires is to be kept dry and out of the frost through the winter. A common practice is to keep the seed in envelopes in a biscuit tin in a garage or frost-free outhouse. Seed can then be sown in spring or early summer, either in a cold frame or out of doors where it is to grow. If grown under glass the seedlings should be well-ventilated to prevent damping-

off. They are liable to the usual pests and problems of young seedlings such as damage by slugs and snails.

Named varieties of grasses should only be increased by division, cool-season growers in spring or autumn, never in the summer, warm-season growers only in the spring or early summer. When grasses are divided in full leaf, the foliage should be cut back to a quarter of its length. The easiest way to divide a grass is to dig up the whole plant and then to break it into smaller pieces. With small grasses such as *Milium* this can easily be done by hand, but with large grasses such as *Miscanthus* more force is needed – some have such tough roots that it is necessary to take an axe or a saw to them. Some grasses, such as the cushion-forming fescues, can be divided into single bundles of leaves with roots, but most of the larger species, *Pennisetum alopecuroides* and *Miscanthus* for example, should never be divided down to the smallest possible pieces but left as quite sizeable sections of roots and growth buds. Grasses that produce runners, such as *Phalaris arundinacea*, can be propagated by detaching rooted pieces and growing them on, either in pots or in the open ground.

One or two grasses can be increased by stem or root cuttings – indeed, cuttings are the usual means of increasing *Arundo donax*, *A. d.* 'Variegata' and *A. pliniana*. The technique is to remove side-shoots with a short length of old stem attached and to lay them obliquely in a shallow pan of water. They will usually send out roots in a matter of days, and can be potted on once they have sufficient. Best results are usually obtained in early summer. Cuttings of sections of the canes of *Saccharum officinarum* (sugar cane) will root at the nodes if laid on their sides half-buried in a potting mix: the cuttings should be taken between the nodes, so that each cutting contains at least one node. *Pennisetum alopecuroides*, *Cymbopogon citratus* and *Miscanthus sinensis* have also been successfully rooted from stem cuttings. *Miscanthus* can also be increased by means of root cuttings and *Cyperus* ssp. can be rooted by inverting their floral heads in water.

Since most grasses are readily increased by division little research or experimentation have gone into methods involving cuttings, but there is a hope that some plants difficult to increase either by seed or division may respond to new techniques.

A small number of grasses are viviparous, that is, they produce plantlets where normal grasses would produce flowers, *Deschampsia caespitosa* 'Fairy's Joke' and *Festuca ovina* var. *vivipara* being two examples. These plantlets will turn into independent plants only if they are brought into contact with earth or potting compost by pegging them down to the soil using wire hoops like small hairpins, or detaching and pegging down into trays of compost. Occasional viviparous spikelets may be found on almost any grass, and may be rooted in the same way.

Newly propagated grasses should be grown on in a position sheltered from wind and if, propagated in summer, also protected from hot sun, for drying out is the greatest danger to young grasses. Obviously attention should be paid to watering, but no amount of overwatering will ever make up for the desiccation caused by wind or sun. Newly propagated grasses are often more vulnerable to frost than they will be once established, and this is particularly true of *Miscanthus*.

Hybridizing

Grasses can be hybridized as easily as other flowering plants. The first step is to remove the pollen sacs from the panicle on the proposed seed parent. This must be done before the pollen sacs start shedding their pollen. The emasculated panicle should then be wrapped in a paper bag or envelope to prevent accidental pollination. Pollen may be collected from the proposed male parent by putting a paper bag or envelope over the panicles and allowing the pollen to fall into it. If the bag protecting the proposed seed parent is then removed and replaced by the bag containing the pollen, pollination can then be achieved by vigorously shaking the bag with the pollen inside it, or indeed by leaving it there and letting the wind shake the bag as it blows. The pollen is dry and can be stored in a refrigerator for many months, and certainly for more than a year, should the need arise, with only a relatively small loss of viability.

PESTS AND DISEASES

Grasses are remarkably untroubled by diseases, though one or two common garden pests may be a nuisance. The only disease that may be a problem, and that only with some grasses, is rust, which is a fungal disease. It usually reveals itself as small, rusty-orange nodules or spots on the leaves. To a certain extent rust can be avoided by paying particular attention to garden hygiene, making sure that dead leaves, especially of affected grasses, are not left lying around but are gathered up and burned. Another factor that will tend to reduce the occurrence of rust is ensuring that there is plenty of air circulation around the grasses, though this is not always easy to achieve. The only real treatment is to use wettable sulphur, applied

several times through the season, beginning before susceptible grasses start into growth. The sulphur should be applied to the ground around the grasses, not to the grasses themselves.

In some districts *Leymus arenarius* (blue lyme grass) will not flower properly due to the presence of stem smut fungus, *Ustilago hypodytes*, producing instead culms that are positively scrofulous with the black spore pustules. Since the fungus infests the tissues throughout the plant, the only remedy is to burn the entire plant.

Aphids sometimes attack the soft new growth of grasses, especially under glass or in tunnels, but the damage is usually not great; grasses grow so vigorously that they soon leave the damaged growth behind, and the aphids cannot keep up. They can be washed off the foliage with a jet of water, or suffocated with a spray of insecticidal soap.

Mealybugs are more serious. If these little white insects are around at all, they will be found down inside the sheaths, where they wrap around the soft part of the culm, which they will eat. They can be destroyed by alcohol applied with a soft brush or cotton-wool swabs.

Slugs and snails can do considerable damage to some grasses and in particular to sedges, though most grasses are never affected. Vulnerable plants are those with soft leaves such as *Milium effusum* and *Carex siderosticha*, as well as some of the subtropical species. There is no absolute cure. Control is best achieved by hand-picking slugs and snails at night, and placing them in a bucket of salt or soapy water. Slug pellets also achieve a measure of control, though they are increasingly seen as ecologically incorrect. Strips of copper and diatomaceous earth (Molbar) have a deterrent effect.

Rabbits can be a serious problem in some gardens, and regard some grasses, *Deschampsia* in particular, as first-rate fodder, though they do not generally bother with grasses with wiry leaves. Rabbit fencing is the only effective strategy, though the cost can be prohibitive.

Deer are not a serious problem of grasses, though they will sample anything that is newly planted, and will sometimes browse on new growth. Generally they leave grasses alone once the leaves have hardened. Like rabbits, they will tend to avoid grasses with tough or wiry leaves. Deer fencing is the ultimate deterrent. Some folk remedies, such as bags of human hair hung on fences, may be effective.

The banded leaves of zebra grasses make intriguing patterns in sunlight.

Appendix I *Grasses for Special Uses*

GRASSES WITH COLOURED FOLIAGE

White
Pleioblastus akebono

Yellow
Carex elata 'Knightshayes'
Deschampsia caespitosa
  'Ladywood Gold'
Deschampsia flexuosa
  'Tatra Gold'
Luzula sylvatica 'Aurea'
L. s. 'Woodsman'
Milium effusum 'Aureum'
Pleioblastus auricomus
  f. chrysophyllus

Brown
Carex berggrenii
C. buchananii
C. comans bronze form
C. dipsacea
C. flagellifera
C. petriei
C. testacea
C. uncifolia
Pennisetum setaceum
  'Burgundy Blaze'
P. s. 'Rubrum'
P. 'Burgundy Giant'
Schoenus pauciflorus
Uncinia egmontiana
U. rubra
U. uncinata (some forms)

Red
Imperata cylindrica 'Rubra'

Black
Ophiopogon planiscapus
  'Nigrescens'

Grey
Arundo donax
Koeleria glauca
Saccharum ravennae
S. arundinoides
Sesleria caerulea

Blue
Alopecurus alpinus
Carex glauca
C. flacca
C. flaccosperma
C. panicea
C. spissa
Corynephorus canescens
Elymus arenarius
E. hispidus
E. magellanicus
Festuca californica
F. cinerea
F. glauca & cvs
F. ovina ssp. coxii
F. valesiaca 'Silbersee'

Helictotrichon sempervirens
H. pratense
Koeleria glauca
K. vallesiana
Leymus racemosus
L. elongatus
Panicum virgatum 'Blue Tower'
P. v. 'Cloud Nine'
P. v. 'Heavy Metal'
P. v. 'North Wind'
P. v. 'Pathfinder'
P. v. 'Prairie Sky'
Poa colensoi
Schizachyrium scoparium
Sorghastrum nutans
  'Indian Steel'
S. n. 'Sioux Blue'

GRASSES WITH STRIPED FOLIAGE

White-striped
Arrhenatherum elatius bulbosum
  'Variegatum'
Arundo donax 'Variegata'
Calamagrostis × acutiflora
  'Overdam'
Carex conica 'Snowline'
C. morrowii 'Variegata'
C. oshimensis 'Variegata'
C. phyllocephala 'Sparkler'
C. saxatilis 'Ski Run'
C. siderosticha 'Variegata'
Cyperus albostriatus 'Variegatus'
C. alternifolius 'Variegatus'
Dactylis glomerata 'Variegata'
Glyceria maxima var. variegata
× Hibanobambusa tranquillans
  'Shiroshima'
Holcus mollis 'Variegatus'
H. 'Albovariegatus'
Luzula sylvatica 'Marginata'
Melica uniflora 'Variegata'
Miscanthus sinensis 'Cabaret'
M. s. 'Cosmopolitan'
M. s. 'Dixieland'
M. s. 'Morning Light'
M. s. 'Rigoletto'
M. s. 'Silberpfeil'
M. s. 'Variegatus'
M. tinctorius 'Nanus Variegatus'
Molinia caerulea 'Claerwen'
Oplismenus hirtellus
  'Variegatus'
Pennisetum alopecuroides
  'Little Honey'
Phalaris arundinacea 'Feesey'
P. a. 'Picta'
P. a. 'Streamlined'
Phyllostachys aurea

'Albovariegata'
Pleioblastus chino
  elegantissimus
P. variegatus
Sasa kurilensis 'Shimofuri'
Schoenoplectus lacustris
  'Albescens'
Stenotaphrum secundatum
  'Variegatum'

Cream-striped
Carex firma 'Variegata'
C. morrowii 'Fisher's Form'
C. 'Evergold'
C. pilulifera 'Tinney's Princess'
Glyceria maxima var. variegata
Hakonechloa macra
  'Albovariegata'
H. m. 'Mediovariegata'
Miscanthus sinensis 'Goldfeder'
Molinia caerulea 'Variegata'
Muhlenbergia japonica
  'Variegata'
Pleioblastus shibuyanus 'Tsuboi'
P. variegatus

Yellow-striped
Alopecurus pratensis
  'Aureovariegatus'
Bromus ramosus
  'Skinner's Gold'
Carex brunnea 'Variegata'
C. elata 'Aurea'
C. 'Evergold'
C. flava
Hakonechloa macra 'Alboaurea'
H. m. 'Aureola'
Pseudosasa japonica
  'Akebonosugi'
Phragmites australis 'Variegatus'
Pleioblastus auricomus
Spartina pectinata
  'Aureomarginata'

Banded
Juncus effusus 'Zebrinus'
Miscanthus sinensis 'Coon Tail'
M. s. 'Hinjo'
M. s. 'Kirk Alexander'
M. s. 'Pünktchen'
M. s. 'Strictus'
M. s. 'Tiger Cub'
M. s. 'Zebrinus'
Schoenoplectus lacustris
  'Zebrinus'

AUTUMN FOLIAGE COLOUR

Yellows
Chasmanthium latifolium
Molinia caerulea ssp. arundinacea
  cvs

M. c. ssp. caerulea cvs
Panicum clandestinum
P. virgatum cvs
Pennisetum alopecuroides cvs
Phragmites australis
Stipa arundinacea
  'Gold Hue'

Orange-reds
Andropogon gerardii
A. glomeratus
A. virginicus
Hakonechloa macra & cvs
Miscanthus oligostachyus
  'Purpurascens'
Saccharum ravennae
Schoenus pauciflorus
Schizachyrium scoparium
Sorghastrum nutans & cvs
Sporobolus heterolepis
Themeda japonica

Bronze-reds
Apera spica-venti
Bouteloua curtipendula
Miscanthus sinensis 'Graziella'
Panicum virgatum
  'Rotstrahlbusch'
Spodiopogon sibiricus
Stipa arundinacea
  'Autumn Tints'
Tridens flavus

Wine reds
Hakonechloa macra & cvs
Imperata cylindrica 'Rubra'
Panicum virgatum
  'Hänse Herms'

WOODLAND AND SHADE

Alopecurus pratensis &
  A. p. 'Aureomarginata'
Arrhenatherum elatius bulbosum
  'Variegatum'
Brachypodium sylvaticum
Briza maxima
B. media & B. m. 'Limouzi'
Bromus ramosus
Calamagrostis × acutiflora
  'Stricta' & 'Karl Foerster'
Carex boottiana
C. conica 'Snowline'
C. 'Evergold'
C. flaccosperma
C. fraseri
C. glauca
C. 'Ice Dancer'
C. morrowii 'Fisher's Form' &
  'Variegata'
C. muskingumensis & cvs
C. ornithopoda 'Variegata'
C. oshimensis 'Variegata'

C. plantaginea
C. pendula & C. p.
 'Moonraker'
C. saxatilis 'Ski Run'
C. siderosticha & C. s
 'Variegata'
C. 'Silver Sceptre'
C. trifida
Chasmanthium latifolium
Deschampsia caespitosa & cvs
D. flexuosa & cvs
Festuca gigantea
Hakonechloa macra & cvs
Holcus 'Alan Cook'
H. mollis 'Albovariegatus'
Hystrix patula
Luzula all
Melica uniflora
M. u. albida
M. u. 'Variegata'
Milium effusum 'Aureum'
Miscanthus oligostachyus 'Africa'
M. o. 'Herbstfeuer'
M. o. 'Purpurascens'
Molinia caerulea ssp. caerulea
 & cvs
Phalaris arundinacea & cvs
Poa chaixii
P. colensoi
Sesleria autumnalis
Spodiopogon sibiricus & S. s.
 'West Hills'
Stipa (Calamagrostis) brachytricha

WATERSIDE GRASSES

These are grasses that need
constant moisture, but will
not necessarily tolerate
submersion of their crowns.
All the grasses listed as
marginals will also grow in
these conditions.
Acorus gramineus & cvs
Alopecurus pratensis &
 A. p. 'Aureovariegatus'
Andropogon glomeratus
Arundo donax
Calamagrostis × acutiflora & cvs
Carex most species & cvs
Chasmanthium latifolium
Cortaderia selloana & cvs
Cyperus eragrostis
C. fuscus
C. ustulatus
Dactylis glomerata & D. g.
 'Variegata'
Deschampsia caespitosa & cvs
Luzula all
Milium effusum & M. e. 'Aureum'
Miscanthus sacchariflorus
M. sinensis & cvs
M. 'Giganteus'
Molinia caerulea ssp. arundinacea
 & cvs
Molinia caerulea ssp. caerulea
 & cvs

Panicum virgatum
 'Hänse Herms'
Phalaris arundinacea & cvs
Spartina pectinata &
 S. p. 'Aureomarginata'

GRASSES FOR MARGINAL WATERS

These are grasses that will
grow with their crowns
submerged (tolerated depth
shown in brackets). None has
an absolute requirement for
submersion, though all need
constant moisture at the root.
Acorus calamus (to 15cm/6in)
Beckmannia eruciformis
 (to 7.5cm/3in)
Carex fascicularis
 (to 2.5cm/1in)
C. glauca (to 2.5cm/1in)
C. riparia & cvs
 (to 7.5cm/3in)
Cyperus involucratus
 (to 15cm/6in)
C. longus (to 15cm/6in)
Eriophorum angustifolium
 (to 2.5cm/1in)
E. latifolium (to 10cm/4in)
E. vaginatum (to 10cm/4in)
Glyceria aquatica & cvs
 (to 2.5cm/1in)
G. plicata (to 7.5cm/3in)
Juncus effusus & cvs
 (to 10cm/4in)
J. glaucus (to 5cm/2in)
Oplismenus hirtellus
 (to 7.5cm/3in)
Oryza sativa (to 10cm/4in)
Phragmites australis & cvs
 (to 60cm/2ft)
Rhynchospora nervosa
 (to 7.5cm/3in)
Schoenoplectus lacustris & cvs
 (to 10cm/4in)
Spartina pectinata & S. p.
 'Aureomarginata'
 (to 10cm/4in)
Typha angustifolia
 (to 30cm/12in)
T. latifolia (to 30cm/12in)
T. minima (to 7.5cm/3in)
T. shuttleworthii
 (to 7.5cm/3in)
Zizania aquatica
 (to 10cm/4in)

GRASSES FOR CLAY SOILS

Calamagrostis × acutiflora cvs
Deschampsia caespitosa & cvs
Elymus glaucus
Phalaris arundinacea & cvs

GRASSES FOR DEEP, RICH, WELL-CULTIVATED SOILS

Miscanthus all

Saccharum ravennae

GRASSES FOR CHALK SOILS

Koeleria glauca
Melica ciliata

GRASSES REQUIRING POOR SOILS

Briza media
Bouteloua gracilis
Festuca most
Phalaris arundinacea & cvs

GRASSES REQUIRING ACID & ALKALINE SOILS

Most grasses grow well on
most soils. However, a small
number have a preference for
acid soils, and rather fewer a
preference for alkaline. Those
listed as needing acid soils
will grow well in soils that
range from neutral (pH 7) to
severely acid (pH 3.5), but
will not flourish in soils on
the alkaline side of neutral.
Similarly, those listed as
needing alkaline soils will
grow in soils that range from
neutral (pH 7) to severely
alkaline (pH 8.5) but will not
flourish in soils on the acid
side of neutral. There are a
few exceptions: Bouteloua
gracilis, Cynodon dactylis and
Phleum pratense will thrive on
acid, alkaline or neutral soils.
For Acid Soils
Anthoxanthum odoratum
Arrhenatherum elatius & A. e.
 'Variegatum'
Bouteloua gracilis
Briza maxima &
 B. m. 'Rhodes Form'
Bromus secalinus
Cynodon dactylon
Deschampsia flexuosa
Holcus 'Alan Cook'
H. mollis 'Albovariegatus'
Molinia caerulea & forms
 & cvs
Oryza sativa
Pennisetum alopecuroides & cvs
Phalaris arundinacea & cvs
Phleum pratense
Poa nemoralis
Stenotaphrum secundatum &
 S. s. 'Variegatum'
For Alkaline Soils
Andropogon gerardii
A. virginicus
Bouteloua curtipendula
B. gracilis
Cynodon dactylon
Koeleria cristata
Milium effusum & M. e. 'Aureum'

Phleum pratense

GRASSES FOR SANDY SOILS

Holcus lanatus 'Variegatus'
Spartina pectinata
 'Aureomarginata'

GRASSES FOR SHADE

Alopecurus pratensis
 'Aureovariegatus'
Arrhenatherum elatius bulbosum
 'Variegatum'
Briza media
Calamagrostis × acutiflora
 'Karl Foerster'
Carex fraseri
Chasmanthium latifolium
Deschampsia caespitosa & cvs
D. flexuosa & cvs
Hakonechloa macra & cvs
Hystrix patula
Luzula all
Melica ciliata
M. uniflora
Milium effusum
Miscanthus oligostachyus
 'Purpurascens'
Molinia caerulea ssp. caerulea
 & cvs
Phalaris arundinacea & cvs
Sesleria autumnalis
S. heufleriana
Spodiopogon sibiricus
Stipa (Calamagrostis) brachytricha

DROUGHT-TOLERANT GRASSES

Andropogon gerardii
Bouteloua gracilis
Eragrostis chloromelas
E. curvula
Festuca punctoria
F. glauca
F. valesiaca
F. dalmatica
F. longifolia
F. mairei
F. californica
Helictotrichon sempervirens
H. filifolius
Holcus 'Alan Cook'
H. mollis 'Albovariegatus'
Koeleria glauca
K. vallesiana
Leymus arenarius
Melica altissima
Muhlenbergia rigens
Oryzopsis miliacea
Panicum virgatum & cvs
Pennisetum all
Sesleria autumnalis
Schizachyrium scoparium
Sorghastrum nutans & cvs
Sporobolus airoides
Stipa barbata
S. calamagrostis

S. capillata
S. gigantea
S. pennata
S. tenuissima
S. tirsa

ANNUAL GRASSES

Agrostis nebulosa
Aira elegantissima
Apera spica-venti
Avena sterilis
Briza maxima
B. minor
Bromus arvensis
B. macrostachys
B. madritensis
Catapodium rigidum
Cynosurus echinatus
Echinochloa crus-galli
Lagurus ovatus
Lamarckia aurea
Lolium temulentum
Lophochloa cristata
Panicum capillare
P. miliaceum
Pennisetum setaceum
Phalaris canariensis
P. minor
Phleum paniculatum
Polypogon monspeliensis
Setaria glauca
S. macrostachya
S. pumila
Sorghum bicolor
S. nigrum
Zea mays

GRASSES FOR TUSSOCK GARDENS

Carex albula
C. berggrenii
C. buchananii & *C. b.* 'Viridis'
C. comans, C. c. bronze form
  & *C. c.* 'Frosted Curls'
C. dipsacea
C. flagellifera
C. forsteri
C. petriei
C. testacea
C. trifida
C. secta var. *tenuiculmis*
C. uncifolia
Chionochloa conspicua
C. flavescens
C. flavicans
C. rigida
C. rubra
Cortaderia fulvida
C. richardii
Uncinia clavata
U. rubra

GRASSES FOR POTS, TUBS AND CONTAINERS OUT OF DOORS

Carex albida

C. berggrenii
C. buchananii
C. comans & *C. c.*
  'Frosted Curls'
C. dolichostachya 'Kaga-nishiki'
C. elata 'Aurea'
C. oshimensis 'Variegata'
C. petriei
C. 'Small Red'
Chasmanthium latifolium
Cortaderia selloana 'Pumila'
Elymus magellanicus
E. hispidus
Festuca amethystina & cvs
F. glauca & cvs
Glyceria maxima & *G. m.*
  var. *variegata*
Hakonechloa macra & cvs
Helictotrichon sempervirens
Holcus mollis 'Albovariegatus'
Imperata cylindrica 'Rubra'
Leymus arenarius
Luzula sylvatica & cvs
Milium effusum 'Aureum'
Miscanthus oligostachyus
  'Purpurascens'
Miscanthus sinensis most cvs
Molinia caerulea ssp. *caerulea*
  & cvs
Phalaris arundinacea & cvs
Pennisetum alopecuroides & cvs
P. setaceum 'Burgundy Blaze'
P. villosum
Pleioblastus auricomus
P. variegatus
Stipa arundinacea
S. tenuissima
Uncinia rubra

GRASSES FOR ALPINE GARDENS

Agrostis canina 'Silver Needles'
Alopecurus alpinus
A. lanatus
Bouteloua gracilis
Carex berggrenii
C. conica 'Snowline'
C. firma & *C. f.* 'Variegata'
C. ulophylla
Festuca gautieri 'Pic Carlit'
F. eskia
F. glacialis
F. punctoria
Holcus mollis 'Albovariegata'
Luzula × borreri 'Botany Bay'
Melica ciliata
Poa alpina nodosa
P. badensis 'Ingelkissen'
P. imbecilla

GRASSES FOR MIXED BORDERS

Ampelodesmos mauritanicus
Andropogon all
Arundo donax
Bouteloua curtipendula

B. gracilis
Bromus most
Briza maxima & *B. m.*
  'Rhodes Form'
B. media & *B. m.* 'Limouzi'
B. minor
Calamagrostis × acutiflora & cvs
Carex baccans
C. pendula & *C. p.*
  'Moonraker'
C. pseudocyperus
Chasmanthium latifolium
Cortaderia fulvida
C. richardii
C. selloana & cvs
Deschampsia flexuosa & cvs
D. caespitosa & cvs
Elymus arenarius
E. hispidus
Eragrostis chloromela
E. curvula
Festuca cushion-forming
  species
Helictotrichon sempervirens
Hordeum jubatum
Hystrix patula
Lagurus ovatus & *L. o.* 'Nanus'
Leymus arenarius
Luzula nivea
Melica altissima 'Atropurpurea'
M. a. 'Alba'
M. ciliata
M. macra
M. transsilvanica
Milium effusum & cvs
Miscanthus floridulus
M. sacchariflorus
M. sinensis & cvs
Molinia most
Panicum virgatum & cvs
Pennisetum alopecuroides & cvs
P. macrourum
P. orientale
P. villosum
Poa chaixii
Schizachyrium scoparium
Sorghastrum nutans & cvs
Spartina pectinata & *S. p.*
  'Aureomarginata'
Spodiopogon sibiricus
Stipa ambigua
S. (Calamagrostis) brachytricha
S. calamagrostis
S. gigantea
S. tenuissima
And most annual grasses

GRASSES FOR MEADOWS

Agrostis canina
A. tenuis
Alopecurus pratensis
Anthoxanthum odoratum
Briza media
Cynosurus cristatus
Deschampsia caespitosa
Festuca arundinacea

F. ovina
F. rubra
F. pratensis
Holcus mollis
Hordeum secalinum
Koeleria macrantha
Phleum pratense
Trisetum flavescens

GRASSES FOR WILDFLOWER LAWNS

Agrostis tenuis
Anthoxanthum odoratum
Cynosurus cristatus
Deschampsia flexuosa
Festuca ovina
F. rubra var. *commutata*
F. r. ssp. *rubra*
F. tenuis
Holcus mollis
H. lanata
Lolium perenna
Phleum bertolonii
Poa trivialis

ORNAMENTAL BRITISH NATIVE SPECIES

Agrostia canina
A. gigantea
Ammophila arenaria
Anthoxanthum odoratum
Apera spica-venti
Briza media
Bromus several
Calamagrostis epigejos
Carex flacca
C. panicea
C. pendula
C. riparia
Cyperus longus
Deschampsia caespitosa
D. flexuosa
Eriophorum
Festuca arundinacea
Glyceria maxima
Juncus all
Koeleria cristata
Lagurus ovatus
Leymus arenarius
Luzula sylvatica
Molinia caerulea ssp. *caerulea*
Phleum pratense
P. bertoloni
Schoenoplectus
Stipa pennata

GRASSES FOR SEASIDE GARDENS

The following grasses will
grow in soils periodically
inundated with salt water and
tolerate salt wind and spray:
Agropyron pungens
Ammophila arenaria
Bromus unioloides
Calamagrostis epigejos

Chloris gayana
Cynodon dactylis
Puccinellia fasciculata
P. maritima
Spartina alterniflora
S. cynosuroides
S. patens
The following grasses tolerate salt wind and salt spray:
Ammophila arenaria
Ampelodesmos mauritanicus
Bromus inermis
Carex testacea
Chasmanthium latifolium
Cortaderia fulvida
C. richardii
C. selloana
Leymus arenarius
Lygeum spartum
Oryza sativa
Panicum virgatum
Phalaris arundinacea & cvs
Phragmites australis & cvs
Spartina pectinata
Sporobolus virginicus
Triticum aestivum
Uniola latifolia

EVERGREEN GRASSES

Ampelodesmos mauritanicus
Bamboos all
Carex albida
C. buchananii
C. caryophyllea 'The Beatles'
C. comans
C. conica 'Snowline'
C. dipsacea
C. flagellifera
C. forsteri
C. fraseri
C. oshimensis & cvs
C. morrowii & cvs
C. pendula
C. petriei
C. pseudocyperus
C. secta
C. testacea
C. texensis
C. trifida
Chionochloa rubra
Cortaderia all
Deschampsia caespitosa & cvs
Juncus all
Koeleria all
Luzula all
Poa chaixii
P. colensoi
Sesleria all
Stipa gigantea
S. papposa
Uncinia all

DROUGHT-TOLERANT GRASSES

Andropogon gerardii

Calamagrostis × *acutiflora*
Carex buchananii
C. caryophyllea 'The Beatles'
C. conica 'Snowline'
C. dipsacea
C. dolichostachya
   'Kaga-nishiki'
C. flaccosperma
C. flagellifera
C. glauca
C. kaloides
C. morrowii & cvs
C. oshimensis & cvs
C. petriei
C. 'Small Red'
C. testacea
C. texensis
Deschampsia caespitosa all
Luzula sylvatica all
Molinia caerulea all
Miscanthus all
Panicum virgatum all
Phalaris arundinacea & cvs
Phyllostachys aureosulcata
   'Spectabilis'
P. bambusoides 'Holochrysa' &
   P. b. 'Castilloni'
P. nigra
P. vivax 'Aureocaulis'
Pennisetum alopecuroides & cvs
Pleioblastus auricomus
P. chino elegantissimus
P. shibuyanus 'Tsuboi'
P. variegatus
Poa colensoi
Pseudosasa japonica
   'Akebonosuji'
Sasa kurilensis 'Shimofuri'
Schizachyrium scoparium
Sorghastrum nutans & cvs
Spartina pectinata
   'Aureomarginata'
Spodiopogon sibiricus
Stipa arundinacea
S. (Calamagrostis) brachytricha
S. tenuissima
Typha most
Uncinia clavata
U. rubra

GRASSES FOR CUTTING

D = good for drying
S = may shatter if not picked early enough
Ss = inclined to shatter even when picked early, and not to be relied upon in permanent arrangements
Aegilops D
Agrostis D
Aira elegantissima D
Ampelodesmos mauritanicus
Apera
Arundo donax D
Avena

Bouteloua gracilis D
Briza all D
Bromus most D
Calamagrostis all
Chasmantium latifolium D
Cortaderia all D
Deschampsia caespitosa & cvs
D. flexuosa & cvs
Echinochloa crus-galli D
Eleusine coracana D
Elymus most
Eragrostis all
Festuca extremiorientalis
Hordeum jubatum Ss
H. vulgare
Hystrix patula S
Koeleria macrantha
Lagurus ovatus D
Lamarckia aurea SS
Leymus
Luzula
Melica altissima & cvs
Milium effusum
Miscanthus all D
Panicum all
Pennisetum all S
Phalaris canariensis D
Phleum pratense
Phragmites australis D
Saccharum ravennae D
Schizachyrium scoparium D
Setaria italica
Sorghastrum nutans & cvs D
Sorghum all D
Spartina pectinata
Stipa (Calamagrostis) brachytricha
S. calamagrostis
S. capillata
Typha all D
Uniola latifolia
Zea mays D
Zizania aquatica

GRASSES FOR HOUSE, GREENHOUSE AND CONSERVATORY

Arundo donax 'Variegata'
Bambusa glaucescens 'Alphonse Karr'
B. g. 'Fernleaf'
Carex brunnea 'Variegata'
C. muskingumensis 'Oehme'
C. oshimensis & cvs
C. phyllocephala 'Sparkler'
Cymbopogon citratus
Cyperus albostriatus
C. alternifolius &
   C. a. 'Variegata'
C. papyrus
Dichromena nervosa
× *Hibanobambusa tranquillans*
   'Shiroshima'
Himalayacalamus hookerianus
Isolepis cernua
Oplismenus africanus &

O. a. 'Variegatus'
Phyllostachys aurea
   'Holochrysa'
P. bambusoides 'Castilloni'
P. b. 'Castilloni Inversa'
P. b. 'Holochrysa'
P. nigra & *P. n.* 'Boryana'
Pleioblastus akebono
P. shibuyanus 'Tsuboi'
P. variegatus
Pseudosasa japonica
   'Akebonosuji'
Saccharum officinarum & cvs
Sasa kurilensis 'Shimofuri'
Setaria palmifolia
Stenotaphrum secundatum
   'Variegatum'

GRASSES FOR FRAGRANCE

Anthoxanthum odoratum
Cymbopogon citratus
Hierochloë odorata
Sporobolus heterolepis
Vetiveria zizanioides

AWARD OF GARDEN MERIT GRASSES

The Award of Garden Merit, as reinstituted in 1992, recognizes plants of outstanding excellence for garden decoration or use, whether grown in the open or under glass.
Carex elata 'Aurea'
C. 'Evergold'
Chusquea culeou
Cortaderia selloana
   'Aureolineata' ('Gold Band')
C. s. 'Pumila'
C. s. 'Sunningdale Silver'
Hakonechloa macra 'Aureola'
Helictotrichon sempervirens
Miscanthus floridulus
M. sacchariflorus
M. sinensis
Molinia caerulea ssp. *caerulea*
   'Variegata'
Pennisetum orientale
Phalaris arundinacea 'Picta'
Phyllostachys aurea
P. bambusoides 'Castilloni'
P. nigra
P. n. var. *henonis*
P. viridiglaucescens
Pleioblastus auricomus
P. variegatus
Pseudosasa japonica
Sasa palmata
Semiarundinaria fastuosa
Sinarundinaria anceps
S. nitida
Thamnocalamus spathaceus

Appendix II *List of Common Names*

African love grass *Eragrostis curvula*
albardine *Lygeum spartum*
alkali dropseed *Sporobolus airoides*
alpine fox-tail grass *Alopecurus alpinus*
American galingale *Cyperus eragrostis*
animated oat *Avena sterilis*
autumn moor grass *Sesleria autumnalis*
bamboo muhly *Muhlenbergia dumosa*
basket grass *Oplismenus africanus*
Bend love grass *Eragrostis trichodes* 'Bend'
big bluestem *Andropogon gerardii*
bird's foot sedge *Carex ornithopoda*
black bamboo *Phyllostachys nigra*
black-flowered sedge *Carex nigra*
black millet *Sorghum nigrum*
blond sedge *Carex comans*
blood grass *Imperata cylindrica* 'Rubra'
blue hair grass *Koeleria glauca*
blue Indian grass *Sorghastrum nutans*
  'Sioux Blue'
blue lyme grass *Leymus arenarius*
blue moor grass *Sesleria caerulea*
blue oat grass *Helictotrichon sempervirens*
blue wheatgrass *Elymus hispidus*
Boer love grass *Eragrostis chloromelas*
bottle-brush grass *Hystrix patula*
Bowles' golden grass *Milium effusum*
  'Aureum'
Bowles' golden sedge *Carex elata* 'Aurea'
broad-leaved snow tussock
  Chionochloa flavescens
brome grass *Bromus* spp.
brown top *Agrostis tenuis*
Buchanan's brown sedge *Carex*
  buchananii
Buddha's belly bamboo *Bambusa*
  ventricosa
bulbous oat grass *Arrhenatherum elatius*
  bulbosum 'Variegatum'
bulbous switch grass *Panicum bulbosum*
bulrush *Schoenoplectus lacustris*
carnation sedge *Carex flacca, C. panicea*
cat's tail grass *Phleum bertolonii*
cat-tails *Typha* spp.
Chewing's fescue *Festuca rubra* var.
  commutata
Chinese goddess bamboo *Bambusa*
  multiplex
Christ's tears *Coix lachryma-jobi*
cloud grass *Agrostis nebulosa*
clubrushes *Schoenoplectus*
common quaking grass *Briza media*
common reed *Phragmites australis*
compact brome *Bromus madritensis*
corkscrew rush *Juncus effusus* 'Spiralis'
corn *Zea mays*
cotton grass *Eriophorum* spp.
creeping soft grass *Holcus mollis*

crested dog's tail grass *Cynosurus cristatus*
crested hair grass *Koeleria macrantha*
crimson fountain grass
  Pennisetum setaceum 'Rubrum'
deer grass *Muhlenbergia rigens*
dropseed *Sporobolus* spp.
esparto grass *Stipa tenacissima*
Ethiopian fountain grass
  Pennisetum villosum
eulalia *Miscanthus sinensis*
European feather grass *Stipa tenuissima*
fairy grass *Deschampsia flexuosa*
feather grass *Stipa pennata*
feather grasses *Stipa* spp.
feather reed grass
  Calamagrostis × *acutiflora*
fern grass *Catapodium rigidum*
flame grass *Miscanthus oligostachyus*
  'Purpurascens'
forest blue grass *Poa chaixii*
fountain grass *Pennisetum alopecuroides*
fountain sedge *Carex dolichostachya*
fox-tail grass *Alopecurus pratensis*
fox-tail millet *Setaria macrostachya*
Fraser's sedge *Carex fraseri*
galingale *Cyperus longus*
giant fescue *Festuca gigantea*
giant reed *Arundo donax*
golden fox-tail grass *Alopecurus pratensis*
  'Aureovariegata'
golden goddess bamboo *Bambusa*
  glaucescens
golden Hakone grass *Hakonechloa macra*
  'Alboaurea' or 'Aureola'
golden toupee fescue *Festuca glauca*
  'Golden Toupee'
goldentop *Lamarckia aurea*
great millet *Sorghum nigrum, S. bicolor*
great weeping sedge *Carex pendula*
greater pond sedge *Carex riparia*
greater quaking grass *Briza maxima*
hair grass *Deschampsia caespitosa*
Hakone grass *Hakonechloa macra*
hard rush *Juncus inflexus*
hare's tail *Lagurus ovatus*
hog millet *Panicum miliaceum*
holy grass *Hierochloë odorata*
Hunangamolio grass *Chionochloa*
  conspicua
idiot grass *Oplismenus africanus*
Indian corn *Zea mays*
Indian grass *Sorghastrum nutans*
Indian rice *Zizania aquatica*
Japanese blood grass
  Imperata cylindrica 'Rubra'
Japanese muhly grass *Muhlenbergia*
  japonica 'Variegata'
Job's tears *Coix lachryma-jobi*

Korean feather reed grass
  Stipa (Calamagrostis) brachytricha
large quaking grass *Briza maxima*
lemon grass *Cymbopogon citratus*
lesser quaking grass *Briza media*
lesser reed mace *Typha minima*
little bluestem *Schizachyrium*
  scoparium
loose silky bent *Apera spica-venti*
lunatic grass *Poa imbecilla*
maiden grass *Miscanthus sinensis*
  'Gracillimus'
mana grass *Glyceria maxima*
Mauritian rope grass
  Ampelodesmos mauritanicus
meadow barley *Hordeum secalinum*
meadow fescue *Festuca pratensis*
meadow fountain grass
  Pennisetum incomptum
Morrow's sedge *Carex morrowii*
mosquito grass *Bouteloua gracilis*
muhly grass *Muhlenbergia* spp.
needle grass *Stipa* spp.
New Zealand blue meadow grass
  Poa colensoi
New Zealand blue sedge *Carex*
  trifida var. *chatamica*
New Zealand everbrown sedge
  Carex buchananii
New Zealand feather grass
  Stipa arundinacea
New Zealand hair sedge *Carex comans*
New Zealand pampas grass
  Cortaderia richardii
North American blue sedge *Carex glauca*
northern sea oats *Chasmanthium*
  latifolium
oriental fountain grass *Pennisetum*
  orientale
oriental hedge bamboo *Bambusa*
  glaucescens
palm grass *Setaria palmifolia*
palm-leaf sedge *Carex muskingumensis*
pampas grass *Cortaderia selloana*
panic grass *Panicum virgatum*
papyrus *Cyperus papyrus*
pendulous sedge *Carex pendula*
perennial quaking grass *Briza media*
perennial rye grass *Lolium perenne*
Petriei's brown sedge *Carex petriei*
pill sedge *Carex pilulifera*
plantain sedge *Carex plantaginea*
plumed tussock grass
  Chionochloa conspicua
prairie cord grass *Spartina pectinata*
Provençal reed *Arundo donax*
purple hog millet *Panicum miliaceum*
  'Violaceum'

purple millet *Panicum miliaceum* 'Violaceum'
purple moor grass *Molinia caerulea* ssp. *caerulea*
purple muhly *Muhlenbergia filipes*
purple top *Tridens flavus*
quaking grass *Briza* spp.
rabbit tail grass *Lagurus ovatus*
Ravenna grass *Saccharum ravennae*
red fescue *Festuca rubra* ssp. *rubra*
red New Zealand hook sedge *Uncinia rubra*
red-seeded switch grass *Panicum virgatum* 'Rubrum'
red tussock grass *Chionochloa rubra*
reed *Phragmites australis*
reed canary grass *Phalaris arundinacea*
reeds *Juncus* spp.
ribbon grass *Phalaris arundinacea*
rice grass *Oryzopsis* spp.

riparian sedge *Carex riparia*
rope grass *Ampelodesmos mauritanicus*
San Diego sedge *Carex spissa*
sand love grass *Eragrostis trichodes*
satintail *Imperata brevifolia*
sheep's fescue *Festuca ovina*
Siberian melic *Melica altissima*
side-oats grama *Bouteloua curtipendula*
silver bluestem *Andropogon saccaroides*
sleepy grass *Stipa robusta*
smilo grass *Oryzopsis miliaecea*
snow grasses *Chionochloa* spp.
snow tussock *Chionochloa rigida*
snowy woodrush *Luzula nivea*
soft rush *Juncus effusus*
soft velvet grass *Holcus mollis*
Spanish oat grass *Stipa gigantea*
spring moor grass *Sesleria heufleriana*
squirrel tail barley *Hordeum jubatum*
sugar cane *Saccharum officinarum*
sweet reed grass *Glyceria maxima*
sweet galingale *Cyperus longus*
sweet vernal grass *Anthoxanthum odoratum*

switch grass *Panicum virgatum*
tall blue sedge *Carex spissa*
tall fescue *Festuca arundinacea*
tall moor grass *Molinia caerulea* ssp. *arundinacea*
Timothy grass *Phleum pratense*
toe-toe *Cortaderia fulvida*
tufted hair grass *Deschampsia caespitosa*
umbrella plants *Cyperus* spp.
vanilla grass *Hierochloë odorata*
velvet bent grass *Agrostis canina*
wavy hair grass *Deschampsia flexuosa*
weeping sedge *Carex pendula*
wild rice *Zizania aquatica*
wood blue grass *Poa chaixii*
wood melic *Melica uniflora*
wood millet *Milium effusum*
woodrush *Luzula sylvatica*
yellow oat grass *Trisetum flavescens*
yellow sedge *Carex flava*
Yorkshire fog *Holcus lanatus*
zebra grass *Miscanthus sinensis* 'Zebrinus'

Golden Hakone grass rimed with frost in mid-winter.

Appendix III *A–Z of Ornamental Grasses*

Legend: LEAVES 🍃 PANICLES ✿

PLANT	PAGE	HEIGHT	SPREAD	Midwinter	Late winter	Early spring	Mid-spring	Late spring	Early summer	Midsummer	Late summer	Early autumn	Mid-autumn	Late autumn	Early winter	WARM/COOL	ZONES
Agrostis canina 'Silver Needles'	151	20cm (8in)	1m (3¼ft)					🍃	🍃✿	🍃✿	🍃✿	🍃	🍃			cool	Z5
A. nebulosa	149	35cm (14in)	35cm (14in)				🍃✿	🍃✿	🍃✿							annual	Z7
A. tenuis	106	70cm (2¼ft)	indefinite						🍃	🍃✿	🍃✿	🍃	🍃			cool	Z5
Aira elegantissima	80	25cm (10in)	25cm (10in)							🍃	🍃✿	🍃✿				annual	Z6
Alopecurus alpinus	150	30cm (12in)	45cm (18in)					🍃	🍃	🍃✿	🍃✿	🍃	🍃			cool	Z5
A. a. ssp. *glaucus*	36	20cm (8in)	30cm (12in)	🍃	🍃	🍃✿	🍃✿	✿	🍃	🍃	🍃	🍃				cool	Z5
A. lanatus	150	10cm (4in)	15cm (6in)					🍃	🍃✿	🍃	🍃	🍃	🍃			cool	Z5
A. pratensis 'Aureovariegatus'	24	30cm (12in)	indefinite			🍃	🍃	🍃✿	🍃✿	🍃✿	🍃					cool	Z4
A. p. 'Aureus'	25	30cm (12in)	indefinite			🍃	🍃	🍃✿	🍃✿	🍃✿	🍃					cool	Z4
Ampelodesmos mauritanicus	67	3m (9ft)	1.8m (6ft)	🍃✿	🍃	🍃		🍃✿	🍃✿	🍃✿	🍃✿	🍃✿	🍃✿	🍃✿	🍃✿	warm	Z8
Andropogon gerardii	69	1.2m (4ft)	60cm (2ft)	🍃✿	🍃✿				🍃		🍃	🍃✿	🍃✿	🍃✿	🍃✿	warm	Z4
A. saccharoides	69	90cm (3ft)	60cm (2ft)	🍃✿	🍃✿				🍃		🍃	🍃✿	🍃✿	🍃✿	🍃✿	warm	Z7
Anthoxanthum odoratum	77	60cm (2ft)	60cm (2ft)				🍃	🍃✿	🍃✿	🍃✿	🍃					cool	Z7
Apera spica-venti	109	1m (3¼ft)	75cm (2½ft)						🍃	🍃✿	🍃✿	🍃✿				annual	Z6
Arrhenatherum elatius bulbosum 'Variegatum'	20	30cm (12in)	30cm (12in)	🍃		🍃	🍃	🍃	🍃✿	🍃✿				🍃	🍃	cool	Z6
Arundinaria gigantea ssp. *tecta*	145	1.8m (6ft)	indefinite	🍃	🍃	🍃	🍃	🍃	🍃	🍃	🍃	🍃	🍃	🍃	🍃	cool	Z6
Arundo donax	29	4.5m (15ft)	indefinite						🍃	🍃	🍃	🍃				warm	Z7
A. d. 'Macrophylla'	115	4.5m (15ft)	indefinite						🍃	🍃	🍃	🍃				warm	Z8
A. d. 'Variegata'	115	2.4m (8ft)	indefinite						🍃	🍃	🍃	🍃	🍃			warm	Z8
A. formosana	34	2.1m (7ft)	1.8m (6ft)	✿	✿			🍃	🍃	🍃	🍃	🍃✿	🍃✿	✿	✿	warm	Z7
A. f. 'Golden Showers'	34	1.8m (6ft)	2.8m (9ft)	✿	✿			🍃	🍃	🍃	🍃	🍃✿	🍃✿	✿	✿	warm	Z7
A. pliniana	117	1.8m (6ft)	indefinite	🍃				🍃	🍃	🍃✿	🍃✿	🍃✿	🍃			warm	Z7
Avena sterilis	81	90cm (3ft)	25cm (10in)						🍃	🍃✿	🍃✿	🍃				annual	Z5
Bambusa glaucescens (syn. *multiplex*)	156	90cm (3ft)	90cm (3ft)	🍃	🍃	🍃	🍃	🍃	🍃	🍃	🍃	🍃	🍃	🍃	🍃	warm	Z9
B. g. 'Alphonse Karr'	156	90cm (3ft)	90cm (3ft)	🍃	🍃	🍃	🍃	🍃	🍃	🍃	🍃	🍃	🍃	🍃	🍃	warm	Z9
Bothriochloa bladhii	76	60cm (2ft)	1m (3¼ft)	🍃✿	🍃				🍃	🍃	🍃✿	🍃✿	🍃✿	🍃✿	🍃✿	cool	Z7
Bouteloua curtipendula	68	80cm (2¾ft)	60cm (2ft)						🍃	🍃	🍃✿	🍃✿	✿			warm	Z6
B. gracilis	68	30cm (12in)	60cm (2ft)						🍃	🍃✿	🍃✿	🍃✿	🍃			warm	Z5
Brachypodium sylvaticum	124	1.2m (4ft)	1m (3¼ft)						🍃	🍃✿	🍃✿	🍃				cool	Z5
Briza maxima	79	30cm (12in)	23cm (9in)	🍃	🍃	🍃	🍃	🍃	🍃✿	🍃	🍃	🍃	🍃	🍃		annual	Z5
B. m. 'Rhodes Form'	79	23cm (9in)	23cm (9in)	🍃	🍃	🍃	🍃	🍃✿	🍃✿	🍃✿	🍃	🍃	🍃			annual	Z5
B. media	123	60cm (2ft)	60cm (2ft)	🍃	🍃	🍃	🍃	🍃	🍃✿	🍃✿	🍃✿	🍃	🍃	🍃		cool	Z5
B. m. 'Limouzi'	90	70cm (2¼ft)	60 cm (2ft)	🍃	🍃	🍃	🍃	🍃✿	🍃✿	🍃✿	🍃	🍃	🍃			cool	Z5
B. minor	79	23cm (9in)	15cm (6in)			🍃	🍃	🍃	🍃✿	🍃✿						annual	Z5
Bromus arvensis	109	90cm (3ft)	60cm (2ft)						🍃	🍃	🍃✿	🍃✿	🍃✿			annual	Z5
B. inermis 'Skinner's Gold'	34	60cm (2ft)	1m (3¼ft)						🍃		🍃	🍃				cool	Z7
B. macrostachys	109	50cm (20in)	50cm (20in)						🍃	🍃✿	🍃✿	🍃✿				annual	Z5
B. madritensis	81	60cm (2ft)	15cm (6in)				🍃✿	🍃✿	🍃✿	🍃						annual	Z5
B. ramosus	124	1.2m (4ft)	1m (3¼ft)						🍃	🍃✿	🍃✿	🍃✿				cool	Z5
Calamagrostis × *acutiflora* 'Karl Foerster'	50	1.5m (5ft)	1m (3¼ft)	✿	✿				🍃✿	🍃✿	🍃✿	🍃✿	🍃✿	✿	✿	cool	Z4
C. × *a.* 'Overdam'	22	1m (3¼ft)	1m (3¼ft)						🍃	🍃✿	🍃✿	🍃✿	🍃✿			cool	Z4
C. × *a.* 'Stricta'	50	125cm (4ft)	1m (3¼ft)	✿	✿				🍃✿	🍃✿	🍃✿	🍃✿	🍃✿	✿	✿	cool	Z4
Carex albida	41	30cm (12in)	45cm (18in)	🍃	🍃	🍃	🍃	🍃✿	🍃✿	🍃	🍃	🍃	🍃	🍃		cool	Z7
C. berggrenii	44	9cm (23in)	23cm (9in)	🍃	🍃	🍃	🍃	🍃✿	🍃✿	🍃✿	🍃✿	🍃	🍃	🍃		cool	Z7
C. boottiana	125	90cm (3ft)	1m (3¼ft)	🍃	🍃	🍃	🍃	🍃✿	🍃✿	🍃	🍃	🍃	🍃	🍃		cool	Z5
C. brunnea 'Variegata'	156	23cm (9in)	30cm (12in)	🍃	🍃	🍃	🍃	🍃	🍃✿	🍃✿	🍃	🍃	🍃			warm	Z8

PLANT	PAGE	HEIGHT	SPREAD	Midwinter	Late winter	Early spring	Mid-spring	Late spring	Early summer	Midsummer	Late summer	Early autumn	Mid-autumn	Late autumn	Early winter	WARM/COOL	ZONES
C. buchananii	43	60cm (2ft)	60cm (2ft)	🌿	🌿	🌿	🌿	🌿✿	🌿✿	🌿✿	🌿✿	🌿✿	🌿✿	🌿	🌿	cool	Z7
C. b. 'Viridis'	137	60cm (2ft)	60cm (2ft)	🌿				🌿	🌿✿	🌿✿	🌿	🌿	🌿	🌿	🌿	cool	Z7
C. caryophyllea 'The Beatles'	45	30cm (12in)	90cm (3ft)	🌿	🌿	🌿	🌿	🌿✿	🌿✿	🌿✿	🌿	🌿	🌿	🌿	🌿	cool	Z7
C. comans	41	60cm (2ft)	1.2m (4ft)	🌿✿	🌿✿	🌿	🌿	🌿	🌿✿	🌿✿	🌿✿	🌿✿	🌿✿	🌿✿	🌿✿	cool	Z7
C. c. 'Bronze Form'	44	30cm (12in)	75cm (2½ft)	🌿	🌿	🌿	🌿✿	🌿✿	🌿✿	🌿✿	🌿✿	🌿✿	🌿✿	🌿		cool	Z7
C. c. 'Frosted Curls'	41	45cm (18in)	1m (3¼ft)	🌿✿	🌿✿	🌿	🌿	🌿	🌿✿	🌿✿	🌿✿	🌿✿	🌿✿	🌿✿	🌿✿	cool	Z7
C. conica 'Snowline'	41	15cm (6in)	30cm (12in)	🌿	🌿	🌿	🌿	🌿✿	🌿✿	🌿	🌿	🌿	🌿	🌿	🌿	cool	Z7
C. dipsacea	45	45cm (18in)	45cm (18in)	🌿	🌿	🌿	🌿	🌿	🌿✿	🌿✿	🌿✿	🌿✿	🌿	🌿		cool	Z7
C. dolichostachya 'Kaga-nishiki'	42	25cm (10in)	38cm (15in)	🌿			🌿	🌿✿	🌿✿	🌿✿	🌿✿	🌿	🌿	🌿	🌿	cool	Z7
C. elata	114	1m (3¼ft)	1m (3¼ft)			🌿	🌿	🌿✿	🌿✿	🌿✿	🌿✿					cool	Z7
C. e. 'Aurea'	118	75cm (2½ft)	90cm (3ft)				🌿✿	🌿✿	🌿✿	🌿	🌿					cool	Z7
C. e. 'Knightshayes'	118	75cm (2½ft)	90cm (3ft)				🌿✿	🌿✿	🌿✿	🌿	🌿					cool	Z7
C. e. 'Sue Ward'	118	75cm (2½ft)	90cm (3ft)				🌿✿	🌿✿	🌿✿	🌿						cool	Z7
Carex 'Everbright'	42	45cm (18in)	60cm (2ft)	🌿	🌿	🌿	🌿	🌿	🌿	🌿	🌿	🌿	🌿	🌿	🌿	cool	Z5
C. 'Evergold'	42	45cm (18in)	60cm (2ft)	🌿	🌿	🌿	🌿	🌿	🌿	🌿	🌿	🌿	🌿	🌿	🌿	cool	Z5
C. firma	151	20cm (8in)	30cm (12in)	🌿	🌿	🌿	🌿	🌿✿	🌿✿	🌿✿	🌿✿	🌿	🌿	🌿	🌿	cool	Z7
C. f. 'Variegata'	151	15cm (6in)	25cm (10in)	🌿	🌿	🌿	🌿	🌿✿	🌿✿	🌿✿	🌿✿	🌿	🌿	🌿	🌿	cool	Z7
C. flacca	43	30cm (12in)	indefinite	🌿	🌿	🌿	🌿	🌿✿	🌿✿	🌿	🌿	🌿	🌿	🌿	🌿	cool	Z5
C. f. 'Bias'	43	30cm (12in)	indefinite	🌿	🌿	🌿	🌿	🌿✿	🌿✿	🌿	🌿	🌿	🌿	🌿	🌿	cool	Z7
C. flaccosperma	42	30cm (12in)	30cm (12in)	🌿	🌿	🌿	🌿	🌿✿	🌿✿	🌿✿	🌿✿	🌿	🌿	🌿	🌿	cool	Z7
C. flagellifera	44	45cm (18in)	1m (3¼ft)	🌿	🌿	🌿	🌿	🌿✿	🌿✿	🌿✿	🌿✿	🌿✿	🌿	🌿	🌿	cool	Z7
C. flava	42	38cm (15in)	60cm (2ft)				🌿	🌿✿	🌿✿	🌿✿	🌿	🌿				cool	Z7
C. fraseri	126	35cm (14in)	60cm (2ft)	🌿	🌿	🌿	🌿	🌿✿	🌿	🌿	🌿	🌿	🌿	🌿	🌿	cool	Z7
C. forsteri	45	90cm (3ft)	1.2m (4ft)	🌿	🌿	🌿	🌿	🌿✿	🌿✿	🌿	🌿	🌿	🌿	🌿	🌿	cool	Z7
C. glauca	42	23cm (9in)	60cm (2ft)	🌿	🌿	🌿	🌿	🌿✿	🌿✿	🌿	🌿	🌿	🌿	🌿	🌿	cool	Z6
C. hispida	45	90cm (3ft)	90cm (3ft)	🌿	🌿	🌿	🌿	🌿✿	🌿✿	🌿	🌿	🌿	🌿	🌿	🌿	cool	Z7
C. 'Ice Dance'	41	60cm (2ft)	1m (3¼ft)	🌿	🌿	🌿	🌿✿	🌿✿	🌿✿	🌿	🌿	🌿	🌿	🌿	🌿	cool	Z7
C. morrowii 'Fisher's Form'	41	75cm (2½ft)	1m (3¼ft)	🌿	🌿	🌿	🌿✿	🌿✿	🌿✿	🌿	🌿	🌿	🌿	🌿	🌿	cool	Z8
C. m. 'Gilt'	41	75cm (2½ft)	1m (3¼ft)	🌿	🌿	🌿	🌿✿	🌿✿	🌿✿	🌿	🌿	🌿	🌿	🌿	🌿	cool	Z8
C. m. 'Variegata'	41	60cm (2ft)	75cm (2½ft)	🌿	🌿	🌿	🌿✿	🌿✿	🌿✿	🌿	🌿	🌿	🌿	🌿	🌿		Z8
C. muskingumensis	125	60cm (2ft)	1m (3¼ft)				🌿	🌿	🌿	🌿✿	🌿✿	🌿✿	🌿	🌿		cool	Z7
C. m. 'Little Midge'	125	15cm (6in)	60cm (2ft)				🌿	🌿	🌿	🌿✿	🌿✿	🌿✿	🌿	🌿		cool	Z7
C. m. 'Oehme'	125	60cm (2ft)	1m (3¼ft)				🌿	🌿	🌿	🌿✿	🌿✿	🌿✿	🌿	🌿		cool	Z7
C. m. 'Wachtposten'	125	75cm (2½ft)	1m (3¼ft)				🌿	🌿	🌿	🌿✿	🌿✿	🌿✿	🌿	🌿		cool	Z7
C. nigra 'Variegata'	42	30cm (12in)	indefinite				🌿	🌿	🌿✿	🌿✿	🌿✿	🌿	🌿			cool	Z5
C. ornithopoda 'Variegata'	41	15cm (6in)	30cm (12in)				🌿	🌿✿	🌿✿	🌿	🌿	🌿	🌿	🌿		cool	Z7
C. oshimensis 'Variegata'	40	25cm (10in)	45cm (18in)	🌿	🌿	🌿	🌿✿	🌿✿	🌿✿	🌿	🌿	🌿	🌿	🌿	🌿	cool	Z6
C. panicea	43	23cm (9in)	indefinite	🌿	🌿	🌿	🌿	🌿✿	🌿✿	🌿	🌿	🌿	🌿	🌿	🌿	cool	Z7
C. pendula	125	90cm (3ft)	1m (3¼ft)	🌿	🌿	🌿	🌿	🌿✿	🌿✿	🌿✿	🌿✿	🌿✿	🌿✿	🌿	🌿	cool	Z8
C. p. 'Moonraker'	42	75cm (2½ft)	1m (3¼ft)	🌿	🌿	🌿	🌿	🌿✿	🌿✿	🌿✿	🌿	🌿	🌿	🌿	🌿	cool	Z8
C. petriei	43	30cm (12in)	30cm (12in)	🌿	🌿	🌿	🌿	🌿✿	🌿✿	🌿✿	🌿	🌿	🌿	🌿	🌿	cool	Z7
C. p. 'Sparkler'	155	30cm (12in)	60cm (2ft)	🌿	🌿		🌿	🌿	🌿✿	🌿✿	🌿✿	🌿	🌿	🌿	🌿	warm	Z8
C. pilulifera 'Tinney's Princess'	41	10cm (4in)	15cm (6in)	🌿			🌿	🌿✿	🌿✿	🌿✿	🌿	🌿	🌿	🌿	🌿	cool	Z6
C. plantaginea	125	20cm (8in)	60cm (2ft)	🌿	🌿	🌿	🌿✿	🌿✿	🌿	🌿	🌿	🌿	🌿	🌿		cool	Z7
C. riparia	113	1.5m (5ft)	indefinite				🌿✿	🌿✿	🌿✿	🌿	🌿	🌿				cool	Z6
C. r. 'Aurea'	118	60cm (2ft)	indefinite			🌿	🌿✿	🌿✿	🌿✿	🌿	🌿					cool	Z6
C. r. 'Variegata'	118	60cm (2ft)	indefinite			🌿	🌿✿	🌿✿	🌿✿	🌿	🌿					cool	Z6
C. saxatilis 'Ski Run'	41	7.5cm (3in)	1m (3¼ft)				🌿✿	🌿✿	🌿	🌿	🌿					cool	Z5
C. secta	118	1m (3¼ft)	1m (3¼ft)	🌿	🌿	🌿	🌿✿	🌿✿	🌿✿	🌿	🌿	🌿	🌿	🌿	🌿	cool	Z7
C. s. var. tenuiculmis	44	75cm (2½ft)	1m (3¼ft)	🌿	🌿	🌿	🌿✿	🌿✿	🌿✿	🌿	🌿	🌿	🌿	🌿	🌿	cool	Z7
C. siderosticha	125	30cm (12in)	60cm (2ft)			🌿	🌿✿	🌿✿	🌿✿	🌿	🌿	🌿				cool	Z7
C. s. 'Variegata'	41	30cm (12in)	60cm (2ft)			🌿	🌿✿	🌿✿	🌿✿	🌿	🌿	🌿				cool	Z7
C. 'Silver Sceptre'	41	45cm (18in)	1m (3¼ft)	🌿			🌿	🌿✿	🌿✿	🌿	🌿	🌿	🌿	🌿	🌿	cool	Z6
C. 'Small Red'	43	60cm (12in)	45cm (18in)	🌿✿	🌿	🌿	🌿	🌿✿	🌿✿	🌿✿	🌿✿	🌿✿	🌿✿	🌿✿	🌿✿	cool	Z7

LEAVES 🌿   PANICLES ✿

PLANT	PAGE	HEIGHT	SPREAD	Midwinter	Late winter	Early spring	Mid-spring	Late spring	Early summer	Midsummer	Late summer	Early autumn	Mid-autumn	Late autumn	Early winter	WARM/COOL	ZONES
C. spissa	43	70cm (28in)	60cm (2ft)	🍃	🍃	🍃	🍃✾	🍃✾	🍃✾	🍃	🍃	🍃	🍃	🍃	🍃	cool	Z7
C. 'Silk Tassel'	41	60cm (12in)	60cm (12in)	🍃	🍃	🍃	🍃	🍃✾	🍃✾	🍃✾	🍃	🍃	🍃	🍃	🍃	cool	Z7
C. testacea	45	45cm (18in)	45cm (18in)	🍃	🍃	🍃	🍃	🍃✾	🍃✾	🍃✾	🍃✾	🍃	🍃	🍃	🍃	cool	Z7
C. texensis	45	23cm (9in)	90cm (3ft)	🍃	🍃	🍃	🍃	🍃✾	🍃✾	🍃✾	🍃✾	🍃	🍃	🍃	🍃	cool	Z7
C. trifida	125	90cm (3ft)	1m (3¼ft)	🍃	🍃	🍃	🍃	🍃✾	🍃✾	🍃✾	🍃✾	🍃	🍃	🍃	🍃	cool	Z7
C. t. var. chatamica	43	60cm (2ft)	1m (3¼ft)	🍃	🍃	🍃	🍃	🍃✾	🍃	🍃	🍃	🍃	🍃	🍃	🍃	cool	Z7
C. ulophylla	151	10cm (4in)	15cm (6in)	🍃	🍃	🍃	🍃	🍃	🍃✾	🍃✾	🍃	🍃	🍃	🍃	🍃	cool	Z7
C. uncifolia	45	23cm (9in)	30cm (12in)	🍃	🍃	🍃	🍃	🍃	🍃✾	🍃✾	🍃	🍃	🍃	🍃	🍃	cool	Z7
Catapodium rigidum	81	25cm (10in)	23cm (9in)							🍃	🍃✾	🍃✾				annual	Z5
Chasmanthium latifolium	123	60cm (2ft)	30cm (12in)	✾	✾				🍃	🍃	🍃	🍃✾	🍃✾	✾	✾	cool	Z6
Chimonobambusa marmorea	140	1.5m (5ft)	indefinite	🍃	🍃	🍃	🍃	🍃	🍃	🍃	🍃	🍃	🍃	🍃	🍃	cool	Z6
Chionochloa conspicua	135	1.8m (6ft)	1.2m (4ft)	🍃	🍃	🍃	🍃	🍃	🍃✾	🍃✾	🍃✾	🍃✾	🍃	🍃	🍃	warm	Z7
C. cunninghamii	135	1.8m (6ft)	1.2m (4ft)	🍃	🍃	🍃	🍃	🍃	🍃✾	🍃✾	🍃✾	🍃✾	🍃	🍃	🍃	warm	Z7
C. flavescens	137	90cm (3ft)	90cm (3ft)	🍃	🍃	🍃	🍃	🍃	🍃	🍃	🍃	🍃	🍃✾	🍃✾	🍃✾	warm	Z6
C. flavicans	137	90cm (3ft)	90cm (3ft)	🍃	🍃	🍃	🍃	🍃	🍃	🍃	🍃	🍃	🍃✾	🍃✾	🍃✾	warm	Z7
C. rigida	137	90cm (3ft)	90cm (3ft)	🍃	🍃	🍃	🍃	🍃	🍃	🍃	🍃	🍃	🍃✾	🍃✾	🍃✾	warm	Z7
C. rubra	137	1m (3¼ft)	1m (3¼ft)	🍃	🍃	🍃	🍃	🍃	🍃	🍃	🍃	🍃	🍃	🍃	🍃	warm	Z7
Chrysopogon gryllus	76	1.2m (4ft)	75cm (2½ft)	✾	✾				🍃	🍃	🍃	🍃✾	🍃	🍃✾	🍃✾	cool	Z7
Chusquea culeou	141	6m (20ft)	1.8m (6ft)	🍃	🍃	🍃	🍃	🍃	🍃	🍃	🍃	🍃	🍃	🍃	🍃	cool	Z7
Coix lacryma-jobi	81	60cm (2ft)	60cm (2ft)						🍃	🍃	🍃	🍃✾	🍃✾			annual	Z9
Cortaderia fulvida	66	2.4m (8ft)	1.8m (6ft)	🍃✾	🍃✾	🍃	🍃	🍃	🍃✾	🍃✾	🍃✾	🍃✾	🍃✾	🍃✾	🍃✾	warm	Z8
C. patagonica	65						new species: no data available										
C. richardii	135	3m (10ft)	3m (10ft)	🍃	🍃	🍃	🍃	🍃✾	🍃✾	🍃✾	🍃✾	🍃✾	🍃	🍃	🍃	warm	Z8
C. selloana	119	3m (10ft)	2.4m (8ft)							🍃	🍃	🍃	🍃✾	🍃✾		warm	Z5
C. s. 'Albolineata'	23	1.2m (4ft)	1.2m (4ft)							🍃	🍃	🍃	🍃✾	🍃✾		warm	Z5
C. s. 'Carminea Rendatleri'	65	3m (10ft)	1.8m (6ft)	✾	✾				🍃	🍃	🍃	🍃	🍃✾	🍃✾		warm	Z5
C. s. 'Carnea'	65	2.4m (8ft)	1.8m (6ft)	✾	✾				🍃	🍃	🍃	🍃	🍃✾	🍃✾		warm	Z5
C. s. 'Gold Band'	26	3m (10ft)	2.4m (8ft)							🍃	🍃	🍃	🍃✾	🍃✾			Z5
C. s. 'Monstrosa'	65	3m (10ft)	1.8m (6ft)	✾	✾				🍃	🍃	🍃	🍃	🍃✾	🍃✾		warm	Z5
C. s. 'Pumila'	65	1.5m (5ft)	1.5m (5ft)	✾	✾				🍃	🍃	🍃	🍃✾	🍃✾	🍃✾		warm	Z5
C. s. 'Roi des Roses'	65	2.4m (8ft)	1.5m (5ft)	✾	✾				🍃	🍃	🍃	🍃	🍃✾	🍃✾			Z5
C. s. 'Rosea'	65	2.4m (8ft)	1.5m (5ft)	✾	✾				🍃	🍃	🍃	🍃	🍃✾	🍃✾			Z5
C. s. 'Silver Beacon'	23	2.4m (8ft)	2.4m (8ft)							🍃	🍃	🍃	🍃✾	🍃✾		warm	Z5
C. s. 'Silver Fountain'	23	2.4m (8ft)	2.4m (8ft)							🍃	🍃	🍃	🍃✾	🍃✾		warm	Z5
C. s. 'Silver Stripe'	46	1.2m (4ft)	1.2m (4ft)							🍃	🍃	🍃	🍃✾	🍃✾		warm	Z5
C. s. 'Sunningdale Silver'	65	3m (10ft)	1.5m (5ft)	✾	✾				🍃	🍃	🍃	🍃	🍃✾	🍃✾		warm	Z5
C. s. 'Violacea'	65	2.4m (8ft)	1.5m (5ft)	✾	✾				🍃	🍃	🍃	🍃	🍃✾	🍃✾		warm	Z5
C. uspellata	65		new species: no data available														
Cymbopogon citratus	149	1.5m (5ft)	1.2m (4ft)	🍃	🍃	🍃	🍃	🍃	🍃	🍃	🍃	🍃	🍃	🍃	🍃	warm	Z9
Cynosurus cristata	106	75cm (2½ft)	60cm (2ft)					🍃	🍃	🍃✾	🍃✾	🍃✾	🍃	🍃	🍃	cool	Z7
C. echinatus	109	1m (3¼ft)	60cm (2ft)						🍃✾	🍃✾	🍃✾	🍃				annual	Z7
Cyperus albostriatus	154	60cm (2ft)	1m (3¼ft)					🍃	🍃	🍃	🍃✾	🍃✾	🍃✾	🍃		warm	Z9
C. eragrostis	119	90cm (3ft)	75cm (2½ft)					🍃	🍃✾	🍃✾	🍃✾	🍃✾	🍃✾	🍃		cool	Z8
C. fuscus	119	30cm (12in)	30cm (12in)					🍃	🍃✾	🍃✾	🍃✾	🍃				annual	Z7
C. involucratus	154	1m (3¼ft)	1m (3¼ft)	🍃	🍃		🍃	🍃	🍃✾	🍃✾	🍃✾	🍃	🍃	🍃		warm	Z10
C. i. 'Variegatus'	154	90cm (3ft)	90cm (3ft)	🍃	🍃		🍃	🍃	🍃✾	🍃✾	🍃✾	🍃	🍃	🍃		warm	Z10
C. longus	113	90cm (3ft)	90cm (3ft)					🍃	🍃	🍃✾	🍃✾	🍃✾	🍃✾	🍃		cool	Z7
C. papyrus	139	3.6m (12ft)	1.2m (4ft)					🍃	🍃	🍃	🍃✾	🍃✾	🍃			warm	Z9
C. p. 'Mexico'	139	3.6m (12ft)	1.2m (4ft)					🍃	🍃	🍃	🍃✾	🍃✾	🍃			warm	Z9
C. ustulatus	119	1.8m (6ft)	1.2m (4ft)	✾	✾			🍃	🍃	🍃	🍃✾	🍃✾	🍃✾	🍃✾		warm	Z8
Dactylis glomeratus 'Variegatus'	31	30cm (12in)	30cm (12in)					🍃	🍃✾	🍃✾	🍃	🍃				cool	Z5
Deschampsia caespitosa	54	90cm (3ft)	75cm (2½ft)	🍃✾	🍃✾	🍃	🍃✾	🍃✾	🍃✾	🍃✾	🍃✾	🍃✾	🍃✾	🍃✾	🍃✾	cool	Z4
D. c. 'Bronzeschleier'	54	90cm (3ft)	75cm (2½ft)	🍃✾	🍃✾	🍃	🍃✾	🍃✾	🍃✾	🍃✾	🍃✾	🍃✾	🍃✾	🍃✾	🍃✾	cool	Z4
D. c. 'Fairy's Joke'	55	1m (3¼ft)	1m (3¼ft)	🍃✾	🍃✾	🍃	🍃	🍃✾	🍃✾	🍃✾	🍃✾	🍃✾	🍃✾	🍃✾	🍃✾	cool	Z4
D. c. 'Goldgehänge'	54	1.2m (4ft)	1m (3¼ft)	🍃✾	🍃✾	🍃	🍃	🍃✾	🍃✾	🍃✾	🍃✾	🍃✾	🍃✾	🍃✾	🍃✾	cool	Z4

LEAVES 🍃   PANICLES ✾

PLANT	PAGE	HEIGHT	SPREAD	Midwinter	Late winter	Early spring	Mid-spring	Late spring	Early summer	Midsummer	Late summer	Early autumn	Mid-autumn	Late autumn	Early winter	WARM/ COOL	ZONES
D. c. 'Goldschleier'	54	1.2m (4ft)	1m (3ft)	🌿❀	🌿❀	🌿	🌿	🌿	🌿❀	🌿❀	🌿❀	🌿❀	🌿❀	🌿❀	🌿❀	cool	Z4
D. c. 'Goldstaub'	55	90cm (3ft)	75cm (2½ft)	🌿❀	🌿❀	🌿	🌿	🌿❀	🌿❀	🌿❀	🌿❀	🌿❀	🌿❀	🌿❀	🌿❀	cool	Z4
D. c. 'Goldtau'	55	90cm (3ft)	75cm (2½ft)	🌿❀	🌿❀	🌿	🌿	🌿	🌿❀	🌿❀	🌿❀	🌿❀	🌿❀	🌿❀	🌿❀	cool	Z4
D. c. 'Ladywood Gold'	34	90cm (3ft)	90cm (3ft)	🌿❀	🌿	🌿	🌿	🌿	🌿	🌿❀	🌿❀	🌿❀	🌿❀	🌿❀	🌿❀	cool	Z4
D. c. 'Northern Lights'	37	90cm (3ft)	90cm (3ft)	🌿❀	🌿	🌿	🌿	🌿	🌿	🌿❀	🌿❀	🌿❀	🌿❀	🌿❀	🌿❀	cool	Z4
D. c. 'Schottland'	55	90cm (3ft)	90cm (3ft)	🌿❀	🌿❀	🌿	🌿	🌿	🌿❀	🌿❀	🌿❀	🌿❀	🌿❀	🌿❀	🌿❀	cool	Z4
D. c. 'Tardiflora'	55	90cm (3ft)	90cm (3ft)	🌿❀	🌿❀	🌿	🌿	🌿	🌿	🌿❀	🌿❀	🌿❀	🌿❀	🌿❀	🌿❀	cool	Z4
D. c. 'Tautraeger'	55	60cm (2ft)	60cm (2ft)	🌿❀	🌿❀	🌿	🌿	🌿	🌿	🌿❀	🌿❀	🌿❀	🌿❀	🌿❀	🌿❀	cool	Z4
D. c. 'Waldschatt'	55	90cm (3ft)	60cm (2ft)	🌿❀	🌿❀	🌿	🌿	🌿	🌿❀	🌿❀	🌿❀	🌿❀	🌿❀	🌿❀	🌿❀	cool	Z4
D. c. var. *parviflora*	55	80cm (31in)	60cm (2ft)	🌿❀	🌿❀	🌿	🌿	🌿	🌿❀	🌿❀	🌿❀	🌿❀	🌿❀	🌿❀	🌿❀	cool	Z4
D. flexuosa	55	75cm (2½ft)	60cm (2ft)	🌿	🌿	🌿	🌿	🌿❀	🌿❀	🌿❀	🌿	🌿	🌿	🌿	🌿	cool	Z4
D. f. 'Tatra Gold'	32	15cm (6in)	15cm (6in)	🌿	🌿		🌿	🌿	🌿❀	🌿❀	🌿	🌿	🌿	🌿	🌿	cool	Z4
D. media	55	90cm (3ft)	90cm (3ft)	🌿❀	🌿❀	🌿	🌿	🌿	🌿❀	🌿❀	🌿❀	🌿❀	🌿❀	🌿❀	🌿❀	cool	Z4
D. setacea	55	45cm (18in)	30cm (12in)	🌿	🌿	🌿	🌿	🌿❀	🌿❀	🌿❀	🌿	🌿	🌿	🌿	🌿	cool	Z4
D. wibelliana	55	30cm (12in)	30cm (12in)				🌿❀	🌿❀	🌿❀	🌿❀	🌿	🌿				cool	Z4
Dichromena nervosa	155	45cm (18in)	30cm (12in)	🌿❀	❀	❀	❀	🌿❀	🌿❀	🌿❀	🌿❀	🌿❀	🌿❀	🌿❀	🌿❀	warm	Z8
Echinochloa crus-galli	109	80cm (2¾ft)	60cm (2ft)						🌿	🌿	🌿❀	🌿❀	🌿❀			annual	Z6
Eleusine indica	109	75cm (2½ft)	60cm (2ft)					🌿	🌿	🌿❀	🌿❀	🌿❀	🌿❀			annual	Z9
Elymus hispidus	28	60cm (2ft)	60cm (2ft)					🌿	🌿❀	🌿❀	🌿❀	🌿❀	🌿❀			cool	Z5
E. magellanicus	28	15cm (6in)	45cm (18in)					🌿	🌿❀	🌿❀	🌿❀	🌿❀	🌿❀			cool	Z5
Eragrostis chloromelas	69	1.2m (4ft)	1.2m (4ft)	❀	❀			🌿	🌿	🌿❀	🌿❀	🌿❀	🌿❀	🌿❀	🌿❀	warm	Z9
E. curvula	68	90cm (3ft)	1.2m (4ft)	❀	❀			🌿	🌿	🌿❀	🌿❀	🌿❀	🌿❀	🌿❀	🌿❀	warm	Z7
E. trichodes	69	90cm (3ft)	90cm (3ft)	❀	❀			🌿	🌿	🌿	🌿	🌿❀	🌿❀	🌿❀	🌿❀	cool	Z7
E. t. 'Bend'	69	90cm (3ft)	90cm (3ft)	❀	❀			🌿	🌿	🌿	🌿	🌿❀	🌿❀	🌿❀	🌿❀	cool	Z7
Erianthus ravennae	109	1.8m (6ft)	1.8m (6ft)	❀	❀			🌿	🌿	🌿	🌿	🌿	🌿❀	🌿❀	🌿❀	warm	Z7
Festuca arundinacea	111	1.8m (6ft)	1.2m (4ft)					🌿	🌿❀	🌿❀	🌿❀	🌿	🌿	🌿		cool	Z5
F. californica	35	30cm (12in)	60cm (2ft)					🌿	🌿❀	🌿❀	🌿	🌿	🌿	🌿	🌿	warm	Z8
F. dalmatica	27	30cm (12in)	60cm (2ft)				🌿	🌿❀	🌿❀	🌿	🌿	🌿	🌿	🌿		cool	Z5
F. eskia	151	15cm (6in)	15cm (6in)				🌿	🌿	🌿❀	🌿❀	🌿❀	🌿				cool	Z5
F. gautieri 'Pic Carlit'	151	10cm (4in)	15cm (6in)				🌿	🌿❀	🌿❀	🌿❀	🌿	🌿				cool	Z5
F. gigantea	124	1.5m (5ft)	1m (3¼ft)					🌿	🌿	🌿❀	🌿❀	🌿❀	🌿			cool	Z5
F. glacialis	150	7.5cm (3in)	30cm (12in)				🌿	🌿❀	🌿❀	🌿	🌿	🌿	🌿			cool	Z3
F. glauca	27	30cm (12in)	60cm (2ft)				🌿	🌿❀	🌿❀	🌿	🌿	🌿	🌿			cool	Z5
F. g. 'Azurit'	27	30cm (12in)	60cm (2ft)				🌿	🌿❀	🌿❀	🌿	🌿	🌿	🌿	🌿		cool	Z5
F. g. 'Caesia'	27	15cm (6in)	30cm (12in)				🌿	🌿❀	🌿❀	🌿	🌿	🌿	🌿	🌿		cool	Z5
F. g. 'Elijah Blue'	27	23cm (9in)	45cm (18in)				🌿	🌿❀	🌿❀	🌿	🌿	🌿	🌿	🌿		cool	Z5
F. g. 'Golden Toupee'	25	23cm (9in)	23cm (9in)				🌿	🌿❀	🌿❀	🌿❀	🌿	🌿				cool	Z5
F. g. 'Harz'	27	23cm (9in)	45cm (18in)				🌿	🌿❀	🌿❀	🌿	🌿	🌿	🌿	🌿		cool	Z5
F. g. 'Meerblau'	27	30cm (12in)	60cm (2ft)				🌿	🌿❀	🌿❀	🌿	🌿	🌿	🌿	🌿		cool	Z5
F. g. minima	27	10cm (4in)	20cm (8in)				🌿	🌿❀	🌿❀	🌿	🌿	🌿	🌿	🌿		cool	Z5
F. heterophylla	114	1m (3¼ft)	75cm (2½ft)					🌿	🌿❀	🌿❀	🌿	🌿				cool	Z5
F. longifolia	35	60cm (2ft)	1m (3¼ft)					🌿	🌿❀	🌿❀	🌿	🌿	🌿	🌿	🌿	warm	Z5
F. mairei	102	41cm (16in)	1m (3¼ft)	🌿	🌿	🌿	🌿	🌿❀	🌿❀	🌿	🌿	🌿	🌿	🌿	🌿	cool	Z5
F. ovina	106	60cm (2ft)	60cm (2ft)				🌿	🌿	🌿	🌿	🌿	🌿	🌿	🌿		cool	Z5
F. o. ssp. *coxii*	27	23cm (9in)	45cm (18in)				🌿	🌿	🌿	🌿	🌿	🌿	🌿	🌿	❀	cool	Z5
F. o. 'Vivipara'	15	25cm (10in)	60cm (2ft)				🌿	🌿	🌿❀	🌿❀	🌿❀	🌿	🌿	🌿	❀	cool	Z5
F. pratensis	114	1m (3¼ft)	1m (3¼ft)					🌿	🌿❀	🌿❀	🌿❀	🌿				Z5	
F. punctoria	34	12.5cm (5in)	45cm (18in)	🌿❀	🌿❀	🌿❀	🌿❀	🌿❀	🌿❀	🌿❀	🌿❀	🌿❀	🌿❀	🌿❀	🌿❀	warm	Z5
F. rubra var. *commutara*	106	60cm (2ft)	90cm (3ft)	🌿❀	🌿❀	🌿❀	🌿❀	🌿❀	🌿❀	🌿❀	🌿❀	🌿❀	🌿❀	🌿❀	🌿❀	cool	Z5
F. r. var. *rubra*	106	80cm (3¾ft)	indefinite				🌿	🌿❀	🌿❀	🌿	🌿	🌿	🌿	🌿	❀	cool	Z5
F. valesiaca 'Silbersee'	27	30cm (12in)	60cm (2ft)				🌿	🌿❀	🌿❀	🌿	🌿	🌿	🌿	🌿	❀	cool	Z5
Glyceria maxima var. *variegata*	24	1.8m (6ft)	indefinite					🌿	🌿❀	🌿❀	🌿❀	🌿❀	🌿			cool	Z5
Graminea sp. Nepal	67	1.2m (4ft)	1m (3¼ft)	❀	❀		🌿	🌿	🌿	🌿❀	🌿❀	🌿❀	🌿❀	🌿❀	❀	cool	Z7
Hakonechloa macra	46	45cm (18in)	1m (3¼ft)	🌿❀	🌿❀			🌿	🌿	🌿	🌿❀	🌿❀	🌿❀	🌿❀	🌿❀	cool	Z5
H. m. 'Alboaurea'	25	23cm (9in)	90cm (3ft)					🌿	🌿	🌿	🌿	🌿❀	🌿❀			cool	Z5
H. m. 'Albostriata'	32	45cm (18in)	1m (3¼ft)					🌿	🌿	🌿	🌿	🌿❀	🌿❀			cool	Z5
H. m. 'Aureola'	26	23cm (9in)	90cm (3 ft)					🌿	🌿	🌿	🌿	🌿❀	🌿❀			cool	Z5
H. m. 'Mediovariegata'	32	45cm (18in)	1m (3¼ft)	❀	❀			🌿	🌿	🌿	🌿	🌿❀	🌿❀	❀	❀	warm	Z5
Helictotrichon filifolius	36	70cm (2¼ft)	60cm (2ft)	🌿	🌿	🌿	🌿	🌿❀	🌿❀	🌿❀	🌿	🌿	🌿	🌿	🌿	cool	Z4

LEAVES 🌿 PANICLES ❀

PLANT	PAGE	HEIGHT	SPREAD	Midwinter	Late winter	Early spring	Mid-spring	Late spring	Early summer	Midsummer	Late summer	Early autumn	Mid-autumn	Late autumn	Early winter	WARM/ COOL	ZONES
H. pratense	36	30cm (12in)	60cm (2ft)	P	P	P	L P	L P	L P	L P	L P	L P	L P	L P	L P	cool	Z4
H. sempervirens	28	1m (3¼ft)	1m (3¼ft)				L	L P	L P	L P	L	L	L			cool	Z4
H. s. pendulum	28	75cm (18in)	1m (3¼ft)				L	L P	L P	L P	L	L	L			cool	Z4
H. s. 'Saphiresprudel'	28	1m (3¼ft)	1m (3¼ft)				L	L P	L P	L P	L	L	L			cool	Z4
× *Hibanobambusa tranquillans* 'Shiroshima'	38	2m (6½ft)	2m (6½ft)	L	L	L	L	L	L	L	L	L	L	L	L	warm	Z8
Hierochloë odorata	77	30cm (12in)	indefinite			L P	L P	L P	L P	L P	L	L	L			cool	Z5
Himalayacalamus hookerianus	156	2.4m (8ft)	indefinite	L	L	L	L	L	L	L	L	L	L	L	L	warm	Z8
Holcus 'Alan Cook'	20	15cm (6in)	60cm (12in)		L	L	L	L	L P	L P	L P	L P	L	L	L	cool	Z5
H. lanatus	106	80cm (3¾ft)	60cm (2ft)			L	L	L P	L P	L P	L P	L	L	L	L	cool	Z5
H. mollis	106	75cm (2⁄ ft)	indefinite			L	L	L	L P	L P	L P	L	L	L	L	cool	Z5
H. m. 'Albovariegatus'	20	15cm (6in)	indefinite		L	L	L	L	L P	L P	L P	L P	L	L	L	cool	Z5
Hordelymus europaeus	114	60cm (2ft)	60cm (2ft)					L P	L P	L P	L P	L				annual	Z5
Hordeum hystrix	80	23cm (9in)	23cm (9in)		L	L	L	L P	L P	L P	L					annual	Z7
H. jubatum	80	30cm (12in)	30cm (12in)		L	L	L	L P	L P	L P	L P	P	P			annual	Z5
H. secalinum	111	75cm (2½ft)	60cm (2ft)					L	L P	L P	L	L				cool	Z5
Hystrix patula	124	1m (3¼ft)	60cm (2ft)	P				L	L P	L P	L P	L P	L P	P	P	cool	Z4
Imperata brevifolia	72	60cm (2ft)	60cm (2ft)	L					L	L P	L P	L P	L P	L	L	warm	Z8
I. cylindrica	32	70cm (2¼ft)	indefinite					L	L	L	L	L	L			warm	Z7
I. c. 'Rubra'	29	45cm (18in)	indefinite					L	L	L	L	L	L			warm	Z7
I. c. variegated	32	70cm (2¼ft)	indefinite					L	L	L	L	L	L			warm	Z7
Indocalamus hamadae	138	90cm (3ft)	indefinite	L	L	L	L	L	L	L	L	L	L	L	L	warm	Z8
Juncus balticus 'Spiralis'	118	30cm (12in)	indefinite	L	L	L	L	L	L P	L P	L P	L P	L	L	L	cool	Z3
J. 'Carmen's Grey'	117	60cm (2ft)	1m (3¼ft)	L	L	L	L	L	L P	L P	L P	L P	L	L	L	cool	Z7
J. concinnus	151	10cm (4in)	10cm (4in)				L	L	L P	L P	L P	L P	L			cool	Z7
J. effusus	118	1m (3¼ft)	1m (3¼ft)	L	L	L	L	L	L P	L P	L P	L P	L	L	L	cool	Z4
J. e. 'Spiralis'	118	30cm (12in)	60cm (2ft)	L	L	L	L	L	L P	L P	L P	L P	L	L	L	cool	Z4
J. e. 'Vittatus'	118	90cm (3ft)	90cm (3ft)	L	L	L	L	L	L P	L P	L P	L P	L	L	L	cool	Z4
J. glomeratus 'Spiralis'	118	15cm (6in)	30cm (12in)	L	L	L	L	L	L P	L P	L P	L P	L	L	L	cool	Z4
J. inflexus 'Afro'	118	30cm (12in)	60cm (2ft)	L	L	L	L	L	L P	L P	L P	L P	L	L	L	cool	Z4
J. pallidus	117	90cm (3ft)	1m (3¼ft)	L	L	L	L	L	L	L P	L P	L P	L	L	L	cool	Z6
Koeleria glauca	35	23cm (9in)	45cm (18in)	L	L	L	L	L	L P	L P	L P	L P	L P	L P	L P	cool	Z4
K. macrantha	111	50cm (20in)	45cm (18in)	L	L	L	L	L P	L P	L P	L	L	L	L	L	cool	Z2
K. nitidula	36	30cm (12in)	45cm (18in)	L	L	L	L	L	L P	L P	L P	L P	L P	L P	L P	cool	Z4
K. vallesiana	35	30cm (12in)	45cm (18in)	L	L	L	L	L	L P	L P	L P	L P	L P	L P	L P	cool	Z4
Lagurus ovatus	80	45cm (18in)	30cm (12in)						L P	L P	L					annual	Z9
L. o. 'Nanus'	80	15cm (6in)	15cm (6in)						L P	L P	L					annual	Z9
Lamarckia aurea	81	30cm (12in)	23cm (9in)					L	L P	L P	L P					annual	Z7
Leymus arenarius	28	1m (3¼ft)	indefinite					L	L P	L P	L P	L	L			cool	Z4
L. elongatus	29	1m (3¼ft)	45cm (18in)					L	L P	L P	L P	L	L			cool	Z7
L. racemosus	29	90cm (3ft)	1m (3¼ft)					L	L P	L P	L P	L	L			cool	Z4
L. secalinus	29	90cm (3ft)	1m (3¼ft)					L	L P	L P	L P	L	L			cool	Z5
Lolium perenne	106	75cm (2½ft)	60cm (2ft)				L	L P	L P	L P	L P	L	L	L		cool	Z5
L. temulentum	109	75cm (2½ft)	60cm (2ft)					L	L P	L P	L P					annual	Z5
Luzula alopecuroides	126	15cm (6in)	45cm (18in)	L	L	L	L P	L P	L P	L	L	L	L	L	L	cool	Z6
L. × *borreri* 'Botany Bay'	126	20cm (8in)	60cm (2ft)	L	L	L	L P	L P	L P	L	L	L	L	L	L	cool	Z6
L. nivea	122	60cm (2ft)	30cm (12in)	L	L	L	L P	L P	L P	L P	L	L	L	L	L	cool	Z5
L. plumosa	126	15cm (6in)	45cm (18in)	L	L	L	L P	L P	L P	L P	L	L	L	L	L	cool	Z6
L. purpureosplendens	126	30cm (12in)	1m (3¼ft)	L	L	L	L P	L P	L P	L P	L	L	L	L	L	cool	Z8
L. sylvatica	126	45cm (18in)	1m (3¼ft)	L	L	L	L P	L P	L P	L	L	L	L	L	L	cool	Z6
L. s. 'Aurea'	126	45cm (18in)	1m (3¼ft)	L	L	L	L P	L P	L P	L	L	L	L	L	L	cool	Z6
L. s. 'Bromel'	126	1m (3¼ft)	1.2m (4ft)	L	L	L	L P	L P	L P	L	L	L	L	L	L	cool	Z6
L. s. 'Gilt'	126	45cm (18in)	1m (3¼ft)	L	L	L	L P	L P	L P	L	L	L	L	L	L	cool	Z6
L. s. 'Hohe Tatra'	126	60cm (2ft)	1m (3¼ft)	L	L	L	L P	L P	L P	L	L	L	L	L	L	cool	Z6
L. s. 'Marginata'	126	45cm (18in)	1m (3⁄ft)	L	L	L	L P	L P	L P	L	L	L	L	L	L	cool	Z6
L. s. 'Taggart's Cream'	126	45cm (18in)	1m (3¼ft)	L	L	L	L P	L P	L P	L	L	L	L	L	L	cool	Z6
L. s. 'Wäldler'	126	45cm (18in)	1m (3¼ft)	L	L	L	L P	L P	L P	L	L	L	L	L	L	cool	Z6
Lygeum spartum	77	75cm (2½ft)	75cm (2½ft)	L	L	L	L P	L P	L P	L P	L	L	L	L	L	cool	Z7
Melica altissima	68	1.2m (4ft)	1m (3¼ft)				L	L	L P	L P	L P	L P	P			cool	Z5

LEAVES (L) PANICLES (P)

Legend: 🍃 = Leaves ❀ = Panicles (🍃❀ = both)

PLANT	PAGE	HEIGHT	SPREAD	Midwinter	Late winter	Early spring	Mid-spring	Late spring	Early summer	Midsummer	Late summer	Early autumn	Mid-autumn	Late autumn	Early winter	WARM/COOL	ZONES
M. a. 'Alba'	68	1.2m (4ft)	3m (3¼ft)				🍃	🍃	🍃❀	🍃❀	🍃❀	❀				cool	Z5
M. a. 'Atropurpurea'	68	1.2m (4ft)	3m (3¼ft)				🍃	🍃	🍃❀	🍃❀	🍃❀	❀				cool	Z5
M. ciliata	151	75cm (2½ft)	75cm (2½ft)				🍃	🍃	🍃❀	🍃❀	🍃❀	❀				cool	Z6
M. macra	58	90cm (3ft)	75cm (2½ft)					🍃❀	🍃❀	🍃❀	🍃	🍃	🍃	🍃		cool	Z6
M. transsilvanica	68	1m (3¼ft)	60cm (2ft)					🍃	🍃❀	🍃❀	🍃❀	🍃❀	🍃❀			cool	Z6
M. t. 'Atropurpurea'	68	1m (3¼ft)	60cm (2ft)					🍃	🍃❀	🍃❀	🍃❀	🍃❀	🍃❀			cool	Z6
M. uniflora 'Variegata'	31	30cm (12in)	30cm (12in)				🍃	🍃	🍃❀	🍃❀						cool	Z7
Merxmuellera macowanii	67	75cm (2½ft)	1m (3¼ft)					🍃❀	🍃❀	🍃❀	🍃❀		🍃	🍃		cool	Z7
Milium effusum 'Aureum'	24	30cm (12in)	30cm (12in)	🍃	🍃	🍃	🍃	🍃❀	🍃❀	🍃			🍃	🍃	🍃	cool	Z6
M. e. var. *esthonicum*	77	1m (3¼ft)	75cm (2½ft)	🍃	🍃	🍃	🍃	🍃❀	🍃❀	🍃❀			🍃	🍃	🍃	cool	Z6
M. floridulus	65	2.4m (8ft)	1.2m (4ft)	❀	❀			🍃	🍃	🍃	🍃	🍃❀	🍃❀	🍃❀		warm	Z6
Miscanthus 'Giganteus'	65	3.3m (11ft)	1.2m (4ft)	❀	❀			🍃	🍃	🍃	🍃	🍃❀	🍃❀	🍃❀		warm	Z4
M. × oligonensis 'Juli'	64	1.2m (4ft)	1.2m (4ft)	❀	❀			🍃	🍃	🍃	🍃❀	🍃❀	🍃❀	🍃❀		warm	Z7
M. × o. 'Wetterfahne'	64	1.2m (4ft)	1.2m (4ft)	❀	❀			🍃	🍃	🍃	🍃❀	🍃❀	🍃❀	🍃❀		warm	Z4
M. × o. 'Zwergelefant'	64	1.8m (6ft)	1.2m (4ft)	❀	❀			🍃	🍃	🍃	🍃❀	🍃❀	🍃❀	🍃❀		warm	Z7
M. oligostachyus 'Africa'	64	90cm (3ft)	1.2m (4ft)	❀	❀			🍃	🍃	🍃	🍃	🍃	🍃❀	🍃❀		warm	Z4
M. o. 'Herbstfeuer'	64	1m (3¼ft)	1m (3¼ft)	❀	❀			🍃	🍃	🍃	🍃	🍃❀	🍃❀	🍃❀		warm	Z4
M. o. 'Purpurascens'	64	1.2m (4ft)	1.2m (4ft)	❀	❀			🍃	🍃	🍃	🍃	🍃❀	🍃❀	🍃❀		warm	Z4
M. o. 'Roterpfeil'	64	1.8m (6ft)	1m (3¼ft)	❀	❀			🍃	🍃	🍃	🍃	🍃❀	🍃❀	🍃❀		warm	Z4
M. sacchariflorus	65	3m (10ft)	indefinite	❀	❀			🍃	🍃	🍃	🍃	🍃❀	🍃❀	🍃❀		warm	Z7
M. sinensis 'Adagio'	63	1.2m (4ft)	1m (3¼ft)	❀	❀			🍃	🍃	🍃	🍃	🍃❀	🍃❀	🍃❀		warm	Z7
M. s. 'Blutenwonder'	63	1.5m (5ft)	1.2m (4ft)	❀	❀			🍃	🍃	🍃	🍃❀	🍃❀	🍃❀	🍃❀		warm	Z7
M. s. 'Cabaret'	23	2.1m (7ft)	1.2m (4ft)						🍃	🍃	🍃	🍃	❀			warm	Z7
M. s. 'China'	63	1.5m (5ft)	1.2m (4ft)	❀	❀			🍃	🍃	🍃	🍃	🍃❀	🍃❀	🍃❀		warm	Z7
M. s. 'Coon Tail'	26	75cm (2½ft)	75cm (2½ft)						🍃	🍃	🍃	🍃❀	🍃❀	🍃		warm	Z7
M. s. 'Cosmopolitan'	23	2.4m (8ft)	1.2m (4ft)						🍃	🍃	🍃	🍃❀	🍃❀	🍃		warm	Z7
M. s. 'Dixieland'	23	1.2m (4ft)	1.2m (4ft)						🍃	🍃	🍃	🍃❀	❀			warm	Z7
M. s. 'Emerald Giant'	63	2.4m (8ft)	2.1m (7ft)	❀	❀			🍃	🍃	🍃	🍃	🍃❀	🍃❀	🍃❀		warm	Z7
M. s. 'Ferne Osten'	62	1.2m (4ft)	1m (3¼ft)	❀	❀			🍃	🍃	🍃	🍃❀	🍃❀	🍃❀			warm	Z7
M. s. 'Flamingo'	62	1.5m (5ft)	1.2m (4ft)	❀	❀			🍃	🍃	🍃	🍃	🍃❀	🍃❀	🍃❀		warm	Z7
M. s. 'Gearmella'	62	1m (3¼ft)	75cm (2½ft)	❀	❀			🍃	🍃	🍃	🍃	🍃❀	🍃❀	🍃❀		warm	Z7
M. s. 'Gewitterwolke'	62	1.5m (5ft)	1m (3¼ft)	❀	❀			🍃	🍃	🍃	🍃	🍃❀	🍃❀	🍃❀		warm	Z7
M. s. 'Goldfeder'	26	1.8m (6ft)	1.2m (4ft)						🍃	🍃	🍃	🍃❀	🍃❀	🍃		warm	Z7
M. s. 'Gracillimus'	59	1.8m (6ft)	1.5m (5ft)	❀	❀			🍃	🍃	🍃	🍃	🍃	🍃❀	🍃❀		warm	Z5
M. s. 'Graziella'	62	1.8m (6ft)	1.2m (4ft)	❀	❀			🍃	🍃	🍃	🍃❀	🍃❀	🍃❀	🍃❀		warm	Z5
M. s. 'Grosse Fontäne'	63	1.8m (6ft)	1m (3¼ft)	❀	❀			🍃	🍃	🍃	🍃	🍃❀	🍃❀	🍃❀		warm	Z7
M. s. 'Hinjo'	26	1m (3¼ft)	75cm (2½ft)						🍃	🍃	🍃	🍃❀	🍃❀	🍃		warm	Z5
M. s. 'Kaskade'	62	1.8m (6ft)	1.2m (4ft)	❀	❀			🍃	🍃	🍃	🍃❀	🍃❀	🍃❀	🍃❀		warm	Z7
M. s. 'Kirk Alexander'	26	1.5m (5ft)	1.2m (4ft)						🍃	🍃	🍃	🍃❀	🍃❀	🍃		warm	Z7
M. s. 'Kleine Fontäne'	62	1.5m (5ft)	1.2m (4ft)	❀	❀			🍃	🍃	🍃	🍃	🍃❀	🍃❀	🍃❀		warm	Z5
M. s. 'Kleine Silberspinne'	63	90cm (3ft)	90cm (3ft)	❀	❀			🍃	🍃	🍃	🍃	🍃❀	🍃❀	🍃❀		warm	Z7
M. s. 'Little Kitten'	64	30cm (1in)	30cm (12in)	❀	❀			🍃	🍃	🍃	🍃	🍃❀	🍃❀	🍃❀		warm	Z5
M. s. 'Malepartus'	62	1.8m (6ft)	1.2m (4ft)	❀	❀			🍃	🍃	🍃	🍃❀	🍃❀	🍃❀	🍃❀		warm	Z7
M. s. 'Morning Light'	46	1.5m (5ft)	1.2m (4ft)	❀	❀			🍃	🍃	🍃	🍃	🍃❀	🍃❀	🍃❀		warm	Z5
M. s. 'Nippon'	63	1.2m (4ft)	90cm (3ft)	❀	❀			🍃	🍃	🍃	🍃❀	🍃❀	🍃❀	🍃❀		warm	Z5
M. s. 'Nishidake'	62	2.4m (8ft)	2m (6½ft)	❀	❀			🍃	🍃	🍃	🍃	🍃❀	🍃❀	🍃❀		warm	Z7
M. s. 'Poseidon'	63	2.1m (7ft)	1.2m (4ft)	❀	❀			🍃	🍃	🍃	🍃	🍃❀	🍃❀	🍃❀		warm	Z7
M. s. 'Pünktchen'	26	1.5m (5ft)	90cm (3ft)						🍃	🍃	🍃	🍃❀	🍃❀	🍃		warm	Z7
M. s. 'Rigoletto'	23	90cm (3ft)	1m (3¼ft)						🍃	🍃	🍃	🍃❀	❀			warm	Z7
M. s. 'Roland'	63	2.4m (8ft)	2.1m (7ft)	🍃❀	🍃❀			🍃	🍃	🍃	🍃	🍃❀	🍃❀	🍃❀		warm	Z7
M. s. 'Rotsilber'	62	1.5m (5ft)	1.2m (4ft)	🍃❀	🍃❀			🍃	🍃	🍃	🍃	🍃❀	🍃❀	🍃❀		warm	Z7
M. s. 'Sarabande'	59	1.2m (4ft)	1m (3¼ft)	❀	❀			🍃	🍃	🍃	🍃	🍃	🍃❀	🍃❀		warm	Z5
M. s. 'Silberfeder'	62	2.4m (8ft)	1.2m (4ft)	❀				🍃	🍃	🍃	🍃	🍃	🍃❀	🍃❀		warm	Z5
M. s. 'Silberpfeil'	23	2.1m (7ft)	1m (3¼ft)						🍃	🍃	🍃	🍃❀	🍃❀	🍃		warm	Z7
M. s. 'Silberspinne'	63	1.2m (4ft)	1m (3¼ft)	❀	❀			🍃	🍃	🍃	🍃	🍃❀	🍃❀	🍃❀		warm	Z7
M. s. 'Silberturm'	63	2.4m (8ft)	1.2m (4ft)	❀	❀			🍃	🍃	🍃	🍃	🍃❀	🍃❀	🍃❀		warm	Z7
M. s. 'Sirene'	62	1.2m (4ft)	1m (3¼ft)	❀	❀			🍃	🍃	🍃	🍃	🍃❀	🍃❀	🍃❀		warm	Z7

PLANT	PAGE	HEIGHT	SPREAD	Midwinter	Late winter	Early spring	Mid-spring	Late spring	Early summer	Midsummer	Late summer	Early autumn	Mid-autumn	Late autumn	Early winter	WARM/COOL	ZONES
M. s. 'Strictus'	26	1.8m (6ft)	75cm (2½ft)	✿	✿	✿	✿	✿	≈✿	≈✿	≈✿	≈✿	≈✿	✿		warm	Z7
M. s. 'Tiger Cub'	26	1m (3¼ft)	75cm (2½ft)							≈	≈	≈✿	≈✿	≈		warm	Z7
M. s. 'Undine'	62	1.4m (4¾ft)	1m (3¼ft)	✿	✿				≈	≈	≈✿	≈✿	≈✿	≈✿		warm	Z7
M. s. 'Variegatus'	23	1.5m (5ft)	1m (3¼ft)						≈	≈	≈✿	≈✿	≈✿	≈		warm	Z6
M. s. 'Vorläufer'	62	75cm (2½ft)	75cm (2½ft)	✿	✿				≈	≈	≈✿	≈✿	≈✿	≈		warm	Z7
M. s. 'Zebrinus'	26	2.4m (8ft)	1.2m (4ft)							≈	≈	≈✿	≈✿	≈✿		warm	Z6
M. tinctoria 'Nanus Variegatus'	32	75cm (2½ft)	indefinite	✿	✿			≈	≈	≈	≈	≈✿	≈✿	✿	✿	warm	Z7
M. transmorrisonensis	63	1.2m (4ft)	1m (3¼ft)	✿	✿			≈	≈	≈✿	≈✿	≈✿	≈✿	≈✿	≈✿	warm	Z7
M. yakushimensis	63	1.2m (4ft)	1.2m (4ft)	✿	✿			≈	≈	≈✿	≈✿	≈✿	≈✿	≈✿	≈✿	warm	Z5
Molinia caerulea ssp. arundinacea	109	1.8m (6ft)	1m (3¼ft)	✿	✿			≈	≈	≈✿	≈✿	≈✿	≈✿	≈✿	≈✿	cool	Z5
M. c. ssp. a. 'Bergfreund'	59	1.8m (6ft)	1.5m (5ft)	✿	✿			≈	≈✿	≈✿	≈✿	≈✿	≈✿	≈✿	≈✿	cool	Z5
M. c. ssp. a. 'Fontane'	58	1.5m (5ft)	1.2m (4ft)	✿	✿			≈	≈✿	≈✿	≈✿	≈✿	≈✿	≈✿	≈✿	cool	Z5
M. c. ssp. a. 'Karl Foerster'	58	1.2m (4ft)	1m (3¼ft)	✿	✿			≈	≈✿	≈✿	≈✿	≈✿	≈✿	≈✿	≈✿	cool	Z5
M. c. ssp. a. 'Skyracer'	58	2.4m (8ft)	1.2m (4ft)	✿	✿			≈	≈✿	≈✿	≈✿	≈✿	≈✿	≈✿	≈✿	cool	Z5
M. c. ssp. a. 'Transparent'	59	1.8m (6ft)	1.2m (4ft)	✿	✿			≈	≈✿	≈✿	≈✿	≈✿	≈✿	≈✿	≈✿	cool	Z5
M. c. ssp. a. 'Windspiel'	58	1.8m (6ft)	1.2m (4ft)	✿	✿			≈	≈✿	≈✿	≈✿	≈✿	≈✿	≈✿	≈✿	cool	Z5
M. c. ssp. a. 'Zuneigung'	58	1.8m (6ft)	1.5m (5ft)	✿	✿			≈	≈✿	≈✿	≈✿	≈✿	≈✿	≈✿	≈✿	cool	Z5
M. c. ssp. caerulea 'Dauerstrahl'	59	90cm (3ft)	90cm (3ft)	✿	✿			≈	≈✿	≈✿	≈✿	≈✿	≈✿	≈✿	≈✿	cool	Z5
M. c. ssp. c. 'Edith Dudszus'	59	90cm (3ft)	90cm (3ft)	✿	✿			≈	≈✿	≈✿	≈✿	≈✿	≈✿	≈✿	≈✿	cool	Z5
M. c. ssp. c. 'Heidebraut'	59	1.5m (5ft)	1.2m (4ft)	✿	✿			≈	≈✿	≈✿	≈✿	≈✿	≈✿	≈✿	≈✿	cool	Z5
M. c. ssp. c. 'Moorflamme'	59	75cm (2½ft)	60cm (2ft)	✿	✿			≈	≈✿	≈✿	≈✿	≈✿	≈✿	≈✿	≈✿	cool	Z5
M. c. ssp. c. 'Moorhexe'	59	90cm (3ft)	60cm (2ft)	✿	✿			≈	≈✿	≈✿	≈✿	≈✿	≈✿	≈✿	≈✿	cool	Z5
M. c. ssp. c. 'Strahlenquelle'	59	90cm (3ft)	90cm (3ft)	✿	✿			≈	≈✿	≈✿	≈✿	≈✿	≈✿	≈✿	≈✿	cool	Z5
M. c. ssp. c. 'Variegata'	24	1m (3¼ft)	60cm (2ft)					≈	≈	≈✿	≈✿	≈✿	≈✿			cool	Z5
M. c. 'Carmarthen'	24	1m (3¼ft)	60cm (2ft)					≈	≈	≈✿	≈✿	≈✿	≈✿			cool	Z5
M. c. 'Claerwen'	24	1m (3¼ft)	60cm (2ft)					≈	≈	≈✿	≈✿	≈✿	≈✿			cool	Z5
M. capillaris	72	90cm (3ft)	90cm (3 ft)	≈✿	≈✿			≈	≈	≈	≈	≈✿	≈✿	≈✿	≈✿	warm	Z9
M. dumosa	139	1m (3¼ft)	1.2m (4ft)	≈	≈	≈	≈	≈	≈	≈	≈✿	≈✿	≈	≈	≈	warm	Z10
M. filipes	72	90cm (3ft)	90cm (3ft)	≈✿	≈✿			≈	≈	≈	≈	≈✿	≈✿	≈✿	≈✿	warm	Z9
Muhlenbergia japonica 'Variegata'	31	20cm (8in)	60cm (2ft)					≈	≈	≈✿	≈✿	≈✿	≈✿			warm	Z7
M. rigens	72	1.2m (4ft)	1m (3¼ft)	≈✿	≈✿			≈	≈	≈	≈	≈✿	≈✿	≈✿	≈✿	warm	Z9
Nassella trichotoma	74	45cm (18in)	1m (3¼ft)	≈✿	≈✿	≈	≈	≈✿	≈✿	≈✿	≈✿	≈✿	≈✿	≈✿		cool	Z7
Oplismenus africanus	153	15cm (6in)	indefinite			≈	≈	≈	≈	≈✿	≈✿	≈✿	≈	≈		warm	Z9
Oryzopsis miliacea	75	60cm (2ft)	60cm (2ft)	≈	≈			≈✿	≈✿	≈✿	≈	≈	≈	≈		cool	Z8
Panicum bulbosum	67	1.2m (4ft)	90cm (3ft)					≈	≈	≈✿	≈✿	≈✿	≈✿	✿		warm	Z5
P. capillare	109	90cm (3ft)	80cm (3¼ft)					≈	≈✿	≈✿	≈✿					annual	Z5
P. clandestinum	67	1.2m (4ft)	1m (3¼ft)					≈	≈	≈✿	≈✿	≈✿	≈✿			warm	Z5
P. miliaceum 'Violaceum'	84	90cm (3ft)	45cm (18in)					≈	≈	≈✿	≈✿	≈✿	≈✿			annual	Z5
P. virgatum	54	1.2m (4ft)	90 cm (3ft)	✿	✿			≈	≈	≈	≈	≈✿	≈✿	≈✿	✿	warm	Z5
P. v. 'Blue Tower'	28	2.7m (9ft)	1m (3¼ft)	✿	✿			≈	≈	≈	≈	≈✿	≈✿	✿	✿	warm	Z5
P. v. 'Cloud Nine'	28	1.8m (6ft)	1.5m (5ft)	✿	✿			≈	≈	≈	≈	≈✿	≈✿	✿	✿	warm	Z5
P. v. 'Forest Snow'	31	1.2m (4ft)	1m (3¼ft)					≈	≈	≈	≈	≈✿	≈✿			warm	Z5
P. v. 'Hänse Herms'	54	90cm (3ft)	75cm (2½ft)	✿	✿			≈	≈	≈	≈	≈✿	≈✿	≈✿	✿	warm	Z5
P. v. 'Heavy Metal'	28	90cm (3ft)	90cm (3ft)	✿	✿			≈	≈	≈	≈	≈✿	≈✿	✿	✿	warm	Z5
P. v. 'Pathfinder'	28	1m (3¼ft)	90cm (3ft)	✿	✿			≈	≈	≈	≈	≈✿	≈✿	✿	✿	warm	Z5
P. v. 'Prairie Sky'	28	90cm (3ft)	90cm (3ft)	✿	✿			≈	≈	≈	≈	≈✿	≈✿	✿		warm	Z5
P. v. 'Red Cloud'	54	90cm (3ft)	90cm (3ft)	✿	✿			≈	≈	≈	≈	≈✿	≈✿	≈✿	✿	warm	Z5
P. v. 'Rehbraun'	54	1m (3¼ft)	90cm (3ft)	✿	✿			≈	≈	≈	≈	≈✿	≈✿	≈✿	✿	warm	Z5
P. v. 'Rotstrahlbusch'	54	1m (3¼ft)	90cm (3ft)	✿	✿			≈	≈	≈	≈	≈✿	≈✿	≈✿	✿	warm	Z5
P. v. 'Rubrum'	54	1m (3¼ft)	90cm (3ft)	✿	✿			≈	≈	≈	≈	≈✿	≈✿	≈✿	✿	warm	Z5

LEAVES ≈   PANICLES ✿

PLANT	PAGE	HEIGHT	SPREAD	Midwinter	Late winter	Early spring	Mid-spring	Late spring	Early summer	Midsummer	Late summer	Early autumn	Mid-autumn	Late autumn	Early winter	WARM/COOL	ZONES
P. v. 'Shenandoah'	29	90cm (3ft)	90cm (3ft)	✿	✿			〰	〰	〰	〰	〰✿	〰✿	✿	✿	warm	Z5
P. v. 'Squaw'	54	1.5m (5ft)	1.2m (4ft)	✿	✿			〰	〰	〰	〰	〰✿	〰✿	〰✿	✿	warm	Z5
P. v. 'Strictum'	54	1.2m (4ft)	90cm (3ft)	✿	✿			〰	〰	〰	〰	〰✿	〰✿	〰✿	✿	warm	Z5
P. v. 'Warrior'	54	1.5m (5ft)	1.2m (4ft)	✿	✿			〰	〰	〰	〰	〰✿	〰✿	〰✿	✿	warm	Z5
Pennisetum alopecuroides	50	1m (3¼ft)	90cm (3ft)	✿	✿			〰	〰	〰	〰	〰✿	〰✿	〰✿	〰✿	warm	Z6
P. a. 'Cassian'	51	1m (3¼ft)	90cm (3ft)	✿	✿			〰	〰	〰	〰	〰✿	〰✿	〰✿	〰✿	warm	Z6
P. a. 'Hameln'	50	45cm (18in)	60cm (2ft)	✿	✿			〰	〰	〰	〰	〰✿	〰✿	〰✿	〰✿	warm	Z6
P. a. 'Little Bunny'	51	30cm (12in)	45cm (18in)	✿	✿			〰	〰	〰	〰	〰✿	〰✿	〰✿	〰✿	warm	Z6
P. a. 'Little Honey'	22	20cm (8in)	41cm (16in)	〰	〰			〰	〰	〰	〰	〰✿	〰✿	〰	〰	warm	Z6
P. a. 'Moudry'	67	60cm (2ft)	1m (3¼ft)	✿	✿			〰	〰	〰	〰	〰✿	〰✿	〰✿	〰✿	warm	Z6
P. a. 'National Arboretum'	67	60cm (2ft)	1m (3¼ft)	✿	✿			〰	〰	〰	〰	〰✿	〰✿	〰✿	〰✿	warm	Z6
P. a. 'Paul's Giant'	51	1.8m (6ft)	1.5m (5ft)	✿	✿			〰	〰	〰	〰	〰✿	〰✿	〰✿	〰✿	warm	Z6
P. a. 'Viridescens'	68	60cm (2ft)	1m (3¼ft)	✿	✿			〰	〰	〰	〰	〰✿	〰✿	〰✿	〰✿	warm	Z6
P. a. 'Weserbergland'	50	75cm (2½ft)	75cm (2½ft)	✿	✿			〰	〰	〰	〰	〰✿	〰✿	〰✿	〰✿	warm	Z6
P. a. 'Woodside'	50	80cm (3¾ft)	80cm (3¾ft)	✿	✿			〰	〰	〰	〰	〰✿	〰✿	〰✿	〰✿	warm	Z6
P. incomptum	51	1.2m (4ft)	indefinite					〰	〰✿	〰✿	〰✿	〰✿	〰✿	〰	〰	warm	Z6
P. i. 'Purple Form'	51	1.2m (4ft)	indefinite					〰	〰✿	〰✿	〰✿	〰✿	〰✿	〰	〰	warm	Z6
P. macrourum	51	1.2m (4ft)	45cm (18in)	✿	✿			〰	〰	〰	〰✿	〰✿	〰✿	✿	✿	warm	Z7
P. orientale	51	90cm (3ft)	90cm (3ft)	✿	✿			〰	〰	〰✿	〰✿	〰✿	〰✿	〰✿	〰✿	warm	Z7
P. setaceum	81	90cm (3ft)	30cm (12in)						〰	〰	〰	〰✿	〰✿	〰✿		annual	Z9
P. s. 'Burgundy Blaze'	81	90cm (3ft)	30cm (12in)						〰	〰	〰	〰✿	〰✿	〰✿		annual	Z9
P. s. 'Rubrum'	81	60cm (2ft)	23cm (9in)						〰	〰	〰	〰✿	〰✿	〰✿		annual	Z9
P. villosum	51	60cm (2ft)	1m (3¼ft)	✿	✿			〰	〰	〰✿	〰✿	〰✿	〰✿	✿	✿	warm	Z8
Phaenosperma globosa	74	1.5m (5ft)	60cm (2ft)	〰				〰	〰	〰✿	〰✿	〰✿	〰✿	〰	〰	cool	Z7
Phalaris arundinacea 'Feesey'	22	1m (3¼ft)	indefinite	〰	〰	〰	〰	〰✿	〰✿	〰	〰	〰	〰	〰	〰	warm	Z4
P. a. 'Picta'	22	1m (3¼ft)	indefinite	〰	〰	〰	〰	〰✿	〰✿	〰	〰	〰	〰	〰	〰	warm	Z4
P. a. 'Streamlined'	22	1m (3¼ft)	indefinite	〰	〰	〰	〰	〰	〰					〰	〰	warm	Z4
P. canariensis	109	80cm (3¾ft)	60cm (2ft)					✿	〰✿	〰✿	〰✿	〰				annual	Z6
P. minor	109	1.2m (4ft)	1m (3¼ft)						〰	〰✿	〰✿	〰✿	〰✿			annual	Z6
Phleum bertoloni	106	50cm (20in)	indefinite				〰	〰	〰✿	〰✿	〰✿	〰	〰	〰	〰	cool	Z5
Phragmites australis	139	2.4m (8ft)	indefinite	〰				〰	〰	〰✿	〰✿	〰✿	〰	〰	〰	warm	Z5
P. a. 'Candy Stripe'	31	2.1m (7ft)	indefinite					〰	〰	〰	〰✿	〰✿	〰✿			cool	Z5
P. a. 'Variegatus'	34	2.1m (7ft)	indefinite	〰✿	✿			〰	〰	〰	〰✿	〰✿	〰✿	〰✿	〰✿	cool	Z5
P. karka 'Variegatus'	31	2.1m (7ft)	indefinite	〰✿	✿			〰	〰	〰	〰✿	〰✿	〰✿	〰✿	〰✿	cool	Z5
Phyllostachys aurea	138	4m (13ft)	1.8m (6ft)	〰	〰	〰	〰	〰	〰	〰	〰		〰	〰	〰	warm	Z6
P. a. 'Albovariegata'	38	3.6m (12ft)	2m (6½ft)	〰	〰	〰	〰	〰	〰	〰	〰	〰	〰	〰	〰	warm	Z6
P. a. 'Holochrysa'	156	3.6m (12ft)	indefinite	〰	〰	〰	〰	〰	〰	〰	〰	〰	〰	〰	〰	warm	Z6
P. bambusoides	156	4m (13ft)	indefinite	〰	〰	〰	〰	〰	〰	〰	〰	〰	〰	〰	〰	warm	Z7
P. b. 'Castilloni'	156	4m (13ft)	indefinite	〰	〰	〰	〰	〰	〰	〰	〰	〰	〰	〰	〰	warm	Z7
P. b. 'Holochrysa' ('Allgold')	156	4m (13ft)	indefinite	〰	〰	〰	〰	〰	〰	〰	〰	〰	〰	〰	〰	warm	Z6
P. decora	141	6m (20ft)	3.6m (12ft)	〰	〰	〰	〰	〰	〰	〰	〰	〰	〰	〰	〰	warm	Z7
P. dulcis	139	9m (30ft)	indefinite	〰	〰	〰	〰	〰	〰	〰	〰	〰	〰	〰	〰	warm	Z7
P. nigra	139	4m (13ft)	1.8m (6ft)	〰	〰	〰	〰	〰	〰	〰	〰	〰	〰	〰	〰	warm	Z7
P. rubromarginata	144	4m (13ft)	3m (10ft)	〰	〰	〰	〰	〰	〰	〰	〰	〰	〰	〰	〰	cool	Z7
P. sulphurea var. viridis	144	4m (13ft)	1.8m (6ft)	〰	〰	〰	〰	〰	〰	〰	〰	〰	〰	〰	〰	cool	Z7
P. viridiglaucescens	144	4m (13ft)	3m (10ft)	〰	〰	〰	〰	〰	〰	〰	〰	〰	〰	〰	〰	cool	Z6
P. vivax	139	3.6m (12ft)	1.8m (6ft)	〰	〰	〰	〰	〰	〰	〰	〰	〰	〰	〰	〰	warm	Z8
P. v. 'Aureocaulis'	38	3.6m (12ft)	2m (6½ft)	〰	〰	〰	〰	〰	〰	〰	〰	〰	〰	〰	〰	warm	Z8
Pleioblastus akebono	156	50cm (20in)	1.2m (4ft)	〰	〰	〰	〰	〰	〰	〰	〰	〰	〰	〰	〰	warm	Z7
P. auricomus	38	1.2m (4ft)	2m (6½ft)	〰	〰	〰	〰	〰	〰	〰	〰	〰	〰	〰	〰	warm	Z7
P. a. f. chrysophyllus	38	1m (3¼ft)	2 m (6½ft)	〰	〰	〰	〰	〰	〰	〰	〰	〰	〰	〰	〰	warm	Z7
P. chino elegantissimus	38	1.2m (4ft)	2m (6½ft)	〰	〰	〰	〰	〰	〰	〰	〰	〰	〰	〰	〰	warm	Z6
P. humilis	145	1.2m (4ft)	indefinite	〰	〰	〰	〰	〰	〰	〰	〰	〰	〰	〰	〰	cool	Z6
P. h. var. pumilus	145	1.2m (4ft)	indefinite	〰	〰	〰	〰	〰	〰	〰	〰	〰	〰	〰	〰	cool	Z6
P. pygmaeus	145	30cm (12in)	indefinite	〰	〰	〰	〰	〰	〰	〰	〰	〰	〰	〰	〰	cool	Z6
P. shibuyanus 'Tsuboi'	38	2m (6½ft)	2m (6½ft)	〰	〰	〰	〰	〰	〰	〰	〰	〰	〰	〰	〰	warm	Z6

PLANT	PAGE	HEIGHT	SPREAD	Midwinter	Late winter	Early spring	Mid-spring	Late spring	Early summer	Midsummer	Late summer	Early autumn	Mid-autumn	Late autumn	Early winter	WARM/ COOL	ZONES
P. variegatus	38	1.2m (4ft)	2m (6½ft)	🍃	🍃	🍃	🍃	🍃	🍃	🍃	🍃	🍃	🍃	🍃	🍃	warm	Z7
Poa alpina nodosa	150	10cm (4in)	15cm (6in)				🍃	🍃❀	🍃❀	🍃❀	🍃	🍃	🍃			cool	Z4
P. badensis 'Ingelkissen'	150	15cm (6in)	15cm (6in)				🍃	🍃	🍃❀	🍃❀	🍃	🍃	🍃			cool	Z4
P. bulbosa	16	30cm (12in)	30cm (12in)			🍃	🍃❀	🍃❀	🍃❀	🍃	🍃	🍃	🍃	🍃	🍃	cool	Z5
P. chaixii	114	1m (3¼ft)	1m (3¼ft)	🍃	🍃	🍃	🍃	🍃❀	🍃❀	🍃❀	🍃	🍃	🍃	🍃	🍃	cool	Z5
P. colensoi	36	30cm (12in)	60cm (2ft)	🍃	🍃	🍃❀	🍃❀	🍃❀	🍃❀	🍃❀	🍃	🍃	🍃	🍃	🍃	cool	Z7
P. glauca	102	20cm (8in)	20cm (8in)				🍃❀	🍃❀	🍃❀	🍃	🍃	🍃	🍃	🍃		cool	Z5
P. imbecilla	150	18cm (7in)	30cm (12in)				🍃	🍃	🍃❀	🍃❀	🍃❀	🍃❀				cool	Z7?
P. labillardieri	36	70cm (2¼ft)	1m (3¼ft)	🍃	🍃	🍃		🍃	🍃❀	🍃❀	🍃❀	🍃	🍃	🍃	🍃	cool	Z7
P. nemoralis	114	80cm (3¾ft)	60cm (2ft)					🍃	🍃❀	🍃❀	🍃	🍃	🍃			cool	Z5
Polypogon monspeliensis	109	60cm (2ft)	45cm (18in)					🍃	🍃❀	🍃❀	🍃❀					annual	Z8
Pseudosasa japonica	141	3.5m (11ft)	2.4m (8ft)	🍃	🍃	🍃	🍃	🍃	🍃	🍃	🍃	🍃	🍃	🍃	🍃	cool	Z6
P. j. 'Akebonosuji'	38	3m (10ft)	2m (6½ft)	🍃	🍃	🍃	🍃	🍃	🍃	🍃	🍃	🍃	🍃	🍃	🍃	warm	Z6
Quiongzhuea tumidinoda	145	1.5m (5ft)	indefinite	🍃	🍃	🍃	🍃	🍃	🍃	🍃	🍃	🍃	🍃	🍃	🍃	cool	Z6
Saccharum arundinaceum	66	4m (13ft)	1.8m (6ft)	❀	❀			🍃	🍃	🍃	🍃	🍃	🍃❀	🍃❀	🍃❀	warm	Z9
S. officinarum	139	3m (10ft)	1.8m (6ft)					🍃	🍃	🍃	🍃	🍃	🍃			warm	Z9
S. o. 'Pele's Smoke'	139	1.8m (6ft)	1.2m (4ft)					🍃	🍃	🍃	🍃	🍃	🍃			warm	Z9
S. ravennae	66	3.6m (12ft)	1.8m (6ft)	❀	❀			🍃	🍃	🍃	🍃	🍃	🍃❀	🍃❀	🍃❀	warm	Z7
Sasa kurilensis 'Shimofuri'	156	2.4m (8ft)	indefinite	🍃	🍃	🍃	🍃	🍃	🍃	🍃	🍃	🍃	🍃	🍃	🍃	warm	Z7
Schizachyrium scoparium	37	1m (3¼ft)	60cm (2ft)	🍃❀	🍃❀			🍃	🍃	🍃	🍃	🍃❀	🍃❀	🍃❀	🍃❀	warm	Z4
S. s. 'Aldous'	37	1m (3¼ft)	60cm (2ft)	🍃❀	🍃❀			🍃	🍃	🍃	🍃	🍃❀	🍃❀	🍃❀	🍃❀	warm	Z4
S. s. 'Blaze'	37	1m (3¼ft)	60cm (2ft)	🍃❀	🍃❀			🍃	🍃	🍃	🍃	🍃❀	🍃❀	🍃❀	🍃❀	warm	Z4
Schizostachyum funghomii	145	1.8m (6ft)	indefinite	🍃	🍃	🍃	🍃	🍃	🍃	🍃	🍃	🍃	🍃	🍃	🍃	cool	Z7
Schoenoplectus lacustris	117	1.5m (5ft)	1.8m (6ft)					🍃	🍃❀	🍃❀	🍃❀	🍃❀	🍃	🍃		cool	Z4
S. l. ssp. *tabernaemontani* 'Albescens'	117	1.5m (5ft)	1.5m (5ft)					🍃	🍃❀	🍃❀	🍃❀	🍃❀	🍃	🍃		cool	Z4
S. l. ssp. *t.* 'Zebrinus'	117	1.5m (5ft)	1.5m (5ft)					🍃	🍃❀	🍃❀	🍃❀	🍃❀	🍃	🍃		cool	Z4
Schoenus pauciflorus	45	90cm (3ft)	60cm (2ft)	🍃	🍃	🍃		🍃❀	🍃❀	🍃	🍃	🍃	🍃	🍃	🍃	cool	Z6
Scirpus cernuus	154	15cm (6in)	30cm (12in)	🍃	🍃	🍃	🍃	🍃	🍃❀	🍃❀	🍃❀	🍃❀	🍃	🍃	🍃	warm	Z8
S. 'Golden Spear'	117	1.5m (5ft)	1.5m (5ft)					🍃	🍃❀	🍃❀	🍃❀	🍃❀	🍃	🍃		cool	Z4
Semiarundinaria fastuosa	139	60cm (20ft)	indefinite	🍃	🍃	🍃	🍃	🍃	🍃	🍃	🍃	🍃	🍃	🍃	🍃	warm	Z7
Sesleria albicans	102	15cm (6in)	30cm (12in)	🍃	🍃	🍃	🍃	🍃❀	🍃❀	🍃	🍃	🍃	🍃	🍃	🍃	cool	Z5
S. autumnalis	72	45cm (18in)	60cm (2ft)	🍃	🍃	🍃	🍃❀	🍃❀	🍃❀	🍃❀	🍃❀	🍃❀	🍃	🍃	🍃	cool	Z5
S. caerulea	36	15cm (6in)	30cm (12in)	🍃	🍃	🍃	🍃	🍃❀	🍃❀	🍃	🍃	🍃	🍃	🍃	🍃	cool	Z4
S. heufleriana	72	75cm (2½ft)	60cm (2ft)	🍃	🍃	🍃❀	🍃❀	🍃❀	🍃❀	🍃❀	🍃	🍃	🍃	🍃	🍃	cool	Z4
S. nitida	36	90cm (3ft)	90cm (3ft)	🍃	🍃	🍃❀	🍃❀	🍃❀	🍃❀	🍃	🍃	🍃	🍃	🍃	🍃	cool	Z4
S. rigida	102	15cm (6in)	15cm (6in)	🍃	🍃	🍃	🍃	🍃❀	🍃❀	🍃❀	🍃	🍃	🍃	🍃	🍃	cool	Z4
Setaria glauca	80	75cm (2½ft)	30cm (12in)						🍃	🍃❀	🍃❀	🍃❀	❀			annual	Z6
S. macrostachya	80	90cm (3ft)	30cm (12in)						🍃	🍃❀	🍃❀	🍃❀	🍃❀			annual	Z6
S. palmifolia	154	1.2m (4ft)	1.8m (8ft)				🍃	🍃	🍃	🍃	🍃	🍃❀	🍃❀			warm	Z9
S. pumila	80	30cm (12in)	23cm (9in)						🍃	🍃❀	🍃❀	🍃❀	❀			annual	Z6
Shibataea kumasasa	140	80cm (2½ft)	1m (3¼ft)	🍃	🍃	🍃	🍃	🍃	🍃	🍃	🍃	🍃	🍃	🍃	🍃	cool	Z6
Sinarundinaria murieliae	141	4m (13ft)	1.8m (8ft)	🍃	🍃	🍃	🍃	🍃	🍃	🍃	🍃	🍃	🍃	🍃	🍃	cool	Z6
S. nitida	141	4m (13ft)	1.8m (6ft)	🍃	🍃	🍃	🍃	🍃	🍃	🍃	🍃	🍃	🍃	🍃	🍃	cool	Z5
S. n. 'Eisenach'	141	2.7m (9ft)	3m (10ft)	🍃	🍃	🍃	🍃	🍃	🍃	🍃	🍃	🍃	🍃	🍃	🍃	cool	Z5
S. n. 'Nymphenburg'	141	2.7m (9ft)	3m (10ft)	🍃	🍃	🍃	🍃	🍃	🍃	🍃	🍃	🍃	🍃	🍃	🍃	cool	Z5
Sorghastrum nutans	75	1.5m (5ft)	1m (3¼ft)	🍃❀	🍃❀				🍃	🍃	🍃	🍃❀	🍃❀	🍃❀	🍃❀	warm	Z4
S. n. 'Indian Steel'	37	1.5m (5ft)	90cm (3ft)	🍃❀	🍃❀				🍃	🍃	🍃	🍃❀	🍃❀	🍃❀	🍃❀	warm	Z4
S. n. 'Sioux Blue'	37	1.8m (6ft)	1m (3¼ft)	🍃❀	🍃❀				🍃	🍃	🍃	🍃❀	🍃❀	🍃❀	🍃❀	warm	Z4
Sorghum bicolor	84	2.4m (8 ft)	1m (3¼ft)						🍃	🍃	🍃❀	🍃❀	🍃❀	🍃❀		annual	Z8
Spartina pectinata 'Aureomarginata'	34	1.5m (5ft)	indefinite	❀	❀			🍃	🍃	🍃	🍃	🍃❀	🍃❀	❀	❀	warm	Z5
S. p. 'Spring Snow'	32	1.5m (5ft)	indefinite	❀	❀			🍃	🍃	🍃	🍃	🍃❀	🍃❀	❀	❀	warm	Z5
Spodiopogon sibiricus	124	1.2m (4ft)	1m (3¼ft)	❀	❀			🍃	🍃	🍃	🍃❀	🍃❀	🍃❀	❀	❀	cool	Z7
S. s. 'West Hills'	124	1.2m (4ft)	1m (3¼ft)	❀	❀			🍃	🍃	🍃	🍃❀	🍃❀	🍃❀	❀	❀	cool	Z7

LEAVES 🍃 PANICLES ❀

Legend: **L** = leaves, **P** = panicles, **LP** = both (leaves and panicles).

PLANT	PAGE	HEIGHT	SPREAD	Midwinter	Late winter	Early spring	Mid-spring	Late spring	Early summer	Midsummer	Late summer	Early autumn	Mid-autumn	Late autumn	Early winter	WARM/COOL	ZONES
Sporobolus airoides	73	90cm (3ft)	90cm (3ft)	P				L	L	L	LP	LP	LP	LP	LP	warm	Z9
S. fertilis	73	1m (3¼ft)	60cm (2ft)	L	L			L	L	L	LP	LP	LP	LP		warm	Z9
S. heterolepis	77	1.m (4ft)	1m (3¼ft)	L	L			L	L	L	LP	LP	LP	LP		warm	Z4
S. s. 'Variegatum'	153	23cm (9in)	indefinite					L	L	LP	LP	LP	L			warm	Z9
Stipa ambigua	57	90cm (3ft)	75cm (2½ft)						LP	LP	LP	LP	LP	LP		cool	Z8
S. arundinacea	75	1m (3¼ft)	1m (3¼ft)	LP	LP				L	L	LP	LP	LP	LP	LP	cool	Z8
S. barbata	74	45cm (18in)	45cm (18in)					L	L	LP	LP					cool	Z8
S. b. 'Ecume d'Argent'	74	45cm (18in)	45cm (18in)					L	L	LP	LP					cool	Z8
S. (Calamagrostis) brachytricha	57	1.2m (4ft)	90cm (3ft)	P	P				L	LP	LP	LP	LP	LP	LP	cool	Z4
S. calamagrostis	56	90cm (3ft)	1m (3¼ft)	P	P				L	LP	LP	LP	LP	LP	LP	cool	Z7
S. c. 'Lemperg'	56	75cm (2½ft)	75cm (2½ft)	P	P				L	LP	LP	LP	LP	LP	LP	cool	Z7
S. capillata	75	90cm (3ft)	60cm (2ft)	L	L		L		L	LP	LP	L	L	L	L	cool	Z7
S. cernua	75	1m (3¼ft)	60cm (2ft)				L		L	LP	LP	L	L			cool	Z9
S. extremiorientalis	75	1.2m (4ft)	1m (3¼ft)	LP	LP				L	L	L	LP	LP	LP	LP	cool	Z6
S. filiculmis	75	75cm (2½ft)	1m (3¼ft)						LP	LP	LP	LP	L	L		cool	Z6
S. gigantea	57	1.8m (6ft)	1.8m (6ft)	L	L	L	L	LP	LP	LP	LP	LP	LP	LP	L	cool	Z8
S. lepida	75	1m (3¼ft)	75cm (2½ft)	P	P		L		L	L		P	P	P	P	cool	Z9
S. offneri	75	1m (3¼ft)	60cm (2ft)						L	LP	LP	LP	LP	L		cool	Z7
S. papposa	102	30cm (12in)	30cm (12in)	L	L	L	LP	LP	LP	LP	L	L	L	L	L	cool	Z7
S. pennata	75	45cm (18in)	45cm (18in)					L	L	LP	LP					cool	Z7
S. pulcherrima	102	80cm (3¾ft)	60cm (2ft)				L	LP	LP	LP	L					cool	Z8
S. pulchra	75	1m (3¼ft)	75cm (2½ft)					L	LP	LP	L	L				cool	Z8
S. robusta	75	1.8m (6ft)	1m (3¼ft)	LP	LP				L	L	LP	LP	LP	LP	LP	cool	Z7
S. tenacissima	57	2m (6½ft)	1.5m (5ft)						LP	LP	LP	LP	LP	L		cool	Z8
S. tenuissima	57	75cm (2½ft)	60cm (2ft)							LP	LP	LP	LP	LP		cool	Z7
S. tirsa	75	30cm (12in)	23cm (9in)					L	L	LP	LP					cool	Z7
S. turkestanica	75	90cm (3ft)	75cm (2½ft)					L	L	LP	LP	LP	L			cool	Z7
S. ucranica	102	80cm (3¾ft)	60cm (2ft)				LP	LP	LP	L	L					cool	Z7
Thamnocalamus crassinodus 'Kew Beauty'	138	4m (13ft)	1.8m (6ft)	L	L	L	L	L	L	L	L	L	L	L	L	warm	Z7
Themeda triandra var. *japonica*	76	75cm (2½ft)	60cm (2ft)					L	L	LP	LP	LP	LP	L		cool	Z9
Tridens flavus	72	1.2m (4ft)	1m (3¼ft)	LP	LP				L	L	L	LP	LP	LP	LP	warm	Z5
Trisetum flavescens	111	60cm (2ft)	60cm (2ft)					L	LP	LP	L	L				cool	Z5
Typha angustifolia	117	1.5m (5ft)	indefinite						LP	LP	LP	LP	LP	L	L	L	cool	Z3
T. latifolia 'Variegata'	117	1.2m (4ft)	indefinite	P	P	P		L	L	LP	LP	LP	LP	LP	LP	warm	Z4
T. minima	117	65cm (26in)	75cm (2½ft)						LP	LP	LP	LP	LP	L	L	cool	Z6
T. shuttleworthii	117	90cm (3ft)	indefinite						LP	LP	LP	LP	LP	L	L	cool	Z5
Uncinia clavata	45	45cm (18in)	90cm (3ft)	L	L	L	L	LP	LP	LP	L	L	L	L	L	cool	Z7
U. rubra	45	30cm (12in)	90cm (3ft)	L	L	L	L	L	LP	LP	LP	LP	LP	LP	LP	cool	Z7
Zea mays	84	2.4m (8ft)	1m (3¼ft)					L	L	LP	LP	LP	LP			annual	Z7
Zizania aquatica	114	1.2m (4ft)	1m (3¼ft)						L	LP	LP	LP				annual	Z6

The seasons shown for leaves and panicles denote the periods when they are of ornamental value and include seedheads as well as flowers.

LEAVES ≈   PANICLES ✿

Appendix IV *Where to See Ornamental Grasses*

UK

Apple Court
Hordle Lane,
Hordle, Lymington,
Hampshire SO41 OHU.

Blooms of Bressingham
Bressingham, Diss,
Norfolk IP22 2AB.

Cotswold Garden Flowers
offices at
1 Waterside, Evesham,
Worcestershire WR11 6BS;
nursery at Sands Lane, Badsey,
Nr. Evesham, Worcestershire.

Green Farm Plants
Bury Court, Bentley,
Farnham, Surrey GU10 5LZ.

Hoecroft Plants
Severals Grange, Holt Road,
Wood Norton, Dereham,
Norfolk NR20 5BL.

Low-growing *Lamarckia aurea*
in early summer.

PW Plants
Sunnyside, Heath Road,
Kenninghall,
Norfolk NR16 2DS.

**The Beth Chatto
Gardens Ltd**
Elmstead Market, Colchester,
Essex CO7 7DB.

The Royal Botanic Gardens
Kew, Richmond, Surrey
TW9 3AE.

**The Campbell-Sharp
Grassery**
Marlborough, Wiltshire
Strictly by appointment only
Tel. 01672 515380.

**The Royal Horticultural
Society's Garden**
Wisley, Woking,
Surrey GU23 6QB.

Windsor Gardens
*including the Savill Garden and
Windsor Great Park at*
Englefield Green, Berkshire.

USA

**Andre Viette Farm &
Nursery**
Route 1, Box 16, Fishersville,
VA 22939.

**Coastal Gardens &
Nursery**
4611 Socastee Boulevard,
Myrtle Beach, SC 29575.

Crystal Palace Perennials
PO Box 154, St John,
IN 46373.

Greenlee Nursery
301 E. Franklin Avenue,
Pomona, CA 91766.

Kurt Bluemel Inc.
2740 Greene Lane, Baldwin,
MD 21013.

**Plant Delights Nursery,
Inc.**
Juniper Level Botanic
Gardens, 9241 Sauls Road,
Raleigh, NC 27603.

Wayside Gardens
1 Garden Lane, Hodges,
SC 29696-0001.

White Flower Farm
PO Box 50, Litchfield,
CT 06759.

Longwood Gardens
Kennett Square, PA 19348.

PepsiCo Headquarters
Purchase, New York
(grass garden designed by
Russell Page).

EUROPE

Arboretum Trompenburg
Groene Wetering 46, 3062
PC Rotterdam, Holland.

Piet Oudolf
Broekstraat 17, 6999 de
Hummelo, Holland.

Appendix V *Where to Buy Ornamental Grasses*

Many nurseries and most garden centres sell some ornamental grasses. However, the following nurseries specialize in ornamental grasses and it is from these that you are likely to be able to acquire the choicer varieties and newer introductions.

UK

Apple Court
Hordle Lane,
Hordle,
Lymington,
Hampshire SO41 OHU.

Birchdale Plants
9 Cowper Road, Moordown,
Bournemouth,
Dorset BH9 2UJ.

Bressingham Plant Centre
Bressingham, Diss,
Norfolk IP22 2AB.

Cotswold Garden Flowers
offices at
1 Waterside, Evesham,
Worcestershire WR11 6BS;
nursery at
Sands Lane, Badsey, Nr.
Evesham, Worcestershire.

Drysdale Garden Exotics
Bowerwood Road,
Fordingbridge, Hampshire
SP6 1BN.

Four Seasons
Forncett St Mary, Norwich,
Norfolk, NR16 1JT.

Green Farm Plants
Bury Court, Bentley,
Farnham, Surrey GU10 5LZ.

Hoecroft Plants
Severals Grange,
Holt Road,
Wood Norton, Dereham,
Norfolk NR20 5BL.

John Chambers Wild Flower Seeds
15 Westleigh Road, Barton
Seagrave, Kettering,
Northamptonshire
NN15 5AJ.

Monksilver Nursery
Oakington Road,
Cottenham, Cambridge
CB4 4TW.

PW Plants
'Sunnyside', Heath Road,
Kenninghall, Norfolk
NR16 2DS.

The Beth Chatto Gardens Ltd
Elmstead Market, Colchester,
Essex CO7 7DB.

The Royal Horticultural Society's Garden
Wisley, Woking, Surrey
GU23 6QB.

USA

Andre Viette Farm & Nursery
Route 1, Box 16,
Fishersville, VA 22939.

Coastal Gardens & Nursery
4611 Socastee Boulevard,
Myrtle Beech,
SC 29575.

Crystal Palace Perennials
PO Box 154, St John,
IN 46373.

Digging Dog Nursery
PO Box 471,
Albion
CA95410

Greenlee Nursery
301 E. Franklin Avenue,
Pomona, CA 91766.

Limerock Ornamental Grasses
70, Sawmill Road
Port Matilda
PA 16870

Niche Gardens
1111 Dawson Road
Chapel Hill NC 27516

Kurt Bluemel, Inc.
2740 Greene Lane, Baldwin,
MD 21013.

Plant Delights Nursery Inc
Juniper Level Botanic
Gardens, 9241 Sauls Road,
Raleigh, NC 27603.

Trans Pacific Nursery
16065 Oldsville Road
McMinnieville
OR 97128

Wayside Gardens
1 Garden Lane, Hodges,
SC 29696-0001

White Flower Farm
PO Box 50, Litchfield,
CT 06759

EUROPE

Piet Oudolf, Broekstraat
17, 6999 de Hummelo,
Holland.

Coen Jansen
Koningsvaren 35, 7721 HM
Dalfsen, Holland.

Staudengartner Klose
Rosenstrasse 10, 3503,
Lohfelden 1, Germany.

Appendix VI *Further Reading*

Brown, Lauren, *Grasses: an Identification Guide*, Houghton Mifflin, New York, 1979.

Burbidge, Nancy T., *Australian Grasses* Angus and Robertson, Sydney, 1966.

Chao, C.S., *A Guide to Bamboos Grown in Britain*, The Royal Botanic Gardens, Kew, London, 1989.

Chapman, G.P., & Peat, W.E., *An Introduction to the Grasses*, C.A.B. International, Oxford, 1992.

Clayton, W.D., & Renvoize, S.A., *Genera Graminum*, Her Majesty's Stationary Office, London, 1986.

Darke, F.P., *Ornamental Grasses at Longwood Gardens*, Longwood Gardens Inc., Kennet Square, Pennsylvania, 1990.

Darke, Rick, *Ornamental Grasses for your Garden*, Michael Friedman Publishing Group, London & New York, 1994.

Fitter, R., Fitter, A., & Farrer, A., *Collins Pocket Guide to Grasses, Sedges, Rushes & Ferns*, Harper Collins, 1984.

Fondation pour L'Architecture, *Les Jardins de Jacques Wirtz* Fondation pour L'Architecture, Brussels, 1993.

Greenlee, John *The Encyclopedia of Ornamental Grasses*, Rodale Press, Pennsylvania, 1992.

Griffiths, Professor D.A., *Grasses & Sedges of Hong Kong*, The Urban Council of Hong Kong, 1983.

Hansen, Richard, & Sachs, Friedrich, *Perennials and their Garden Habitats*, Cambridge University Press, Cambridge, 1993.

Hitchcock, A.S., *Manual of the Grasses of the United States*, Dover Publications, Inc., New York, 1971.

Hubbard, C.E., *Grasses* Penguin Books, 2nd edition, London, 1968.

Jermy, A.C. and Tutin, T.G., *British Sedges* The Botanical Society of the British Isles, London, 1968.

King, Michael & Oudolf, Piet *Prachtig Gras*, Uitgeverij Terra, Warnsveld, Den Haag, 1996.

Kingsbury, Noel, *The New Perennial Garden*, Frances Lincoln, London, 1996.

Loewer, Peter, *Ornamental Grasses*, Brooklyn Botanic Garden, New York, 1988.

Loewer, Peter, *Ornamental Grasses*, Better Homes and Gardens Books, Des Moines, 1995.

Meyer, Mary Hockenberry, *Ornamental Grasses*, Charles Scribner's Sons, New York, 1975.

Oakes, A. J. *Ornamental Grasses and Grasslike Plants* Van Nostrand Reinhold, New York, 1990.

Oehme, Wolfgang and van Sweden, James, *Bold Romantic Gardens*, Acropolis Books Ltd, Reston, Virginia, 1990.

Ottesen, Carole, *Ornamental Grasses, The Amber Wave* McGraw-Hill, New York, 1989.

Philips, Roger, *Grasses, Ferns, Mosses and Lichens of Great Britain and Ireland*, London, Pan Books Ltd, 1980.

Philips, Roger & Rix, Martin, *Perennials*, Pan Books Ltd, London, 1991.

Recht, Christine, & Wetterwald, Max F., *Bamboos*, Timber Press, Portland, Oregon, 1992.

Reinhardt, Thomas A., Reinhardt, Martina, and Moskowitz, Mark, *Ornamental Grass Gardening* Macdonald Orbis, New York, 1989.

Romanowski, Nick, *Grasses, Bamboos and Related Plants in Australia*, Thomas C. Lothian Pty Ltd, Melbourne, 1993.

Rose, Francis, *Grasses, Sedges, Rushes and Ferns of the British Isles and North-western Europe*, Viking, London, 1989.

Royal Horticultural Society, The, *Award of Garden Merit Plants*, The Royal Horticultural Society, London, 1993.

Ryves, T.B., Clement, E.J. & Foster, M.C., *Alien Grasses of the British Isles*, Botanical Society of the British Isles, London, 1996.

Speichert, Greg, *Miscanthus Checklist*, Crystal Palace Perennials, St John, Illinois, 1994.

Taylor, Nigel J., *Ornamental Grasses, Bamboos, Rushes and Sedges*, Ward Lock, London, 1992.

Walters, S. M. et al *The European Garden Flora*, Vol II, Cambridge University Press, Cambridge, 1984.

Sheaths on *Chusquea culeou.*

Appendix VII *Plant Hardiness Zone Map*

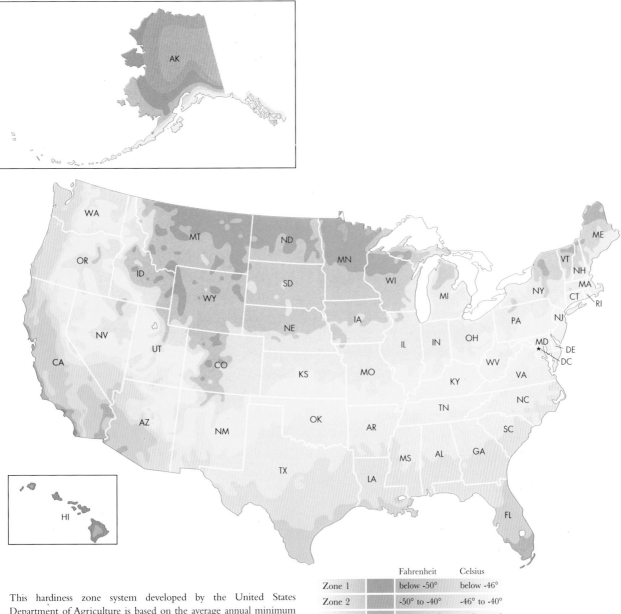

This hardiness zone system developed by the United States Department of Agriculture is based on the average annual minimum temperatures for each zone. All plants in the A–Z of Ornamental Grasses (pages 174–183) are rated with a zone indicating the coldest temperatures they will reliably survive and perform consistently. The plant may also be grown in all zones warmer than the one indicated. However, the zone system is only a guide. Microclimates within each zone may mean you can grow plants from a warmer zone, or conversely, some plants hardy to your zone may not survive in your garden. This is particularly true toward the upper and lower limits of each zone. Gardeners living outside the USA can deduce the zone in which they live based on their own average minimum temperature.

		Fahrenheit	Celsius
Zone 1		below -50°	below -46°
Zone 2		-50° to -40°	-46° to -40°
Zone 3		-40° to -30°	-40° to -34°
Zone 4		-30° to -20°	-34° to -29°
Zone 5		-20° to -10°	-29° to -23°
Zone 6		-10° to 0°	-23° to -18°
Zone 7		0° to 10°	-18° to -12°
Zone 8		10° to 20°	-12° to -7°
Zone 9		20° to 30°	-7° to -1°
Zone 10		30° to 40°	-1° to 4°
Zone 11		above 40°	above 4°

Index

ACKNOWLEDGEMENTS

This book is not just the product of the time it took to write but rather the fruit of the decades that went before, during which many people opened my eyes to new wonders in the world of grasses and their uses in gardens, and to all these people I am deeply grateful. In this respect I should particularly like to thank the following: Rick Darke, Greg Speichert, Trevor Scott, Alan Cook, Kurt Bluemel, Wolfgang Oehme, David Crampton, John Coke, Jill Butcher, John Trinder, David McClintock, Neil and Gerry Campbell-Sharpe, Peter Hall, Richard Loader, Piers Trehane, Dr Ullrich Fischer, Gert Fortgens, Peter Addington, Joe Sharman and Piet Oudolf.

I should also like to thank the following for allowing us to photograph in their gardens: John and Pamela Southwell of Sherborne Gardens at Litton, Near Wells, Somerset; David and Sue Ward of 53 Ladywood in Eastleigh; John Coke and Marina Christopher of Green Farm Plants at Bury Court, Bentley, Farnham, Surrey; Mark and Marianne Barker of Box Cottage, Newtown, Fareham, Hampshire; Mr and Mrs Ian Pasley-Tyler of Coton Manor, Nr Guilsborough, Northamptonshire; David Crampton of Drysdale Exotics, Bowerwood Road, Fordingbridge, Hampshire; Mr and Mrs R. Paice of Bourton House Garden, Bourton-on-the-Hill, Gloucestershire; the Curator, the Royal Horticultural Society's Garden at Wisley, Woking, Surrey; the Director, the Royal Botanic Gardens, Kew; and, in the USA, Tony & Michelle Avent of Plant Delights Nursery, Inc. at Juniper Level Botanic Gardens, 9241 Sauls Road, Raleigh, North Carolina.

I should like to give special thanks to those whose photographs have done so much to make this book inspirational, particularly Marie O'Hara, who took most of the photographs, Neil Campbell-Sharp for photographs including those of his own grassery, Noel Kingsbury for photographs of Westpark in Munich and others showing naturalistic ways of using grasses, Piet Oudolf for photographs of his own, unique garden at Hummelo, Wolfgang Oehme for photographs of the New Wave gardens of the Oehme, van Sweden partnership, Patrick Taylor for photographs of Jacques Wirtz's garden at La Petite Garenne near Schoten in Belgium, Howard Rice, and Karl Adamson, who took the studio shots.

My thanks go also those involved in the making of this book, particularly Diana Vowles, who edited my manuscript and asked many searching questions; Ali Myer, who was responsible for the design; and Anna Mumford, who had the dire responsibility of overseeing it all.

Finally I should like to thank my wife Diana for allowing me to dig up the lawn and grow grasses where she would much rather have had daylilies, and for all her help and encouragement, without which I would never have got around to writing this book at all.